Jane Rosser

AMAZON ODYSSEY

AMAZON ODYSSEY

Ti-Grace Atkinson

First Printing
Standard Book Numbers:
0-8256-3016-9 softcover edition
0-8256-3023-1 hardcover edition
Library of Congress Catalog Card Number: 73-80394
Printed in the United States of America

Book and cover art by Barbara Nessim
Back cover photographs by Bettye Lane

to those who fought
and got away—

but never went home

(and for Charlotte
August 1936 – January 1973)

CONTENTS

LIST OF CHART ILLUSTRATIONS
(STRATEGIC AND TACTICAL MAPS)

FOREWORD

The essays and speeches included in this volume are only a small fraction of my writings abstracted from the years 1967 through 1972. Nonetheless, I believe this collection represents my work of those years fairly.

I never had an opportunity, prior to this, to consider my work—even an abstraction of my work—as a whole. I have always been in the midst of battle, and, so seemingly, necessarily transfixed on the moment. I have always been aware, however, that I was probing deeper and deeper into the *roots* of the oppression of women.

I originally thought of this volume as a sort of compromise. I have been working on my "serious" book, *Women and Oppression,* since the spring of 1968. I have yet to find a publisher for it. Recently, however, it was suggested that the comparatively easy pieces included in this volume might open the way to the publication of what I view as my major work (and what I've come to label, my "dream" book). But as I've edited these pieces, and now see them together for the first time, I find that I must reassess what has transpired over the last six years. And I have been forced to reassess the significance of this collection as well. I no longer see it as a "compromise," but as a work in its own right—with its own special value.

I have always been aware that I had two distinct, yet, in some ways, interlocking concerns. The "ideological"—or, "*what* is the problem?"—and the "tactical"—or, "*how* can this problem be solved?" Exactly how the "ideological" and "tactical" interact and relate is an enormously important and intricate philosophical issue.

The "ideological" concerns the definition of a problem, and a plumbing of its depths. In the essays and speeches which follow, sometimes the "problem" is barely suggested. Sometimes only the appropriate *questions* concerning the definition of the relevant problem are raised. And sometimes, simply questioning the accepted answers is the beginning of a new process of definition.

The "tactical" concerns, above all, organizational structures and methods for change. What instruments can effect the changes sought for? Of these instruments, which are available to the Oppressed? What are the mode/s of these instruments relevant to the particular group within the

Oppressed of concern?

Oversimplification within an ideological framework can badly snarl any *modus operandi.*

At least two things are clear from these pieces.

First, I perceived and stated, very early, that female oppression was essentially a class confrontation.

(I should add here that I always understood that it was male *behavior* that was the enemy and that it was crucial to identify and analyze this behavior as an aspect of the phenomenon of oppression. It could well be that the failure to do this led to future confusion and error.)

Second, I saw from the first that feminism raised fundamental philosophical issues, such as the distinction between "function" and "capacity."

Because of the first point, that of class confrontation, I thought my title for this collection should include something relating to the Amazons. For *that* reason, and also because I'm always being denounced, even within the Women's Movement, for being so "warlike."

(Unlike most women in the Movement, my world, very early, became restricted to women. By choice.)

But this early Amazonian position also led to an early realization that women operated among themselves in apparent "class" relationships. And since the *instru-ment* for change had questionable effectiveness if corrupted, much effort in this early period of my work was spent in a recognition and confrontation with this corruption within the Women's Movement.

This "probing" constantly led to more and more fundamental questions. Questions about sex, and how power was woven into the fabric of that.

Questions about love. And how "love," as a psychological phenomenon, operates as a response and support to power, and, thus, to oppression.

Inevitably, the question arose of the nature and concept of power itself. This is the "answer," the *conceptual* structure, on which all *political* structures are built. Without questioning this "answer," no fundamental changes can occur.

And, yet, how few are willing to give up the power relationship. Even the power*less* cling to the ideology, in the hope that as long as the *idea* exists they have hope of escaping power*less*ness by achieving *some*way, *some*how, power*ful*ness. Of course, as long as the conceptual framework of "power" itself is valued (especially, if valued by the Oppressed!), *none* of us has *any* hope.

In trying to understand what seemed irrational—oppressed people clinging to the root cause of their oppression, I stumbled onto the issue of identity, and invented what I called my theory of metaphysical cannibalism.

From a suggestion of this problem, I tried to rough out the direction of a solution—an internally controlled method of identity construction.

I call this collection *Amazon Odyssey.* After drawing up the lines of battle very early, I've apparently spent at least five years bumbling around, ricocheting off false solutions, searching for solid ground.

Obviously, "change" can never occur *in situ.* But at least some fundamental, solid, and reasoned direction should be in hand. And some methodology for reaching the charted destination should be consciously in process. These two minimal—and somewhat modest—basics are what I consider, at present, the end of my Odyssey.

I know the current feminist analysis is badly flawed. Even the radical feminist analysis fails in its lack of refinement and lack of strategy. *Both* analyses fail to probe the *foundations* of the sex institutions.

And all "flaws," in political theory, translate into human fatalities.

We are all still imprisoned by Marx. Perhaps the very notion of "class" is irrelevant to revolutionary political theory. (But, if "class" *is* irrelevant, how could we still even *refer* to the oppression of "women"?)

At this point, I'm not sure. But my suspicion of "class" as a base concept of the analysis of *any* oppression grows.

The political maneuverings of the Women's Movement prove, without doubt, that the ideological boundaries maintaining women as an oppressed class have not been touched. We swirl in circles, building in frenzies, that can only solidify—and lock in even more securely—the oppression of women into our political system.

The issue of "power" leads quickly to the problem of "identity." Identity is the foundation of "free will" and "responsibility." The *choice,* the *decision* to fight any given oppression depends upon "identity."

As my awareness and perception of these fundamental concepts grew, I found myself seeing other movements as I had not seen them before. I began seeing certain parallel interests—the desire to plumb these deeper issues—reflected in the words of a few individuals within other groups.

At the same time, I began to see a larger tactical battlefield.

Of course, there were many flaws in my *own* analysis. And I lacked the courage to stand as totally alone as I sensed I might be, if I pursued my Odyssey honestly—wherever it might lead me.

In the end, I betrayed myself. In the deepest and most total sense. For a long time, I felt I had no right to speak or write.

I wasn't able to take that final step—from ideology to life. I wasn't able to stand by an individual—not as a man, but as a revolutionary—who was bumbling toward the same conclusions as was I. I was so afraid of betraying that Amazonian battle-field.

Now that I see this collection together —my first collection—I see what a long way and how many shores I have touched since that first drawing up of lines. For the Movement as a whole, that Battle is much more recent and the lines still fresh.

I hope I have learned sufficiently the price of self-deception. It is the ultimate collaboration.

The test of one's humanity is to stand with the truth as best one can make it out, even if totally alone, and to fight *for* that truth. This is the measure of liberation.

I am still an Amazon, although much battered. Science has done very little for ideological transport over the centuries.

My odyssey continues. Perhaps I must retrace my steps. I must return to that first battlefield and survey what remains of it. Perhaps now is the time to itemize and re-construct the process of that battle.

I hope the shores I have touched since 1967 will deepen my insights.

April 11, 1973
New York City

AMAZON ODYSSEY

ABORTION

PAPER NUMBER II[1]

The reproductive function of a woman is the only innate function which distinguishes women from men. It is the critical distinction upon which all inequities toward women are grounded. It is, therefore, crucial for women to understand clearly what the nature of this function is, how it is to be defined, and in what relationship the reproductive function stands to a woman.

The reproductive function is a special ability, capacity, or talent held by women. This function is a property which determines their womanhood. The distinction between this function and the usual sense of property is that the latter is static, or primarily spatial, while the former is operational, or exists over time. The reproductive function has the status of property because of its definitive nature.

Since any discussion of the woman's reproductive function is at the moment clouded over by emotion, the notion of function in the definitive sense will be discussed here by justified analogy to allow an objective analysis.

A sculptor is a sculptor by virtue of his capacity to sculpture. Sculpturing is the function which distinguishes him from the rest of mankind; it is the property which defines his essence. (The sculptor gives some sign of his capacity; e.g., a woman's menstruation is a sign of her capacity to bear children.) The sculptor controls his function: he can choose not to exercise it at all; he can experiment with it by operating it without any intention of creating a work; he can destroy a work in process of the operation of his capacity upon it; he can complete a work.

The question—"when is a work completed?"—is important. When you say that a work is complete, you indicate some notion of finish, end, breaking off, independence.

Once you establish independence, questions arise as to the object's rights to existence.

As long as material owned by the artist is operated upon by him, the artist has the rights of ownership over the artistic process, e.g., cessation of the process. But what criteria might be applied to the work giving it independent, non-property status? Two criteria could be used:

1

[1] [November 18, 1967; National Conference, National Organization for Women; Washington, D.C.]

(1) the sculptor states that that is his idea of a statue of a person, or

(2) the work meets some objective criteria of what it is to be a statue of a person.

The woman is the artist. The property which distinguishes her as a woman is her reproductive function. She may choose not to exercise her function at all, or she may choose to exercise it. The man may try to give her certain material which would then become her property. She can accept or reject the gift. Once accepting the gift, she can choose to exercise her special capacity on this material or not. It is at this stage that the initial choice is made by the woman whether or not to exercise her reproductive process on the sperm.

The method of implementing her choice might be some contraceptive technique such as a pill, injection, diaphragm, coil, foam, jelly, or any other adequate technique. (Definition of "adequate technique" = a technique that works at least 95 percent of the time, i.e., a technique intended to be effective, considering the range of techniques available.)

Both the raw material gift and the special reproductive function are properties of the woman. She may decide to permit the one, i.e., the special function, her function, to operate upon her raw material gift. An embryo (definition of "embryo" = product of reproductive process in the womb in the first three months after conception [for a human]) may begin to take shape through her process. The woman may decide to stop the process: the embryo is destroyed.

But perhaps the woman does not make this decision, and, through her special capacity, the embryo may be transformed into a fetus. (Definition of "fetus" = product of reproductive process in the womb from the end of the third month of pregnancy until birth.) There is a six-month span here during which a woman may choose to exercise her reproductive function on the fetus. Both her reproductive function and the fetus within this function constitute her property. She may decide at any time during this period that she does not want to exercise this function any longer, at which time she is free not to do so.

It is only when the fetus ceases to be the woman's property (her reproductive process ceases at natural terminations) *that the choice to exercise or not to exercise her reproductive function on that fetus can be interfered with.* The fetus ceases to be property when

(1) certain minimal criteria are met defining what it is to be a person: the denotative definitive characteristic is existence as a single *separate* man, woman or child, or

(2) the woman decides to give the fetus child-status.

The woman can confer child-status in one of two ways:

(1) she can arbitrarily give the fetus child-status by naturally and/or voluntarily expelling the fetus from her body, thereby declaring personhood on the fetus, i.e., existence as a single separate being. This may occur any time during the embryonic or fetal stages of her reproductive process. Or

(2) what is more usual, child-status is conferred on the fetus when it's come full term, i.e., nine months, to birth.

Birth is defined as the transformational event between fetus- and child-status and is characterized by one of two conditions:

(1) the voluntary (on the part of the woman) expulsion of the fetus from the woman's body *accompanied by her stated intention of giving birth to a child,* or

(2) the natural (without any form of outside interference) expulsion of the fetus from the woman's body.

The Constitution of the United States, in the Fourteenth Amendment, clearly protects the life, liberty, and property of every person. Any legislation interfering in any way with any woman's self-determination of her reproductive process is clearly unconstitutional. It would interfere with her life by interfering with her person; it would interfere with her liberty by interfering with her freedom of choice as regards her own person; it would interfere with her property since her reproductive process constitutes, in the most integral and strictest sense, her property.

VAGINAL ORGASM AS A MASS HYSTERICAL SURVIVAL RESPONSE[1]

I suppose we all have put aside the speeches we prepared before last night. In the face of Martin King's death, one must tell the truth as plain as one can.

I was asked by the Medical Committee for Human Rights to speak on sex. All right, I really will.

The oppression *of* women *by* men is the source of *all* the corrupt values throughout the world. Between men and women we *brag* about domination, surrender, inequality, conquest, trickery, exploitation. Men have *robbed* women of their lives.

A human being is not born from the womb; it must create itself. It must be *free, self*-generative. A human being must feel that it can grow in a world where injustice, inequity, hatred, sadism are not directed at *it.* No person can grow into a life within these conditions; it is enough of a miracle to survive as a *functioning* organism.[2]

Now let's *talk* about function. Women have been *murdered* by their so-called *function* of childbearing exactly as the black people were murdered by their *function* of *color.* The *truth* is that childbearing *isn't* the function of women. The *function* of *childbearing* is the *function* of *men* oppressing women.

It is the *function* of men to oppress. It is the *function* of men to exploit. It is the *function* of men to *lie,* and to *betray,* and to *humiliate,* to *crush,* to *ignore, and the final insult:* it is the *function* of men to tell women that *man's iniquities* are *woman's function!*

I'm telling it to you as straight as I can. Marriage and the family are as corrupt institutions as slavery ever was. They must be abolished as slavery was. By definition they *necessarily* oppress and exploit their subject groups. If women were free, free to grow as people, free to be self-creative, free to *go* where they like, free to *be* where they like, free to *choose* their lives, there would be no such institutions as marriage or family. If slaves had had those freedoms, there wouldn't have been slavery.

Until DNA[3] or something similar comes through, women are the only source of new organisms. Men cannot continue to force women to produce children. The society as a whole can decide what it wants to do about its birthrate, and then the women can be asked to contribute their special capacities. But if women don't want to, that's the breaks. If a woman decides to

5

[1] [April 5, 1968; National Conference, Medical Committee for Human Rights; Philadelphia.

I requested and was ceded that the following be included within any introductory remarks: "Miss Atkinson is not representing her organization tonight; N.O.W. has no policy on the issues discussed in her paper."]

[2] [I recall a slip of the tongue here: I pronounced "organism" as "orgasm." There was much laughter at the time, although those same people are probably laughing less now.]
[3] [A reference to "test-tube" babies.]

help out, she has absolutely no responsibility for the child. The child is not hers, it belongs to society. It is society even *now,* or rather men, that decides whether or not women have children; children are the whole society's responsibility.

I'm not going to fall into the male-supremacy[4] trap tonight of "who's going to take care of the children," and the "working-mother-delinquent-child" blues. Last night's events reminded me that there's no more time for injustice, euphemistically known as "social justice." It's irrelevant to the emancipation of women what happens when women free themselves from the institutions that maintain them in their oppressed state. It wasn't the responsibility of the slaves to think up, develop, experiment, and prove superior a new economic system for the South before they were emancipated, and it's not our job to figure out what happens to the kiddies before women free themselves. And *women will free* themselves. I'm just here to tell you men about it so you can expose your sadistic hostility toward your wives and mothers a little more, a little sooner, so they'll revolt quicker. I don't see why women should lose any more of their lives than they have already.

I'm assuming as I write this that I'll be reading it to liberal men. You're a real prize bunch. You quiver with horror over Vietnam because you identify your hide with the boy sent over there. You pontificate, but mostly just shake your head, over black people because you know if they get too uppity, you outnumber them nine to one, and *you* know that *they* know it. That's an extra kick. But do you get uptight about women! There are those of you who try to *lay* a woman to put down her protests. (I expect nervous laughter here.)[5]

Then there are those who pat her on her ass and say, "Gee, baby, it's too bad you're inferior, but that's your function, and I think that's great." *What's* great? *She's* great? Of course that's not what you mean. You mean it's great that it's her function to be inferior. But she can't face *that* so she twists it to mean that you think that she's great. And because she's the cheapest maid going and sleeps in your bed, you let it go—more or less. We all know how uncomfortable it is to be around disgruntled maids nowadays, and as for hostile sex, what other kind is there?

Oh yes, sex. Your kind. The kind you wanted me to titillate you with by speaking here tonight. What could be more amusing than a feminist talking about sex? Obviously, if feminism has any logic in it at all, it must be working for a sexless society. But sex you want? Sex you're going to get.

Vaginal orgasm is an excellent illustration of the way men oppress and exploit women. It's ironic that you insist men and women respond the same in the one place no one can deny men and women are different—in their genitals. This difference is

---

[4] [I still prefer the concept of "male-supremacy" to "male chauvinism." "Supremacy" refers more to *actual* conditions. "Chauvinism" connotes more of a *mental* condition. "Supremacy" is the more political of the two references.]

[5] [Nobody was laughing. They were in shock.]

the basis for the whole distinction between men and women and the ground for the inequities that are heaped on women by men. But men have no shame.

That's what power does for you—like Johnson raping Vietnam. And Johnson has the gall to say the Vietnamese want us to be there, to keep the free world safe for democracy. He means, as your enlightened pocket books now know, that we're there to *maintain* the oppression of the *Vietnamese* to keep the world, by object lesson, safe to exploit for the United States. And as we have seen the little life left in the country being burned out of it, Johnson had the gall to tell us the Vietnamese were loving it. Try that argument with women, baby, and you'll be home free.

A man's penis and a woman's vagina are obviously different. Male orgasm is analogous to clitoral orgasm. Where, then, does vaginal orgasm come from? People say it's learned. And by God you'd better learn it, lady, especially if you're with a liberal man; you'd better learn to shuffle, nigger, because if you don't you won't get the job. And you want to eat, don't you? Why *should* she learn vaginal orgasm? Because that's what men want. How about a

facial tic? What's the difference?

And love. As long as we're on sacred cows, let's finish them. What is love but the payoff for the consent to oppression?[6] What is love but need? What is love but fear? In a just society, would we need love?

In a free society, you cannot have the family, marriage, sex, or love. You will have your Vietnams, and more, you will have your murdered Martin King's, and more, you will have your Revolution unless your wives and mothers free themselves, because that's where the foundations of oppression and exploitation are laid. You are going to have to have your power wrenched away from you right where you live, and you're not going to like it. And that's tough shit.

To the women in the audience, I say: think about these things with the man you love and want the most. Scratch *his* love, and you'll find *your* fear.[7] You'll be afraid you'll die, and the *woman* will die, but *your* life will be born, and *you'll* begin to be *free*.

To the men in the audience, I say: move on over, baby, or we'll move on over you—'caus al de *good* niggers is daide!!

7

---

[6] [The "consent to oppression" is a concept *within* the phenomenon of oppression. I am indebted to Florynce Kennedy for the idea.]
[7] [I have had more women tell me they related to this one sentence than to any other statement I have made.]

RESIGNATION FROM N.O.W.[1]

FROM: Ti-Grace Atkinson, President
       New York chapter
       N.O.W. (National Organization for
       Women)

FOR IMMEDIATE RELEASE

NEW YORK, October 18—Ti-Grace Atkinson, President of the New York chapter of N.O.W., has resigned as President. Miss Atkinson announced her resignation today after a fiery meeting last night at which her attempt to modernize the chapter by-laws was defeated.

Miss Atkinson gives her reasons for resigning the office she holds which would normally expire in December:

"I am convinced that there are irreconcilable ideological conflicts in N.O.W. Since the beginning there have been bitter schisms over taking unequivocal positions on certain issues: abortion, marriage, the family, the support of persons in the cause who have crossed the law (e.g., Bill Baird, Valerie Solanas), the inextricable relationship between caste and class.

"The disagreement has often been on the issues, but the division has always also been on whether or not one stands publicly on them. One group would say, the public isn't ready for this The other group would say, but that's our purpose: to say the truth as soon as we see it, as best we can, so that the public will *get* ready for it.

"I think that until last night I made the mistake of thinking that any person *could* believe something, *could* have certain values, and at the same time not represent these values. It was with that mistaken notion that I accepted offices in N.O.W., particularly the office of President of the New York chapter (the New York chapter, one of 45 chapters, contains 30 percent of the national membership in N.O.W.).

"I thought that we all shared the same values, that it was an issue of timidity, and that someone as President who was less afraid might be able to pull the movement along faster.

"My false assumption was that the issues now dividing the feminist movement were minor ones and not deep-rooted value conflicts concerning such fundamental issues as (1) what is feminism about? (2) what are its goals?

"In a small (of 8) group last Tuesday evening (10/15/68, 220 East 60th Street, New York City) some of us were trying to resolve the factionalism in N.O.W. The leader of N.O.W. (Betty Friedan), in the

9

[1] [Written October 18, 1968; mailing sent out to press on October 21, 1968, announcing my resignation from N.O.W.]

discussion of feminist goals, said 'I want to get women into positions of power.'

"Some of the rest of us saw this statement as representative of the opposite side to our differences. We said, each in our own way, 'We want to destroy the positions of power. To alter the condition of women involves the shifting of over half the population. We complain about the unequal power relationships between men and women. To change that relationship requires a redefinition of humanity, of all the relationships within humanity. We want to get rid of the positions of power, not get up into those positions. The fight against unequal power relationships between men and women necessitates fighting unequal power everyplace: between men and women (for feminists especially), but also between men and men, and women and women, between black and white, and rich and poor.'

"Well, those lines are pretty strongly drawn. I began to see that the positions were irreconcilable.

"Last night at the New York chapter's monthly membership meeting, we discussed and voted on the By-Laws Committee's new Implementing By-Laws. The younger dissenting faction of which I am a member has been trying for a long time to change the unequal power relationships within the organization, i.e., the power hierarchy represented by officers: Executive Committee, Board of Directors, membership.

"We thought that these laws within the organization had critical symbolic importance for two reasons: (1) implementing by-laws are within our power to change easily, unlike the laws in the world at large, and (2) the power relationships we have among ourselves are a good indication of what we *really* want in the world at large. In other words 'charity begins at home.'

"We were stopped at every turn: our original idea of simply eliminating offices altogether was stopped legalistically. We then attempted to diffuse the office powers by increasing the number of persons within each office. Thus, our program of last night 'A N.O.W. Version of Participatory Democracy: Multiple and Cyclical Presidents.'

"The new Implementing By-Laws were defeated 2 to 1. The speeches against the by-laws revealed unmistakably that the division in N.O.W. as well as in the feminist movement as a whole is between those who want women to have the opportunity to be oppressors, too, and those who want to destroy oppression itself.

"I am resigning my office because, after last night as the final proof, I realize that by holding this office I am participating in oppression itself. You cannot destroy oppression by filling the position of the oppressor. I don't think you can fight oppression 'from the inside'; you either *are* on the inside or the outside and you fill one of those two ranks by your presence. Since I have failed to get rid of the power position

I hold, I have no choice but to step out of it."

Ti-Grace Atkinson announced that, simultaneously with her resignation as President of the New York chapter, she was resigning her other offices in N.O.W.: elected member of the National Board of Directors, Finance Chairman of the National Organization for Women, member of N.O.W.'s 1968 National Nominating Committee.

Miss Atkinson has been active in N.O.W. since the first organizing meeting of the New York chapter in February, 1967.

THE INSTITUTION OF SEXUAL INTERCOURSE[1]

our "society," . . . if it's not deflected from its present course
and if the Bomb doesn't drop on it, will hump itself to death.
—Valerie Solanas

The debate on vaginal orgasm is not central to feminism as a whole. The theory of vaginal orgasm was created quite recently to shore up that part of the foundation of a social institution[2] that was being threatened by the increasing demand by women for freedom for women. The political institution I am referring to is the institution of sexual intercourse. The purpose, i.e., the social function, of the institution is to maintain the human species.

It used to be that the construct[3] of marriage guaranteed the institution of sexual intercourse. It is still true that, when and where marriage in any of its original variants is properly entered into and protected, the activities sufficient to the definition of this construct and, thus, the purposes of the institution of sexual intercourse, are protected. The substitute theoretical construct of vaginal orgasm is necessary only when marriage is threatened.

The theory of vaginal orgasm was the concoction of a man, Freud, whose theories generally place women in an inhumane and exploited role. His theory of vaginal orgasm reaches the apex of these. This theory was inspired by his confrontations with women who were sick to death of the female role, and it adjusted women back into this female role by conning them that it was in a woman's interest, *by her very nature* (i.e., it is in the interest of her vagina), to be dehumanized and exploited. While Freud's theory is inconsistent with female anatomy, it is excellent evidence in support of the theory that the concept of sexual intercourse is a political construct, reified into an institution.

The construct of vaginal orgasm is most in vogue whenever and wherever the institution of sexual intercourse is threatened. As women become freer, more independent, more self-sufficient, their interest

13

[1] [November, 1968; published by *The New York Free Press*, December 13, 1968; reprinted in *Notes from the Second Year,* Shulamith Firestone and Anne Koedt, eds. (New York; 1970), pp. 42-47.]
[2] The definition of "institution" used in this article—(John Rawls's df. of "practice" = any form of activity specified by a system of rules which defines offices, roles, moves, penalties, defenses, and so on, and which gives the activity its structure) + (*Webster*'s df. of "institutional" = organized so as to function in social, charitable, and educational activities).
[3] [My usage of the words "construct" and "institution" in this article has confused some readers. I have already defined my use of "institution" in the preceding footnote.

I use "construct" to mean a kind of sub-institution within another institution. It is a product of the systematic evolution of its original institution. Thus, marriage is a "construct" within the "institution" of the family. And vaginal orgasm is a "construct" within the "institution" of sexual intercourse. Obviously, there are an infinite number of ways related institutions and constructs (for example, all those institutions and constructs within the male-female class system) can interrelate.

All "institutions" have at one time been "constructs." The converse is not true. Therefore, when I refer to certain construct-institutional entities, such as marriage and the family, I refer to both as "constructs."]

in (i.e., their need for) men decreases, and their desire for the construct of marriage which properly entails children (i.e., a family) decreases proportionate to the increase in their self-sufficiency. It is for this reason that the construct of *vaginal* orgasm is coming under attack among women radicals in the feminist movement (as opposed to radical feminists[4]) while at the same time the construct of *marriage* is coming under attack among women in the feminist movement who are either politically conservative, or liberal-to-the-right (e.g., a McCarthyite [Eugene]), or, as is the case with most women, apolitical in the main. The latter group is both presently and potentially far larger than the former which is the only reason the debate on the marriage–family[5] construct is central to feminism as a whole, whereas its more recent substitute, vaginal orgasm, is not.

I

Vaginal orgasm is, then, a substitute construct for marriage. Unfortunately for those women who are accepting the substitute, vaginal orgasm as a political construct is less in their interests than marriage. It takes time for women, simply because they are so much weaker politically, to build in compensations for themselves in any political construct in which they are a necessary member.

It is interesting to compare the correlative structures of these two political constructs. (I will not consider those protections built in at a later date into marriage so that the two constructs can be compared in their original and definitive forms.) The salient feature of both is that both constructs (marriage and vaginal orgasm) are in the interests of the male and against the interests of the female, and both constructs were, not surprisingly, conceived of by men. Both constructs limit a woman's human possibilities (the double standard is built into any double-role theory). Both constructs incorporate attempted justifications (excuses?) for the role assigned to women in sexual intercourse, which, however, in no way mitigates the initial exploitation.

A. Both constructs contain conveniently supportive theretofore unknown or unrecognized biological theories:
1. in marriage, the supportive biological theory is the theory of maternal instinct. The biological argument for the maternal instinct goes something like this: women *need* to have children, it's part of their *nature.*

14

[4] [My first public use of the concept of "radical feminism" appeared in a press release concerning Valerie Solanas (Criminal Court, New York City, June 13, 1968).]
[5] This article is not on the interdependence of the two political constructs of marriage and the family, but the comments on the biological theory contained in the construct of marriage assumes this interdependence. The goal of the institution of sexual intercourse, i.e., childbearing by women, is the bridge between the two constructs of marriage and family. If this article were not concentrating on political constructs by definition limited to two persons and as pertains to the institution of sexual intercourse, it might be more accurate to refer to the marriage-family construct. At the present time and in the foreseeable future, without the construct of the family, the marriage construct would serve no political purpose, i.e., there would be nothing to protect, and it would evolve out.

Can't you see that that's what their bodies were built for? And if women didn't *like* to have children, they wouldn't; this proves women *choose* to have children. And since they choose to have children in such large numbers, having children must come naturally to women. It's an *instinct,* the *maternal* instinct.

    a. there's a confusion of priorities here: a *capacity* for some activity is not the same as a *need*[6] for that activity, so that even if women's bodies were suitably formed for the activity of childbearing, this in no way necessarily entails that they *want* to bear children, much less *need* to. Unfortunately for women, childbearing wreaks havoc on their bodies and can hardly be defended as healthy.

        1. Pregnancy and birth distend and tear women's bodies out of their natural forms as women (as opposed to mothers), so that it hardly can be held that women's bodies are con-structed appropriately for the activity of child-bearing.

        2. Reliable estimates indicate that in the U. S., the maternal death rate was 29.1 out of every 1,000; the *female* death rate in 1966 was 8.1 out of every thousand. (U. S. Vital Statistics.) Maternity more than triples the risk of death for the average woman in the years of her pregnancy. The maternal death rate for the entire world in 1966 was at least twice that of the U. S., so that the average woman, appropriately enough, more than sextupled her chance of death by becoming pregnant. (U. N. figures.) There is no other activity in the world, short of war, with that high a mortality rate that would be legalized. (It's interesting, albeit chilling, that the maternal death rate is almost never publi-

15

---

6 [Again, as in *Abortion: Paper Number II,* pp. 1–3, I make the distinction between a *capacity* and a *function.* The biological notions of "need" and "instinct" are preliminaries to the bio-political concept of "function."]

cized, whereas the infant mortality rate is often seen; this is another indication of the low value placed on women.)

b. at this point, it might be countered that while it might not make *sense* to engage in such an activity as pregnancy, this is in itself proof that maternity is indeed an instinct: it is an activity engaged in, in spite of its being contrary to the interests of the agent.

(It is easy to see how nicely this argument feeds the theory of innate masochism into female psychology. The institutional strangleholds that coerce women into childbearing are always overlooked here, but it is in fact these institutions that transform the alleged maternal instinct from what would appear to be a kind of death wish into an instinct for her own political survival.)

It is claimed then that women enjoy having or, at least, wish to have children. The evidence is against this, too.

1. does anyone wish to try to hold that the blood-curdling screams that can be heard from delivery rooms are really cries of joy?

2. how are you going to account for the fact that as much as two-thirds of the women bearing children suffer post-partum blues, and that these depressions are expressed in large numbers by these women killing their infants, or deserting them, or internalizing their hostility to such an extent that the women must be confined in mental hospitals for "severe depression" (often a euphemism for attempted murder). Either it's necessary to fall back on some physiological explanation which will irrevocably damage the claim that childbear-

ing is good for a woman's health, or it's necessary to admit that an overwhelming number of women do not *like* to bear children regardless of whether or not there is some theory that it is a woman's natural function to bear children.

3. as for women wishing to possess children, it will be necessary to account for the fact that parents (and we all know who that is) are the second-highest cause of children's deaths ("accidents" rank first). If the theory is still maintained that women by their nature like to have, or take care of, children, and that this constitutes at least a necessary part of what is called "maternal instinct," it would seem that it is the duty of men, i.e., society, to protect children from women's care just because of this instinct.

c. it seems clear that there is far too large a body of counterevidence to try to maintain any biological theory of maternal instinct.

2. in vaginal orgasm, the supportive biological theory is that the institution of sexual intercourse is in the interests of woman's sexual instinct. The argument goes something like this: man has a sexual instinct, and we know this because men like to have sexual intercourse so much. Since male desire for sexual intercourse is not determined by the recipient, it must be the activity itself which is desired. The activity is defined essentially as the penetration by the penis into the vagina. But the man may have an intense experience, called "orgasm," caused by some activity of his own within the particular environment of the vagina. The completion of his experience, or orgasm, is indicated by certain signs, e.g., ejaculation. This experience has been judged by society to be pleasurable.

The environment of the vagina is necessary for sexual intercourse. Either a woman must be forced to provide this environment or it must be in her interests to do so. It's illegal to force her: that's called rape.[7] Therefore, it must be in her interest to provide this environment. Therefore, it must be that she experiences the same experience that the man does because of the same activity. This will be called "vaginal orgasm" to distinguish it from the original sense of "orgasm," i.e., male orgasm. And it is pleasurable for the woman. If it is the same experience as the male orgasm, there should be no discrepancy between either the amount or conditions of the experience. Therefore, woman also has a sexual instinct.

    a. the maternal instinct is obviously too indirect an interest to justify sexual intercourse to a free woman. There has to be some direct connection between the act and the woman's interests. As exterior coercion lessens, it must be projected inside the victim.

    b. the construct of vaginal orgasm as even a second-order biological need for women has been absurd from the beginning. First of all, animals don't have this need, that is, they don't have vaginal orgasm. The whole point of vaginal orgasm is that it supports the view that vaginal penetration, i.e., a necessary condition of the institution of sexual intercourse, is in the direct interests of women. Since a necessary condition for a biological need is that it cover the genus of living beings, the fact that animals do not experience vaginal orgasm is an extremely strong argument against its biological nature. Secondly, women don't possess the receptors in the vagina for any sensations that could *cause* anything like a male orgasm, that is, what has been proposed as vaginal orgasm.

B. Both the construct of marriage and the construct of vaginal orgasm contain conveniently supportive

<hr />

[7] [A wife cannot legally be said to have been "raped" by her husband. Only if a husband were to hold his wife down while *another* man raped her, could the wife's husband be included in a rape charge.

The construct of vaginal orgasm is the substitute coercion for the laws making up the construct of marriage.]

psychological theories to justify the institution of sexual intercourse to the female. These psychological theories are dependent on their respective physiological theories; without the biological basis, the psychological theory, instead of justifying, exposes the exploitative nature of the institution of sexual intercourse.

1. in marriage, the psychological theory is an analysis of the psychological characteristics inherent in the alleged maternal instinct. This varies somewhat from time to time depending on what sacrifices society deems necessary from the parents to keep the child in line, and how the political system needs, or regards as a liability, women in the outside world. The main constants are that a woman, i.e., a mother, whether actual or potential, is adaptable and giving. It is the woman's role in marriage to meet the needs of others, and her joy to do so. But in the circular argument of the marriage construct, the woman's role is called her will and from there is transformed into her essential nature.

2. in vaginal orgasm, the psychological theory is based on the assumption of the physiological fact of vaginal orgasm, and the further assumption that that orgasm is *caused,* not psychologically but physiologically, by the penetration of the penis into the vagina. There is an equivocation at this point in the argument for the theory that even further assumes that what was defined by a male as vaginal orgasm is analogous to the orgasm the male experiences by penetration. It is only by claiming some such responsive equivalence that the institution of sexual intercourse can be justified between free parties.

19

II

So far here, sexual intercourse has been referred to as an *institution.* Since our society has never known a time when sex in all its aspects was not exploitative and relations based on sex, e.g., the male–female relationship, were not extremely hostile, it is difficult to understand how sexual intercourse can even be salvaged as a *practice,* that is, assuming that our society would desire positive relationships between individuals.

The first step that would have to be taken before we could see exactly what the status of sexual intercourse is as a *practice* is surely to remove all its institutional aspects: we would have to eliminate the *functional* aspect. Sexual intercourse would have to cease to be society's *means* to population renewal. This change is beginning to be within our grasp with the work now being done on extrauterine conception and incubation. But the possibilities of this research for the Women's Movement have been barely suggested and there would have to be very concentrated research to perfect as quickly as possible this extrauterine method of prenatal development so that this could be a truly *optional* method, at the very least.

This step alone would reduce sexual intercourse, in terms of its political status, to a practice. But the biological theories as well as the psychological ones would fall with the institutional purposes: sexual "drives" and "needs" would disappear with their *functions.* But since a practice must have some sort of structure, and without a social function sexual relations would be individually determined and socially unpatterned, sexual intercourse could not be a practice either.

It is necessary to at least speculate on just what the status or place of sexual relations would be once the institutional aspects disappeared. If for no other reason, it is necessary to figure out some sort of projection because an idea like this frightens people so badly. Because of the implications of such a change, people must have some idea of a possible future. It should still be understood, however, that such projections must be very tentative guesswork because so many possible variables could appear later that can't be foreseen now.

Having lost their political function, one possibility is that perhaps we could discover what the nature of the human sensual characteristics are from the point of view of the good of each individual instead of what we have now which is a sort of psychological draft system of our sexualities. Perhaps the human sensual characteristics would have the status of a sense organ; they might even properly be called a sort of "sixth sense." This sense organ, like the other five, would receive stimuli via the brain and the more direct contact appropriate to that sense. In the case of the sexual organs (although they would probably not be called that anymore since the term "sexual organs" assumes two sexes: the purpose of transforming that distinction into a definitive property has been the procreative function of the sexual organs), the direct stimuli would be tactile and the indirect stimuli would be the thought of someone or something that you would like to touch or be touched by.

Now, for the sake of the argument, let's assume that the direct stimulus is a living being, even a human being, and that this human being is other than the human being stimulated. If the procreative function of the activity is absent even in the concept of the activity (that is, it is not regarded as a practice since it is not a structured activity), why should there be this tactile contact with another person? We assume at this point that sexual contact is not a biological need and was formerly only the means to satisfy the social need of survival of the species.

It will be argued, no doubt, that this tactile contact is pleasurable. But what exactly is meant by this? Why is it more pleasurable than auto-contact? In whose interest is this physical contact between two persons, and what are the grounds of this interest? If masturbation has such strong arguments in its favor (assuming the sexual organs are a kind of sense organ) such as technical proficiency, convenience, egocentricity, on what grounds is an outside party involved? On what grounds is this party a positive addition to the experience?

Must this alleged pleasure be mutual? and if so, why? What motivates the desire to touch other people? Without the procreative function of sex, what would distinguish (for the average person) touching a child and touching an adult in whom one had an alleged "sexual" interest? Would you want to make an important distinction between an erotic and a sexual contact? Isn't it crucial, to the argument for tactile contact as innately pleasurable, whether or not you can hold the claim that touching the other person is directly pleasurable to the toucher, not only indirectly pleasurable to the toucher by witnessing the pleasure of the touched? How could it be claimed that the fingertips are as sensitive as the alleged erogenous areas of the body? Or would you have to establish some separate-but-equal synchronized system of mutual indirect/direct stimuli? But wouldn't that force you back into a practice? And under what justification? Wouldn't you be institutionalizing sex again? Given the nature of sex, once you de-institutionalize it and it has no social function, and there is no longer any need for a cooperative effort, and when the physical possibilities of this sense can be fully realized alone, on what possible grounds could you have anything remotely like what we know today as "sexual relations"?

III

If the sense of touch alone were under discussion, it would be surely less complicated simply because there would be only one, in any way relevant to our discussion, fluctuating (i.e., changeable) party. And even more important to any ethical consideration, it wouldn't matter whether the touched wished to be touched. (The constructs of marriage and of vaginal orgasm as supportive practices to the institution of sexual intercourse are both based on the assumption that "it wouldn't matter whether or not the touched wished to be touched." The construct of vaginal orgasm differs from marriage only in that the coercive aspect is internalized in the female.)

The important distinction between "the sense of touch" and what is being called here the "sixth sense," the "sense of *being* touched," or the "sense of feeling" is the addition of a strong passive element. Since what is being received cannot be a technical or physical improvement on that same auto-experience, any positive external component must be a psychological component. It must be some attitude or judgment held by the person doing the touching, or the agent, about the person being touched. This attitude is satisfactory to the person being touched most of the time and at other times is supportive to the person being touched. In short, the agent is trusted to either add to or to reinforce and diffuse the pleasure of the sensual experience.

The contribution of the agent is firstly to extend the area of the sensual experience in the quite literal way of touching the recipient's body and being touched by it. This reinforces the auto-erotic senses by extending the feelings of pleasure and of well being. The second, more important, contribution is that the recipient must make a psychological extension from the agent touching and giving pleasure and the attitude of good will the recipient deduces from that action to the outside world and its attitude toward the recipient. The extension of the recipient's intention for its own pleasure to the world's intentions toward the recipient must be at least one good motive for the socialization of the sensual experience.

IV

The most difficult component to define in this projected, seemingly gratuitous, co-operative act is the psychological attitude of the participants each to the other. What is it about this psychological attitude, the two attitudes together transmitted through various physical contact being the relationship, that could render the two-party experience

1. relevant to what is essentially an independent experience, and
2. an improvement upon such an independent experience.

The first step might be to determine what the components of such a cooperative experience would be: two individuals and their respective erotic sensibilities. Since neither individual can *add* to the physical experience of the other, it must be that the contribution is a mental one, that it consists of the agent forming certain concepts and expressing these concepts in statements to the recipient. These statements, or thoughts, are not translated into a verbal medium but into a medium of gestures (or physical actions). These gestures are most fully understood when they are received directly, that is in physical contact, by the person to whom they are addressed. This is because of the nature of the language, that it is not primarily heard but *felt* through being touched.

The most plausible explanation for a theory of cooperative sensual experience is probably some theory of psychic language, that is, a mime expressive of the agent's attitude toward the recipient and transcribed into gestures appropriate to a particular experience. (It must be remembered that this is the roughest sketch of some alternatives to institutionalized sex.) Some account must be given of this language which would be common to many different cultural languages, such as, that it is emotive, that it is expressed by touch, et cetera. Some account must be given of its structure, perhaps whether or not some attitudes are required or some emotions must be expressed before someone could claim the use of the language. Some account must be given of how the concept of style is relevant to the language; for example, at what point do you have a dialect? and, what would count as a metaphor?

The agent is present to convey certain feelings. Assuming a healthy relationship, it's probably safe to say that these feelings would be positive toward the recipient. But what would "positive" mean? It would have to satisfy the recipient, since the gesture would be received by that person and simultaneously interpreted. But why would such feelings have to be expressed by touching instead of verbally? What is significant about the connection between certain emotions and the sense of touch? But most important, what is the significance of this combination to the recipient?

How is the expression of approval related to the sensual experience? It must mean something that it is a joining of extreme examples of the public (approval being a conventional judgment) and of the private (the auto-erotic). It must be that this mime has a symbolic aspect, and that in this essentially private act the outside participant expresses by its presence an identification with the recipient's feelings for itself. This could serve as a reinforcement to the ego and to a generalization from the attitude of the agent (toward the recipient) to the attitude of the public as a whole (toward the recipient).

These are only a few suggestions. Our understanding of the sense of feeling, or intuition, is almost nonexistent, and few people probably even realize that there is such a sense. It is as if our understanding of the sense of sight were modeled on the experience of being punched in the eye instead of on experiences such as seeing a Tunisian watercolor by Paul Klee. One might infer the possibility of assault from the art but not the possibility of art from the assault. We are unfortunately in the latter position, and there's not much hope of inferring an understanding of the sense of feeling from the institution of sexual intercourse. It has to be approached from some other direction. I have tried to suggest a possibility.

JUNIATA I

THE SACRIFICIAL LAMBS[1]

I had a very difficult time bringing myself to write this speech. Since I usually enjoy figuring out just the right presentation of the issues in feminism to a new kind of group, and since a college group is no doubt the least threatening audience I've ever had to face, I have spent most of the time I would normally spend developing a special approach and language for you in trying to figure out why I was having trouble beginning work on it at all. In discussing my hesitations with several other radical feminists, one woman suggested that the most likely method for my making feminism in some way personal and meaningful to you would be for me to bring my difficulties of exposition before you and take them and feminism wherever they might lead us.

Before I continue I should add that I am addressing this speech primarily to the women in the audience. It's the only way I could possibly be effective. I am a woman. I am a feminist. I see the problem of women from the woman's point of view. Women who empathize with the male role, that is, women who grasp the male point of view more than momentarily, are not feminists.

The point of speaking before a group, as opposed to the members of that group reading what that person has published, is for the speaker to reach the audience in some personal way. The men in the audience will have to try to understand what I am saying from an oblique angle.

Feminism[2] is usually not relevant to any woman before she has left college. If it is, she is probably technically a lesbian, that is, she has recognized that the male role is maintained at her expense, and she turns her back on it. The lesbian solution to the problem of women is to evade it, that is, to opt for an apolitical solution. Feminism is, of course, a political position. When the term is used in any pure sense, it refers to the view that women form a class and that this class is political in nature, that is, to some degree artificial. Feminism means that the class of women was created for exploitative purposes, and that to the degree that women exist, these individuals, that is, these women, are exploited.

I think that feminism must seem irrelevant to women in college because of the particular political function women serve.

25

[1] [February 20, 1969; Juniata College, Huntingdon, Pennsylvania. My first speech at a college.]

[2] ["Feminism" is by definition "radical," so I sometimes use these terms "feminism" and "radical feminism" interchangeably.]

Women, unfortunately for them, are the only reproductive factories science has seen fit to develop. Their political function is to maintain whatever population rate their respective governments, i.e., men, decide is appropriate, to whatever ends that government considers appropriate at that particular moment. A woman's importance is her reproductive function; the "mother" is the most politically, socially, and economically catered to woman in our society. God help her when she's passed her fertile years; not only does she cease being a mother, but there is reluctance to define her as even a woman. The college girl, or any woman prior to her early twenties, is money in the bank, and the Man is not about to blow it. Try comparing the young woman's treatment with that of the darling little pickaninnies of the plantation; the whip was rarely applied before the black became serviceable.

Before a woman leaves college she has had very few crudely overt signs of the exploitation and oppression of women, and for good reason, "good" that is, naturally, in the interests of the oppressor. Looking back now I can see certain clues I had myself, such as a certain vagueness about my future in relationship to my studies. Somehow, my studies seemed in some ways a kind of exercise, but it became increasingly unclear what I was exercising *for*.

Finally in an hysterical state of ennui, I decided to get married. But please don't misunderstand me. My husband was very good to me; I had known him for several years; he had finished college and was on his way to graduate school. But I did have this feeling of despair, of closing the door on my life. What has since that time taken on for me a political significance is that I remember quite clearly that at the time there was no mental alternative for me to marriage. If I left the institution[3] of the family, it could only be to the institution of marriage. If I had been a boy with my particular spirit for adventure, no doubt I would have left home and wandered about the world for a bit; I would have lived as I could and where I liked. But because I was a woman, with the female role obliterating any human possibility I might have, leaving the family or the daughter role left one alternative: wife or prostitute. What I saw as my life and destiny at 17 intuitively, I see now to be, in popular phraseology, the "correct analysis." A woman by definition has no life, no destiny, no identity. The woman of the twentieth century has no hope, for She has no future. The twentieth-century woman is in what our motherfucking-loving sociologists call "transition": from death to death. She was dead as the functional coordinate between father and son, and, to the degree that any human being of the future is human, it will not be able to be called "woman."

I can understand now why I dreaded coming here. It's easier to speak before a

---

3 [In this speech, I use "institution" in the popular sense without applying the more careful distinctions I made in *The Institution of Sexual Intercourse*, pp. 13–23.]

convention of psychiatrists because we're running a sophisticated game on each other, and feminism has an old debt to settle with psychoanalytic theory; it's easier to speak to women in their thirties and forties because they know the score and it's all a matter of figuring out the solutions and coasting downhill.

But there is no game for me here, nor I think are you likely to know the score. I feel as if I'm speaking to myself as I was ten years ago, and I don't want to remember how I was tricked, how I thought that I was at the beginning of my *real* life, of what it was to be a woman: to be loved, and to have a life of a kind of elaborate fun. I don't want to remember the game that was run on me ten years ago and be forced to compare the promise I was made then in exchange for my humanity with the reality I now see in place of that promise. What I feared in coming here was to see myself from before, bewildered and compelled, and to feel again the bitterness and hate for the injustice done to me and my kind, women.

I felt in coming here that it was analogous to campaigning for a bill soon to appear before the legislature on the prevention of cruelty to animals. My audience is as if made up of lambs about to be led to the slaughter; the lambs have been led to believe that it is part of their divine destiny to be the stars of their culture's religious rites, while in reality it is their divine destiny to be the traditional dish for Sunday dinner.

What I am trying to say is that feminism, thank God for your sake, is not quite yet relevant for you, and that I am not at all convinced that to come here to tell you about it can, first of all, possibly be comprehended, and second, to the degree you do understand feminism, I'm not sure that it is in your present interests to understand its issues.

I would like to ask the women in the audience to raise their hands now in appropriate response to my two questions:

1. how many of you plan to marry within the next two years? and
2. how many of you plan to marry as part of your future?

Why, then, those of you who plan to marry, did you come to college? Don't you realize it's against your interests? What does going to college have to do with getting married?

Women usually respond in answer to this question that education develops them as human beings, so that they can enjoy their lives more. But first, it's not clear that education does develop humanness; at best, it develops the student's intelligence and, usually, simply tacks on some pieces of information to the individual's prior store of information, none of which, incidentally, is necessarily in the interests of what we like to think of as humane capacities. But second, and more important, in what way is education relevant to the female role? Maybe instruction in cooking, diaper-changing, or sexual intercourse would be relevant but hardly the *study* of any subject by definition outside the female role such as art history, literature, economics, or, God forbid, philosophy. The serious "study" of any subject with the exception of "how to destroy any characteristics that could possibly resemble the human" is off-limits to women by their definition, and the confusion of roles is undoubtedly the cause of the high rate of mental breakdowns among college-educated women.

It has always fascinated me that when you pose a feminist question to men and women the answer is usually divided by the class difference. In reply to the question "Why bother to educate women?" men usually reply that they'll make better mothers. And when this line of reasoning is pursued and the men are asked how and what college courses are relevant to mothering, they usually, when pushed to the wall, reply "psychology." Now it is certainly not clear that even professional psychologists have contributed much if anything to the mental stability of the population, old or young, so that the thesis that a couple of courses in psychology will make a better mother is hardly plausible. This theory is, however, interesting, as are so many of men's theories, in that it reveals the maliciousness of their intentions toward women.

Women do have at least a perverted human potential. Their attitudes and behavior toward others depend primarily on their feelings about themselves. Psychology is the last place women can develop an attitude of self-respect toward themselves. And, moreover, the question has been left unasked whether motherhood itself is by its nature a self-respecting role or occupation. Why should pregnancy, with all the distortion of the body, discomfort and pain, particularly endear the resulting child to that particular woman? And if it did, then surely the fact of post-partum blues in two-thirds of women after childbirth and the incredibly high rate at which women are killing their children, just now being investigated under the "battered child syndrome," would be fatal counterevidence to the maternal instinct. If being a mother is so wonderful, why are women rejecting the fact so violently? It is not the hired nurse who is murdering the infants in her charge, but the mother, perhaps because the nurse had some small degree of choice in her occupation.

But it's fascinating to study the problem of women from the point of view of what men say women like. It's something like Stokely Carmichael said: it's the people in power who make up the definitions, and they sure aren't going to make them up in *your* interests. When women seem fuzzy on some political issue or institution relevant to themselves, it's always enlightening to ask and hear the response of the male wrap-up, and it's always clear. The only reservation I would suggest is you need a strong stomach for that kind of truth.

For instance, ask a man sometime what it means to be a woman. Or try to be serious in some professional field sometime and maintain serious discussions with the men in that field and you won't even have to ask any questions, they'll tell you. Your definition *is* that you're a woman and your function is to either get knocked up or to get laid. If you make it clear that this definition is unacceptable, which is almost impossible to make clear over any period of time, then your other function is to be ignored. (In a field such as philosophy which I know, alas, intimately, the lack of serious discursive relationships with colleagues is almost fatal intellectually.) Intellectual development in a woman, or any kind of self-development, is of value to men only insofar as it is an addition to her value as a sexual object, like big breasts, only of course it is understood that big breasts are much more important to sexiness than a Ph.D. And there is no question that intelligence in a woman is a liability to any sexual relationship. So that my earlier comment that a Ph.D. might be of some sexual value would not of course hold if the woman were also intelligent.

Men often claim that it is women who want to be married, and this is usually said as some sort of justification and with the implication that if it had been up to Him, and at this point you're treated to a deprecating leer, there wouldn't be any marriage. As with so much that men say, there is a great deal of truth in this. If it were up to men there probably wouldn't be marriage—witness the New Left—and it is also true that it is women who usually insist on the legal contract. What is not mentioned, however, is that men want and demand, one way or another, all the services from women that the legal marriage contract is payment for, and like any free enterpriser, if he can get these services for nothing, so much the more profit for him.

I am not going to go through my usual analysis of the problem of women, which is a breakdown and unpacking of the particular social institutions peculiar to women. I think that if you have not been married, or had a family, or come across a certain number of men in some way such as any woman of 25 and over has, that this analysis would have no meaning for you. You have to have picked up the pattern for yourself to recognize its description. If you are interested in this kind of analysis I suppose I have done more of it than any other feminist in this country. Some of it has been published and more of it is coming out soon. Simone de Beauvoir's *The Second Sex* is undoubtedly the definitive work on women. For those of you who know you want to begin your own study into the problem of women, I would suggest *The Second Sex,* a good history of the feminist movement such as Eleanor Flexner's *Century of Struggle,* Valerie Solanas' *SCUM Manifesto,* and the latest publications from the Citizens' Advisory Council on the Status of Women.

For some reason quite suspect to me at this time, many people just love to hear the statistics proving women are oppressed, such as that the average white man makes over half again as much as the average black man, and that the average white woman makes slightly over half that of the average black man and slightly over one-quarter of that of the average white man, and that the average black woman makes slightly less than the average white woman. That the percentage of women going to graduate school now is less than that going forty years ago. And so on and so forth.

But since the average woman I've met is well aware that she is desperate, this numbers game seems pretty trivial to me at this point. And since none of these studies have been done by feminists, that is, people in whose interest it is to muckrake, I have a pretty good idea that the studies that will be done on such items as mental health studies on women,[4] and more detailed studies and breakdowns of the battered child syndrome, will convince society, that is, men, that the oppression of women amounts to a public health hazard, that is, subriotous conditions, and that to get its own ass out of a sling society had better get off the backs of women. I am a great believer in self-interest and the inspiration it can give to philanthropy.

As far as other theoretical work that might be helpful to a better understanding of feminism, I don't think there is any. The issue of women challenges all of political philosophy. Since the oppression of women is generally agreed to be the beginning of the class system and women the first exploited class, every culture or institution or value developed since that time contains that oppression as a major foundational ingredient and renders all political constructs after that initial model of human oppression at the very least suspect. This would include the family, sexual intercourse, motherhood or the concept of functionalism, love, the appearance structure of the male/female role system, marriage. Of course all religious structures are built on and dependent upon the oppression of women. Most of political philosophy is irrelevant to women and irrelevant philosophy because of this omission.

I thought that toward the end of my statement one of the best ways of reaching you on feminism and giving you some sense of your true position in society would be to recount some of my own recent experiences with feminism and women in colleges:

I. *Linda LeClair.* As you may know I am a graduate student in philos-

4 [Phyllis Chesler, *Women and Madness* (Doubleday, 1972), scratched the surface.]

30

ophy at Columbia University. Until there was a split in the feminist movement in October of last year, I was president of the New York chapter of the National Organization for Women, the first and until recently the largest civil-rights group for women in this country. We had made repeated efforts to organize Barnard as well as other coeds with no more success than the earlier feminist movement had had with women under 21. The issues we had been pushing on campuses were those such as equal educational opportunities; equal employment benefits; establishment of university-run nurseries; abolition of nepotism rules; academic reform; equalization of all dormitory hours; sign-out requirements and social regulations; integration of student facilities; equality of initiative and responsibility in dating; sex equalization or abolition of the draft; birth control.

Linda LeClair appeared on the front pages of newspapers all over the country in the late spring of last year, in the midst of the tail end of the Columbia brawl. Miss LeClair was a student at Barnard; her boyfriend, Peter Behr, was a student at Columbia. Like many of her classmates, Linda LeClair was living with her boyfriend off campus. Miss LeClair had filled out a Barnard residence card, giving a false address, which was known to be part of the game at Barnard since they have the *in loco parentis* system. Unlike the many other students at Barnard exercising similar individual rights, Linda LeClair and one other student there appeared in the slightest of disguises (after being promised virtual anonymity) on the women's page of the *New York Times* as part of the new wave of emancipated students. Curiously enough, I mean by this that I'm not clear just what the connections were, one of the stodgiest members of the Barnard Trustees is Mrs. Arthur Hays Sulzberger, wife of the chairman of the board of the *New York Times,* and by rumor one of the most vehement and unrelenting seekers after Linda's blood. Barnard's administration asked Linda to leave quietly, or I believe it was put something to the effect that she would probably be happier someplace else. Linda decided that she would stick it and demanded a hearing. The general attitude around Barnard at that time was that Linda was being overly dramatic about nothing since the administration was understood to be trying to save face by putting on a little show suggesting that Linda should leave but that it would soon blow over and Linda could stay.

But slowly little facts became known, such as that over the past several years several women *had* left quietly for the same "offense" as Linda's, and that Barnard was bringing Linda before Barnard's Judicial Council. I had brought the matter before my organization and asked two members of the Executive Committee, who also happened to be members of the Barnard faculty, to do something for Miss LeClair for us. But I too had underestimated how seriously Barnard was taking this case. The Barnard administration brought considerable pressure on all the members of my organization at either Barnard or Columbia with the exception of myself, and without my knowledge, so that the LeClair case was without any kind of organizational support until I caught on that something was wrong and took care of things myself some few days before the hearing.

The Barnard Council found Linda LeClair guilty but recommended the punishment of not eating with the other girls and not going to the Barnard dances. I felt that the judges should have found Linda not guilty by virtue of the unfairness of the law she was being held to. Furthermore, the penalty assigned, while I understand it was considered witty, struck me as rather unwholesome. It confused sex and food and reminded me of a throwback to a kind of nineteenth-century ostracism of the female pariah who becomes, by her act, recognized by none and touchable by all. I was uncomfortable because I am not convinced we have left behind the nineteenth century on women, but my uneasiness was not shared by others.

Martha Peterson, the Barnard president, has veto power over penalties passed on by the Barnard Judicial Council, although this veto power was said never to have been used. The veto power is only over the penalty and its severity, but I'm not sure that, if it had been necessary, it wouldn't have somehow been extended to the verdict as well. Martha Peterson would not accept the penalty, noting, profoundly, that it was absurd. She further let it be known that she planned to expel Linda, that the judicial panel needed some reviewing itself as to its structure, and that, although not in these exact words, house niggers who don't know how to play "house" *properly,* won't be allowed to play "house" at all anymore.

From my point of view of organizing women, nothing better could have happened. All the self-righteous ladies who had theretofore been, in my view, extremely petty about Linda's culpability were suddenly struck with profound insight and comprehension into the problem of women. They immediately organized a housing committee and arranged to meet at Barnard; they asked me to be the first speaker. The meeting was, at the last minute, banned from the campus by Barnard's Dean, and I was personally banned as an "outside agitator." We held the meeting in the religious hall at Columbia, my own "foreign" base of operations across the street from Barnard. Dormitories were organized, petitions set up, and a strategy planned. Two-thirds of the entire student body at Barnard signed the petition in support of Linda LeClair and the abolishment of the housing regulations. Martha Peterson overruled these too.

You may wonder just how this was a feminist issue and not a student issue. Peter Behr, Linda's boyfriend, was a student at Columbia. Boys' schools do not have the same restrictive housing regulations as do girls' or the same *in loco parentis* attitude. Even within a coed university, the regulations for men and women are frequently different. This is fairly well known.

Where I and everyone else involved in Linda's case misjudged was that we assumed that this inequity was an outdated oversight; we did not understand the powerful political taboos still operant behind these rules. Linda LeClair was stoned in the press; Peter was billed as the cute boy across the street with initiative. Finally, also in the *Times,* an interviewer got Linda's parents to publicly disown her (her father was vice-president of the local bank in a small New Hampshire town). Linda in the end, for all her initial élan, was broken. She finally was allowed to stay at Barnard, but by the time that came through she was too exhausted to cope with the scene in any way.

What came out of it for Barnard women was a premature cold view that if you touch the fence you're "instant nigger." And if any woman crosses over any line of that female role, the uglies are let loose on you, and nobody else is home. For the first time it was possible for coeds to understand the hassle in the United Nations, repeated just a few months before, on the freedom of movement clause in the U.N.'s Declaration on the Elimination of Discrimination Against Women. The denial of freedom of movement rights to women is justified on the grounds that these rights, if granted to women, would destroy the family. But until Linda LeClair, Barnard women thought restriction on this most basic human right to women was limited to South America and Egypt.

Barnard women came to understand that as long as you have women in society, that society cannot have human rights. Not only are coeds denied these rights but, in all but five states in this country, married women are denied full rights of domicile. Lack of domicile rights means that a woman's legal place of residence is wherever her husband chooses to be, and wherever he might go and she not follow would qualify as legal desertion with the appropriate legal penalties. In many countries a woman cannot leave the country without her husband's or father's signature on her visa or passport, and women cannot in some places even journey

out of their villages without written permission from their husbands or fathers. But I don't see any significant difference between our situation without domicile rights and these others.

II. *The Columbia Arrests.* Some fifty-six women were arrested and booked at the 13th Precinct House during the second Columbia bust. Most of these women were Barnard students and of the average age of 19.

One of the S.D.S. girls had mentioned to me in passing after the first bust that the police performed vaginal examinations on those arrested for trespass or disorderly conduct. I was taken aback, as I could see no connection between female trespassing and vaginas. I mentioned this to one of our lawyers, the well-known attorney for lost causes, Florynce Kennedy, and she too was surprised since she said that this humiliating tactic is usually reserved for black women.

I functioned as an observer during the second detention period and, while my presence no doubt prevented the most extreme forms of harassments, the detention period primarily served as yet another unwelcome addition to my education. The policewomen were sadists; like the male police, their function in society seems to be to serve as our Red Guards or terrorist weaponry. And for some psychological reason, the presence of an observer forced the Barnard women to look objectively at what was being done to them. Unlike before, when they didn't seem to have any sense of their being, they were now outraged.

III. *Joan Bird.* I'm not going to try to recreate what happened at the 13th Precinct last spring, partly because I don't think I could make it vivid enough. Instead, I will read you the sworn statement of another girl in New York City, dated January 29, 1969:

"I, JOAN BIRD, being duly sworn, deposes and says:

"That I am 19 years of age, and presently a student at Bronx Community College.

"That on Friday evening, January 17, 1969, at about nine o'clock P.M., I was in a car on Harlem River Drive, New York City, that was approached by police without any provocation. Guns were fired and I remained in the car that was being fired

upon. I did not participate in the gunfire. Then one of the police told me to 'crawl out of that car bitch,' so I proceeded to do as instructed. Then, Patrolman McKenzie said, 'Let me take this—bitch, you better tell me the truth.' At this point McKenzie and another dragged me by my arms, while on the ground on my back. McKenzie then with a short black club beat me across my face and head, at which point I became dizzy; I also noticed that my mouth was bleeding.

"At this time they put handcuffs on me and turned me over face down to the ground and my hands cuffed behind me. Then they began to kick me and walk on my back and legs. Then McKenzie put a gun to my head and stated, 'I ought to kill you, you motherfucker,' then proceeded to take my right-hand fingers and bend them back and said, 'You better talk or I'll break your fingers.' I screamed. Then they were all talking about how they should take me to the woods in the park and shoot me, and nobody would know the difference. I screamed. Then McKenzie and another picked me up and put me into a car.

"On the way to the station house, at about 160th Street and Edgecombe Avenue, McKenzie got out of the car and stopped a black man, and searched him, then put the black man in the car and we proceeded to the 34th Precinct. Then we entered the station house, with the black man. I never saw this man before and I do not know his name, and I never saw him again.

"Then I sat downstairs for about five minutes, seated facing a wall, then I was taken upstairs to another room, filled with what I believed to be plainclothes police. At this time, a tall white plainclothes policeman told me, 'Unless you tell the truth, I will take you upstairs and throw you out the window and it will look like suicide.' This person also stated during the evening that, 'I will stick this size ten up your cunt until it comes out your throat if you don't stop this bullshitting.'

"Also, during the evening, a short, white plainclothes policeman with beige suede shoes, or short boots on, said, 'I'd better say that the others with me beat me up or that I tripped.' Then on the way to an erroneous address I gave them, the cop who stated he would use his 'size ten' stated, 'I'm a bastard and unless you tell the truth I'll show you how much of a bastard I can be.'

"After we returned to the station from the erroneous address, at about 3:30 A.M., a white, short, heavy-set plainclothes policeman with black-rim glasses called me 'bitch' and pushed me against the wall and threatened me with his fist closed, and I screamed, and he said, 'You better shut up, or I'll punch your face in some more.' At this time, about 4:00 A.M., I screamed for my mother, and they let her come in; they did not do anything to me after that point.

"They never asked me if I needed medical attention nor did they allow me to call my attorney. I was not placed under arrest, until 19 hours later. I was told I was being held as a material witness, and they were going to let me go home with my mother. They took me to court at about 12:00 P.M. the next day, after being held all night. I was still not under arrest.

"I finally got to see my attorney, Mr. Arthur F. Turco, Jr., when he arrived at court, 100 Centre Street, New York, at about 3:30 P.M. Saturday. He demanded to see me in private, at which time I told him what had happened to me. Then we were called into the courtroom, at which time the Assistant D.A. asked that I be held in $50,000 bail as a material witness, because my life was in danger. Mr. Turco objected to the bail and demanded my immediate release, it was now 19 hours I was being held. He also questioned by whom my life would be in danger by, the police or my own black people? At this time, the judge called both my attorney and the D.A. to the bench, and he suggested since he could not hold me as a witness that the D.A. should arrest me, which he then did. I was not arraigned until 26 hours after I was picked up."

Next time somebody tries to con you that women are protected, and that the woman is the most idolized and best treated member in our society, you just close your mouth and remember Linda LeClair and Joan Bird. And whatever you do, don't touch the fence. And, oh yes, lie down.

Photo by William David, *The Juniatian*

STATEMENT
BY
TI-GRACE ATKINSON
JUNIATA COLLEGE, FEBRUARY 21, 1969

Last night some 50 boys assaulted the South Hall dormitory where several hundred women were meeting. As far as I could gather from the shouts and pounding against glass and the sign "Atkinson's panties," the boys were attempting a political attack in retaliation for what they seem to view as an attack on their masculinity.

I said yesterday that it was men alone who could convince women that women are a politically oppressed group. The boys last night demonstrated my point. The panty raid mentality cannot in my opinion be dismissed as a meaningless prank. It is clearly sexual and degrading; it reveals the prostitute attitude toward women that many men have. It also, in the case of last night, bears out what I said yesterday, that if you're a woman you'd better not touch the fence. There are only two possible political stances for women: helpless and silent, or sexually assaulted, that is, raped.

I think that women as a political group should have a dialogue with men, but a feminist's first obligation is to women and the raising of women's awareness. In good conscience, I don't believe a feminist can spend time with men who are not ready for civilized verbal behavior. The men at Juniata proved last night that they were not ready, so that I cannot remain here for this discussion with you today.

I do not know which of you were there last night but I suspect that of those of you who were not, most were gratified at their colleagues' behavior. Those of you who reject the panty raid mentality, I suggest you address yourselves to your brothers and try to prepare them for political discussion. I, for one, cannot continue with you until that time.

39

RADICAL FEMINISM AND LOVE[1]

Radical feminism is a new political concept. It evolved in response to the concern of many feminists that there has never been even the beginnings of a feminist analysis of the persecution of women. Until there is such an analysis, no coherent, effective program can be designed to solve the problem. The October 17th Movement[2] was the first radical feminist group, and it has spent a great deal of its first five months working out the structure and details of a causal class analysis.

The analysis begins with the feminist *raison d'être* that women are a class, that this class is political in nature, and that this political class is oppressed. From this point on, radical feminism separates from traditional feminism.

The class of women is one-half of a dichotomized class definition of society by sex. The class of women is formed by positing another class in opposition: the class of men, or the male role. Women exist as the corollaries of men, and exist as human beings only insofar as they are those corollaries.

Without women, men would be limited only as to *re*production, not as to human existence itself. Similarly as women to men, nonwhites could not exist as human beings without the positing of whites. Of course, both the terms "men" and "whites" are role definitions, but that is, after all, what political definitions are all about.[3]

Oppression is an ongoing activity. If women are a political class and women are being oppressed, it must be that some other political class is oppressing the class of women. Since the very definition of women entails that only one other class could be relevant to it, only one other class could possibly be oppressing women: the class of men.

Since it is clear that men oppress women, and since this oppression is an ongoing process, it was clear to radical feminists that women must understand the *dynamics* of their oppression. Men are the *agents* of the oppression of individual women, and these agents use various means to achieve the subordination of their counterclass.

But over thousands of years, men have created and maintained an enclosure of institutionalized oppression to fortify their domination of women by using many insti-

41

---

[1] [April 12, 1969; I was asked to write something special for a feminist issue of the Barnard College newspaper. I have long understood that the only way to reach people on feminism is to go for that aspect that is *their* jugular.

In *Juniata I,* pp. 25–39, I sketch out the problem of reaching women under the age or situation of the major female institutions: marriage, motherhood, prostitution. However, college women are approaching that twilight zone just prior to these major traps: they are about to fall in love. Or they are at least looking to do so.

Voila! Love. The feminist jugular for the college"girl."]
[2] [Later renamed The Feminists.]
[3] The situation is not improved by substituting the biologically functional term "female" for the sociologically functional "woman"—both terms serve essentially political functions.

tutions and values as *vehicles* of oppression, e.g., marriage, family, sexual intercourse, love, religion, prostitution. Women are the *victims* of this oppression.

The class of women[4] has several peculiar political characteristics:

(1) the class of women, or the female role, is generally agreed to be the largest single political class in history

(2) the oppression of the class of women *qua* women is stable historically and similar geographically

(3) the political class of women, or the female role, is generally agreed to be the earliest political class in history, therefore all known cultures are constructed with the oppression of women as the major foundational ingredient (i.e., the class of women is the key functional unit in all of our social, economic, and political institutions and values)

(4) the class of women has been dispersed over time, thereby further suppressing it, throughout later class systems: e.g., chron-

ological, familial, religious, racial, economic.

These special characteristics of the class of women affect the radical feminist analysis in two major directions. First, it is clear that the male and female roles do not comprise a simple class confrontation. While class confrontation, with the consequence of mutually exclusive interests *qua* male and female role interests, is an important element in the dynamics of the oppression of women, it is complicated by the institutions and values, created by men to consolidate their roles as Oppressors. These institutions form unnatural alliances or contracts between men and women against the interests of the victims' basic class identification.

It is in the interests of the Oppressor to "unite" with the Oppressed; the key to maintaining the Oppressor role is to *prevent the Oppressed from uniting.* As long as the Oppressor has some kind of "contract," be it "marriage" or "love," with the Oppressed, he can bring pressure within that private or individual contract, in which he has unequal power because of his political class identification, to keep his subordinate "partner" subordinate. A woman can only change her political definition by organizing with other women to change the definition

---

[4] I distinguish between the "class of women" and the "woman class." The "woman class" refers to what might be called the sex-class or the "s-class": society dichotomized by sex. The class of women, or one half of the s-class, is primarily defined by the s-class.

The class of men is further dichotomized in important political ways, e.g., by color, economics, and so forth.*

An oppressed individual is assigned its role through its primary class dichotomy, thus, from the "s-class" to the "woman class." An oppressed individual also transfers its individual identity to its dichotomy in the context

of other class systems, as in the case of the woman class and the black class.

The "class of women" refers to the class of individual women within the s-class. It is this sense of class that women must deal with first.

* [See my development of class divisions within both the male and female classes in *Juniata II: The Equality Issue*, pp. 65–75.

I distinguish between "identification" classes (within the female class) and "power" classes (within the male class).]

of the female role, eventually eliminating it, thereby freeing herself to be human.

These cross-sexual alliances, because they are definitively inequitable, and because they thus necessarily alienate women from their natural class interest, are antifeminist. The tension created by the male/female role confrontation and the pseudo-alliances across these role interests has the structural appearance of a web of boxes with a single woman trapped in each one. The tension between these two conflicting interests has frustrated the natural consequence of confrontation (the annihilation of the role system) and maintained the oppression of women as stable.

Second, because the class of women is slightly larger than its oppressor class, and because the oppression of women has not been changed significantly either over time or place, it follows that either

(1) women are biologically subhuman and feel, therefore, that they are not oppressed but naturally assume a subordinate role (this explanation is outside any possible feminist interpretation), or that

(2) a large part of the policing of the oppression of women has to be internalized not only into the female role but into the female as well. There has to be a blurring between the biological class of females (a human being with the *capacity* to bear children, *period*) and the sociological class of women (a human being who *must* bear children, *should* rear them, et cetera, the rest of the female role follows from the first point).[5]

Since radical feminists assume that the source of the necessity within the female to maintain the female role lies within the male in his political role as Oppressor, it must be that the internal coercion within the female to maintain the female role is not essentially biological in nature but psychological.

I propose that the phenomenon of love is the psychological pivot in the persecution of women. Because the internalization of coercion must play such a key functional part in the oppression of women due to their numbers alone, and because of the striking grotesqueness of the one-to-one political units "pairing" the Oppressor and the Oppressed, the hostile and the powerless, and thereby severing the Oppressed from any kind of political aid, it is not difficult to conclude that women by definition must exist in a special psycho-pathological state of fantasy both in reference to themselves and to their manner of relating to their counterclass. This pathological condition, considered the most desirable state for any woman to find herself

43

[5] [Reference again as in *Abortion: Paper Number II*, pp. 1–3, and *The Institution of Sexual Intercourse*, pp. 13–23, to the capacity/function distinction.]

in, is what we know as the phenomenon of love.

Because radical feminists consider the dynamics of their oppression the focal point of their analysis, it was obvious that some theory of "attraction" would be needed. Why do women, even feminists, consort with the enemy? For sex? Very few women ever say that; that's the male-role reason. What nearly all women mutter in response to this is: "for love."

I distinguish between "friendship" and "love." "Friendship" is a rational relationship which requires the participation of two parties to the mutual satisfaction of both parties. "Love" can be felt by one party; it is unilateral by nature, and, combined with its relational character, it is thus rendered contradictory and irrational.

There has been very little analytic work done on the notion of "love." This is remarkable, considering the importance of it in ethics and political philosophy. Philosophers usually skirt it or brush it aside by claiming it's "irreducible," or "irrational." Or they smile and claim it's the *"sine qua non."* All these things may be true and are clues to the political significance of "love": it's basic; it's against individual human interest; a great deal rests upon it.

Any theory of attraction could begin with the definition of the verb "to attract": the exertion of a force such as magnetism to draw a person or thing, and susceptibility in the thing drawn. Magnetism is caused by friction or conflict, and the primary relationship between men and women of class confrontation or conflict certainly suffices for the cause of magnetism. Usually the magnetized moves toward the magnet in response to the magnet's power; otherwise the magnetized is immobile.

The woman is drawn to ⟶ attracted by ⟶ desirous of ⟶ in love with ⟶ the man. She is power*less,* he is power*ful.*

The woman is instinctively trying to recoup her definitional and political losses by fusing with the enemy. "Love" is the woman's pitiful deluded attempt to attain the human: by fusing, she hopes to blur the male/female role dichotomy, and that a new division of the human class might prove more equitable. She counts on the illusion she has spun out of herself in order to be able to accept the fusion, to be transferred to the whole and, thus, that the new man will be garbed now equally in her original illusion.

Unfortunately, magnetism depends upon inequity. As long as the inequity stands, the fusion may hold (everything else relevant remaining the same). If the inequity changes, the fusion and the magnetism fall with the inequity.

A woman can unite with a man as long as she is a woman, i.e., subordinate, and no longer. There's no such thing as a "loving" way out of the feminist dilemma: that it is as a *woman* that women are oppressed, and that in order to be free she must shed what keeps her secure.

The October 17th Movement recently devoted one of its meetings to a discussion of "love" and tried to analyze together how this phenomenon operated. The main difficulty was, and was left at, understanding the shift from the woman desiring an alliance with the power*ful* to the woman being *in love with* the man.

It's clear that love has to do with some transitional or relational factor. But from what to what? It is a psychological state the woman feels she must enter into. But why, exactly?

She is going from the political, the power*less* identification, to the individual, one-to-one unit. She is disarming herself to go into the enemy camp.

Is love a kind of hysterical state, a *mind*less state therefore a *pain*less state, into which women retreat when the contradiction between the last shreds of their human survival and the everyday contingencies of being a woman becomes most acute?

Is love a kind of frenzy, or something like a Buddhist immolation, to unite with the One? The love women feel for men is most akin to religious love.

But hysteria might be a more useful paradigm for us since it's limited almost exclusively to women (the word "hysterical" derives from the Greek word for "uterus") and the condition is marked by certain characteristics strikingly similar to those of "love": anxiety converted into functional symptoms of illness, amnesia, fugue, multiple personality.

45

RADICAL FEMINISM

DECLARATION OF WAR[1]

Almanina Barbour, a black militant woman in Philadelphia, once pointed out to me: "The Women's Movement is the first in history with a war on and no enemy." I winced. It was an obvious criticism. I fumbled about in my mind for an answer. Surely the enemy must have been defined at some time. Otherwise, what had we been shooting at for the last couple of years? into the air?

Only two responses came to me, although in looking for those two I realized that it was a question carefully avoided. The first and by far the most frequent answer was "society." The second, infrequently and always furtively, was "men."

If "society" is the enemy, what could that mean? If women are being oppressed, there's only one group left over to be doing the oppressing: men. Then why call them "society"? Could "society" mean the "institutions" that oppress women? But institutions must be maintained, and the same question arises: by whom? The answer to "who is the enemy?" is so obvious that the interesting issue quickly becomes "why has it been avoided?"

The master might tolerate many reforms in slavery but none that would threaten his essential role as master. Women have known this, and since "men" and "society" are in effect synonymous, they have feared confronting him. Without this confrontation and a detailed understanding of what *his* battle strategy[2] has been that has kept us so successfully pinned down, the "Women's Movement" is worse than useless. It invites backlash from men, and no progress for women.

There has never been a feminist analysis. While discontent among women and

47

[1] [April, 1969; written at the request of *MacLean's* magazine (Canada's version of *Life*); rejected as too esoteric; published in *Notes From the Second Year,* Shulamith Firestone and Anne Koedt, eds. (New York: 1970), pp. 32-37.]

[2] [See *Strategy and Tactics: A Presentation of Political Lesbianism,* pp. 135–189, for a fuller development of the concept of "strategy."]

the attempt to resolve this discontent have often implied that women form a class, no political or *causal* class analysis has followed. To rephrase my last point, the persecution of women has never been taken as the starting point for a political analysis of society.

Considering that the last massing of discontent among women continued some 70 years (1850-1920) and spread the world and that the recent accumulation of grievances began some three years ago here in America, the lack of a structural understanding of the problem is at first sight incomprehensible. It is the understanding of the *reasons* for this devastating omission and of the *implications* of the problem that forces one to "radical feminism."

Women who have tried to solve their problems as a class have proposed not solutions but dilemmas. The traditional feminists want equal rights for women with men. But on what grounds? If women serve a different *function* from men in society, wouldn't this necessarily affect women's "rights"? For example, do *all* women have the "right" not to bear children? Traditional feminism is caught in the dilemma of demanding equal treatment for unequal functions, because it is unwilling to challenge political (functional) classification by sex.

Radical women, on the other hand, grasp that women as a group somehow fit into a political analysis of society, but err in refusing to explore the significance of the fact that women form a class, the uniqueness of this class, and the implications of this description to the system of political classes. Both traditional feminists and radical women have evaded questioning any part of their *raison d'être:* women are a class, and the terms that make up this initial assumption must be examined.

The feminist dilemma is that it is as women—or "females"—that women are persecuted, just as it was as slaves—or "blacks"—that slaves were persecuted in America. In order to improve their condition, those individuals who are today defined as women must eradicate their own definition. Women must, in a sense, commit suicide, and the journey from womanhood to a society of individuals is hazardous. The feminist dilemma is that we have the most to do, and the least to do it with. We must create, as no other group in history has been forced to do, from the very beginning.

The "battle of the sexes" is a commonplace, both over time and distance. But it is an inaccurate description of what has been happening. A "battle" implies some balance of powers, whereas when one side suffers all the losses, such as in some kinds of raids (often referred to as the "rape" of an area), that is called a *massacre*. Women have been massacred as human beings over history, and this destiny is entailed by their definition. As women begin massing together, they take the first step from *being* massacred to *engaging in* battle (resistance). Hopefully, this will eventually lead to negotiations—in the *very* far future—and peace.

When any person or group of persons is being mistreated or, to continue our metaphor, is being attacked, there is a succession of responses or investigations

(1) depending on the severity of the attack (short of an attack on life), the victim determines how much damage was done and what it was done with

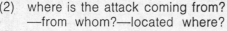

(2) where is the attack coming from? —from whom?—located where?

(3) how can you win the immediate battle?—defensive measures? —holding actions?

(4) why did he attack you?

(5) how can you win (end) the war? —offensive measures. —moving within his boundaries.

These first five questions are necessary but should be considered diplomatic maneuvers. They have never been answered by the so-called "Women's Movement," and for this reason I think one cannot properly call that Movement "political." It could not have had any direction relevant to women as a class.

If diplomacy fails, that is, if your enemy refuses to stop attacking you, you must force him to stop. This requires a strategy, and this strategy requires a map of the relevant landscape, including such basic information as

(1) who is the enemy?

(2) where is he located?

(3) is he getting outside support? — material? —manpower? —from whom?

(4) where are his forces massed?

(5) what's the best ammunition to knock them out?

(6) what weapons is he using?

(7) how can you counteract them?

(8) what is your plan of attack on him to force diplomatic negotiations? —program of action (including priorities). —techniques.

I am using some military terminology, and this may seem incongruous. But why should it? We accept the phrase "battle of the sexes." It is the proposal that *women* fight *back* that seems incongruous. It has been necessary to program women's psychic structure to nonresistance on their own behalf—for obvious reasons—they make up over half the population of the world.

Without a programmatic analysis, the "Women's Movement" has been as if running blindly in the general direction of where they *guess* the last missile that just hit them was based. For the first two years of the last organizing, I was very active in this running-blind approach. It's true that we were attacking evils, but why *those* particular evils? Were they the central issues in the persecution of women? There was no map so I couldn't be sure, but I could see no reason to believe that we knew what the key issues were, much less that we were hitting them.

It became increasingly clear to me that we were incorporating many of our external problems (e.g., power hierarchies)[3] into our own movement, and in understanding this and beginning to ask myself some of the obvious questions I've listed above, I came to the conclusion that at this time the most radical *action* that any woman or group of women could take was a feminist analysis. The implications of such an analysis is a greater threat to the opposition to human rights for women than all the actions and threatened actions put together up until this time by women.

With this introduction to the significance of a feminist analysis, I will outline what we have so far.

As I mentioned before, the *raison d'être* of all groups formed around the problem of women is that women are a class.

[3] [See *Resignation from N.O.W.*, pp. 9–11.]

What is meant by that? What is meant by "women" and what is meant by "class"?

Does "women" include all women? Some groups have been driven back from the position of *all* women to some proposed "special" class such as "poor" women and eventually concentrated more on economic class than sexual class.[4] But if we're interested in women and how women *qua* women are oppressed, this class must include *all* women.

What separates out a particular individual from other individuals as a "woman"? We recognize it's a sexual separation and that this separation has two aspects, "sociological" and "biological." The term for the sociological function is "woman" (wifman); the term for the biological function is "female" (to suckle). Both terms are descriptive of functions in the interests of someone other than the possessor.

And what is meant by "class"? We've already briefly covered the meaning as the characteristic by which certain individuals are grouped together. In the "Women's Movement" or "feminism," individuals group together to *act* on behalf of women as a class in opposition to the *class* enemies of women. It is the interaction between classes that defines political action. For this reason I call the feminist analysis a *causal class analysis*.

We have established that women are a political class characterized by a sexual function. It is clear that women, at the present time at any rate, have the *capacity* to bear children. But the question arises: "how did this biological classification become a political classification?"[5] How or why did this elaborate superstructure of coercion develop on top of a capacity (which normally implies choice)?

[4] [See footnote 4 in *Radical Feminism and Love*, p. 42.]

[5] [Back to functionalism versus a capacity theory. See *Abortion: Paper Number II*, pp. 1–3, and *The Institution of Sexual Intercourse*, pp. 13–23.]

It is generally agreed that women were the first political class. (Children do not properly constitute a political class since the relevant characteristic of its members [namely, age] is unstable for any given member by definition.) "Political" classes are usually defined as classes treated by other classes in some special manner distinct from the way other classes are treated. What is frequently omitted is that "political" classes are *artificial;* they define persons *with* certain capacities *by* those capacities, changing the contingent to the necessary, thereby appropriating the *capacities* of an individual as a *function* of society. (Definition of "political class" = individuals grouped together by other individuals as a function of the grouping individuals, depriving the grouped individuals of their human status.) A "function" of society cannot be a free individual: exercising the minimal human rights of physical integrity and freedom of movement.

If women were the first political class, and political classes must be defined by individuals outside that class, who defined them, and why, and how? It is reasonable to assume that at some period in history the population was politically undifferentiated; let's call that mass "Mankind" (generic).

The first dichotomous division of this mass is said to have been on the grounds of sex: male and female. But the genitals *per se* would be no more grounds for the human race to be divided in two than skin color or height or hair color. The genitals, in connection with a particular activity, have the *capacity* for the initiation of the reproductive process. But, I submit, it was because one half the human race bears the *burden* of the reproductive *process* and be-

53

cause man, the "rational" animal, had the wit to take advantage of that that the childbearers, or the "beasts of burden," were corralled into a political class. The biologically contingent burden of childbearing was equivocated into a political (or necessary) penalty, thereby modifying those individuals' definition thereby defined from the human to the functional—or animal.

There is no justification for using any individual as a function of others. Didn't *all* members of society have the right to decide if they even *wanted* to reproduce? Because one half of humanity was and still is forced to bear the burden of reproduction at the will of the other half, the first political class is defined not by its sex—sexuality was only relevant originally as a means to reproduction—but by the function of being the *container* of the reproductive process.

Because women have been taught to believe that men have protective feelings toward women (men have protective feelings toward their functions [property], *not* other human beings!), we women are shocked by these discoveries and ask ourselves *why* men took and continue to take advantage of us.

Some people say that men are naturally, or biologically, aggressive. But this leaves us at an impasse. If the values of society are power-oriented, there is no chance that men would agree to be medicated into an humane state.

The other alternative that has been suggested is to eliminate men as biologically incapable of humane relationships and therefore a menace to society. I can sympathize with the frustration and rage that leads to this suggestion.

But the proposal to eliminate men, as I understand it, assumes that men constitute a kind of social disease, and that by "men" is meant those individuals with certain typical genital characteristics. These genital characteristics are held to determine the organism in every biochemical respect thus determining the psychic structure as well. It may be that as in other mental derangements, and I do believe that men behave in a mentally deranged manner toward women, there is a biochemical correspondence, but this would be ultimately behaviorally determined, not genetically.

I believe that the sex roles—both male and female—must be destroyed, not the individuals who happen to possess either a penis or a vagina, or both, or neither. But many men I have spoken with see little to choose from between the two positions and feel that without the role they'd just as soon die.

Certainly it is the master who resists the abolition of slavery, especially when he is offered no recompense in power. I think that the *need* men have for the role of Oppressor is the source and foundation of all human oppression. Men suffer from a disease peculiar to Mankind which I call "metaphysical cannibalism." Men must, at the very least, cooperate in curing themselves.

METAPHYSICAL CANNIBALISM[6]

Perhaps the pathology of oppression begins with just that characteristic which distinguishes Mankind from the other species: rationality. It has been proposed before that the basic condition of Man is *Angst:* the knowledge and constant awareness that He will die. Man, so the theory goes, is thus trapped by existence in an inescapable dilemma. My proposal is more fundamental.

Man is not aware of the possibility of death until He is able to put together certain abstractions, e.g., descriptions of events, with the relevant descriptive connectives. It requires a fairly sophisticated intellect to be able to extrapolate from the description of an event to one's own condition, that is, from another person's *experience* to one's own essential definition. If, instead of asking ourselves what particular conclusion rationality might arrive at, we ask what the nature of this distinguishing human characteristic is, we come to a more fundamental question.

The distinction between the nature of the animal and human brain seems to be that while an animal can imagine, that is, can mentally image some object before its eyes in some familiar situation, an animal cannot *construct* with its imagination. An animal cannot imagine a new situation made up of ingredients combined together for the first time with each ingredient initiating consequences for the other ingredients to produce the new situation.

Man's rationality is distinguished by its "constructive imagination,"[7] and this constructive imagination has been a mixed blessing. The first experience of Man in His existence is usually called "awareness" or "consciousness"; we are *sensible;* our senses are operating unrestricted by exter-

57

[6] [May, 1969; see Footnote 1, p. 47.]

[7] [The notion of a "constructive imagination" is further developed in *Juniata II: Metaphysical Cannibalism or Self-Creativity,* pp. 76–81, and in *Untitled: Some Notes Toward a Theory of Identity,* pp. 109–116.]

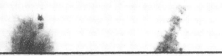

nal coercions. (So far our description is also true of animals.)

What probably is first *known* to us as a distinct thing is our own body, since it is the object most consistently within our perception.[8] As we see other objects with parts similar to our first object of perception, I think we can observe our first operation of rationality. We "imagine" that the second observation has *consequences* for the first observation. We see another human being as physically complete and autonomous (powerful) and ourselves as abbreviated thus incomplete (powerless). We can never see ourselves as fleshly integral units. We feel and sense and analogize that we are each independent units, but we can never completely perceive *ourselves* as such. Each of us begins with this initial insecurity.

Rational action (intention) requires some sense of individual autonomy. We have choice only to the degree that we are physically free, and every Man by His nature feels ambiguity on this point. In addition, Man realizes early in His maturity that there is an enormous gap between what He can do and what He can *imagine* done. The powers of His body and the powers of His mind are in conflict within one organism; they are mockeries of each other. This

---

[8] [Apparently, what I thought was obvious is not obvious to all my readers. As in *The Institution of Sexual Intercourse,* my point is to eliminate what is currently accepted—sexual intercourse as synonymous with sex and, in this case, *Angst,* as one of the primary causes of the frustration which leads men to oppress.

My point (and for those for whom I am being redundant, I apologize) is that before *Angst* is possible, the foundations for the need to oppress are laid down. *Angst* then becomes a "front."

I use examples as a means to illustrate the forms or questions any ultimate answers must satisfy. I could have used the straight form I used in *The Institution of Sexual Intercourse,* but I thought that rather boring.

However, for those who need it, here is a "pony":

1. with what kind of experience does knowledge begin
2. what is the first operation or process of knowledge
3. what are the parts of this process
4. how do these parts inter-connect
5. how do these parts affect each other
6. is anything produced by this process, such as additional parts of the process
7. are there any consequences of this process which then exist apart from this process

Whatever the answers to these questions, one consequence of the nature of human rationality has been a psychological insecurity.

I hope that this parallel exposition makes it possible for my reader to extrapolate sufficiently from here.]

second factor adds frustration to the first factor of insecurity.

We now posit Man as insecure and frustrated. He has two needs:

(1) substance, as autonomous body —necessarily outside Himself, and

(2) the alleviation of His frustration (the suppression of feeling) through anger—*oppression.*

When we understand these two consequences peculiar to Man's nature, we can begin to understand the nature of "politics."[9]

Man feels the need of something, like Himself, as an "extension." This presents a problem since *all* Men suffer this same need. All Men are looking for potency—the substantive power to close the gap between their bodily and mental powers. It seems clear that, once the resolution takes this external direction, some Men—ideally half (thus, one for each)—would have to catch *other* Men in some temporary depression of consciousness (when matured, rationality or constructive imagination) and at some physical disadvantage. This temporary depletion of Self provides the opportunity to simultaneously devour the mind of a member of the selected class and to appropriate their substance to oneself.

It is this process that I call "metaphysical cannibalism." It is to eat one's own kind, especially that aspect considered most potent to the victim while alive—its constructive imagination. This process absorbs the free will of the victim and destroys the evidence that the aggressor and the victim are the Same. The principle of metaphysical cannibalism seemed to meet

59

[9] [While I cannot go into it here in detail, I want to make clear that we must use our constructive imagination to devise a moral alternative. Such an alternative must provide an internal solution to the feelings of inadequacy. The solution would probably depend upon just that faculty that initiated the original dilemma, the human imagination. Rationality will have to construct the substance sufficient for individual autonomy from the inside. This would resolve both the problem of substantive incompleteness and be a step in the reconciliation of mind and body.]

both needs of Man: to gain potency (power) and to vent frustration (hostility).

Some psychic relief was achieved by one half the human race at the expense of the other half. Men neatly decimated Mankind by one half when they took advantage of the *social* disability of those Men who bore the burden of the reproductive process. Men invaded the being of those individuals now defined as functions, or "females," appropriated their human characteristic, and occupied their bodies. The original "rape" was political, the robbing of one half of Mankind of its humanity. The sexual connotations to the term no doubt grew out of the characterizations made later of the Men in the original action.

This original rape in its essential features has been reenacted and rationalized and justified ever since. First, those Men called women have been anchored to their position as victim by men devising numerous direct variations on women's capture, consolidating women's imprisonment. Second, men have devised indirect variations on the original crime via the principle of oppression against other Men. But all of these variations—what we call class systems and their supportive institutions—are motivated by Man's nature, and all political change will result in nothing but other variations on metaphysical cannibalism—rape —until we find a human and equitable alternative to Man's dilemma.

The male-female distinction was the beginning of the role system, wherein some persons function for others. This primary distinction should properly be referred to as the Oppressor (male) — Oppressed (female) distinction, the first political distinction. Women were the first political class and the beginning of the class system.

Certainly in the pathology of oppression, it is the agent of oppression who must be analyzed and dealt with. He is responsible for the cultivation and spread of the disease.

Still a question arises: how is it that, once the temporary susceptibility to disease (aggression) has passed, the patient does not spontaneously recover? It must be that the external attack aggravates in the victim a latent disorganization which grows and flourishes in response to and finally in tandem with the pathology imposed from outside. This disease, drawn out and cultivated from within, can finally maintain the original victim in a pathological state with fewer external pressures.

I propose that the latent disorganization in "females" is the same disorganization—dilemma—from which "males" opted for metaphysical cannibalism. The role of the Oppressor (the male role) is to attempt to resolve his dilemma at the expense of others by destroying their humanity (appropriating the rationality of the Oppressed). The role of the Oppressed (the female-woman role) is to resolve her dilemma by self-destruction (bodily destruction or insanity).

Given an Oppressor—the will for power—the natural response for its counterpart, the Oppressed (given any shade of remaining Self-consciousness), is Self-annihilation. Since the purpose and nature of metaphysical cannibalism is the appropriation *of* and extension *to* substance, bodily self-destruction is uncommon in comparison with mental escapes.

While men can "cannibalize" the consciousness of women as far as human Self-construction for the woman is concerned, men get no direct use from this except insofar as they *believe* it gives them magic powers. But rationality imprisoned must destroy itself.

Metaphysical cannibalism does not solve the dilemma posed by human rationality for either the Oppressor or the Oppressed. The Oppressor can only whet his appetite for power by external measures (like drugs to dull the symptom of pain) and thus increases his disease and symptoms. The Oppressed floats in a limbo of un-Consciousness—driven there by the immobilization of her vital organ, rejecting life but not quite dead, sensible enough to still feel the pain.

The most common female escape is the psychopathological condition of love. It is a euphoric state of fantasy in which the victim transforms her oppressor into her redeemer. She turns her natural hostility toward the aggressor against the remnants of herself—her Consciousness—and sees her counterpart in contrast to herself as all-powerful (as he is by now at her expense).

The combination of his power, her self-hatred, and the hope for a life that is self-justifying—the goal of all living creatures—results in a yearning for her stolen life—her Self—that is the delusion and poignancy of love. "Love" is the natural response of the victim to the rapist.

What is extremely difficult and "unnatural," but necessary, is for the Oppressed to cure themselves (destroy the female role), to throw off the Oppressor, and to help the Oppressor to cure himself (to destroy the male role). It is superhuman, but the only alternative—the elimination of males as a biological group—is subhuman.

Politics and political theory revolve around this paradigm case of the Oppressor and the Oppressed. The theory and the practices can be divided into two parts: those institutions that directly reinforce the paradigm case of oppression, and those systems and institutions that reinforce the principle later extrapolated from this model.

JUNIATA II

THE EQUALITY ISSUE[1]

The equality issue is both the basis and measure of the Women's Movement. It could be viewed as a radical interpretation and implementation of "participatory democracy."

The issue of equality is ostensibly the basis of all political movements. It is the most obvious issue but also, I hope to show, one of the least observed.

"Equality" within the context of political theory would seem to have an obvious meaning. All individuals participating in some activity together share equally in the rights and responsibilities together. In that activity known as "society," all citizens must contribute an equal amount of labor and are entitled to an equal amount of what is produced thereby.

Now, an obvious example is the factory in which every member is a participant. Everyone is both "employee" simultaneously and, later, "employer" simultaneously. Every member works the same amount of time and receives an equal amount of the profits.

But a factory producing, say, automobiles requires within it different jobs. And while a participant might contribute an equal amount of time, it might be argued that one job differed in some significant way from some other job, such as in degree of interest.

Would you want to count as equal in *kind* the number of hours spent assembling a car with that of designing it? Isn't there some intrinsic difference between the two tasks, and, if so, what is it?

One reply might be that the two tasks are different in that they require different backgrounds or experiences. But is that really accurate? Isn't it that to *assemble* a

65

[1] [February 19, 1970; Juniata College, Huntingdon, Pennsylvania.]

car requires no background and that to design it requires *some* experience of a specific kind? This experience is usually referred to as "education."

But if there is some quantity in a society some degree of which is denied to some persons, isn't it more to the point to say the person with the lesser of the unequal shares has been assigned a handicap?

"Education" is a two-edged sword. Doesn't all experience "educate"? Then why do we call positive experience "education" and give no such name ordinarily to negative experience?

Doesn't assembling the same parts day in day out "educate" a person? Doesn't "education" really refer to the artificial shaping of the mind? And isn't crushing the natural flexibility of the mind, its intellectual functioning, to give an artificial shape to the mind, as much "education" as to add a facet to the mind by contributing certain information concerning the history of a discipline?

Doesn't the word "education" really stand for the *least* "education," the least amount of crushing out the natural vitality of the human mind? Isn't then, the assembler the most "educated" person in the factory?

Isn't all work repetitive by nature (popularly known in the Movement as "shitwork") potentially dangerous? certainly more dangerous than drugs? And yet one might say that shitwork is the most potent drug of all to the human mind. Guaranteed to destroy it.

Shouldn't we admit that shitwork should be labeled as the dangerous task that it is? Shouldn't it be removed from the market as much as possible? And shouldn't whatever part of it which is not liquidable be borne equally by all participants in any given society?

It is, of course, out of the question for any individual/s to be forced to bear the dangers of this drug unequally for the community at large. But isn't this what the class system is all about? Isn't this its motivating force?

Isn't this really what it means to be a woman? *Shitwork reincarnated?*

In the first part of this section on the equality issue, I want to concentrate on the significance of the equality issue, both within the major sex institutions and, more especially, within the class of women operant in feminist groups.

The institution of the male-female relationship has a fairly simple formalized structure. Marriage or some variant of it is the prototype institution of this class system structure. The family is the natural consequence of the definitive sex institution of marriage. Sex and love are the dynamics of the male and female roles respectively.

Marriage is definitively unequal: man and *wife*. There is only one role change here—that of *wife*. Within the family, the role change from wife to mother is to doubly burden the woman. Sex, because it is genitally determined, is in the interests of the male and against the interests of the female. Love is the female ballast to the male dynamic of sex within the male-female structure. (Insofar at least as love is inequitable, that is, as long as it is not by definition reciprocal, love will not survive the liberation of women.)

My primary interest here is to deal

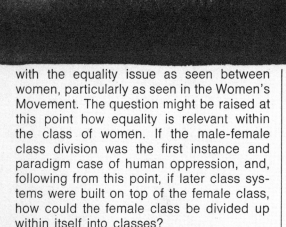

with the equality issue as seen between women, particularly as seen in the Women's Movement. The question might be raised at this point how equality is relevant within the class of women. If the male-female class division was the first instance and paradigm case of human oppression, and, following from this point, if later class systems were built on top of the female class, how could the female class be divided up within itself into classes?

I don't think I could have made the discoveries I am about to present to you if I had not spent the last three years in the Women's Movement.

When I was president of New York N.O.W. I noticed, first, how inefficient the organization was. N.O.W. is structured and operates according to standard parliamentary procedure, that is, *Robert's Rules of Order.* Authority stems from the peak of the pyramidal structure. No matter how much the organization grew, since all moves had to be cleared by the president, efficiency decreased in direct relation and proportion to membership increase.

This standard hierarchical structure entailed that the decisions, thus the views of a few, determined the labors of the majority. This was unfair and thus demoralizing to the bulk of the membership. This general depression caused the organization to, at best, move by jerks—at worst, to drag to a near standstill.

My primary goal at that time was to foment a Revolution. My interest in the lower classes within the organization grew out of the organization's inefficiency and the detrimental effect of that inefficiency on my primary goal of major societal change. I attempted in 1968 to abolish the representational hierarchical system in N.O.W.

by introducing the "lot" system as our operating principle.

(The lot system is one of the most ancient governmental systems. Representatives of the people are chosen for short terms from the people as a whole by lot. Representation is random and, eventually, completely fair, since every citizen at some time represents the "people" by representing himself.)

The rest of the officers in N.O.W. banded together to defeat the lot system by packing the meeting and buying up votes in the worst American tradition. Moving speeches were presented castigating me as an unnatural traitor to my class and appealing to the great American dream (or nightmare, depending on your point of view).

The lot system was defeated two to one, and those of us who were most con-vinced of the centrality of the equality issue left N.O.W. and formed the radical feminist wing of the movement—based on the equality issue.

If you can't destroy the positions of power, you certainly can't participate in them.

Within Women's Liberation,[2] there is no formal hierarchy. But demagoguery is immediately evident. A few women dominate all meetings. While lip service is paid to participatory democracy, it is no more a reality than what I've observed in S.D.S. meetings.

A few people scattered throughout the room dominate the discussion. Then a vote is taken which supports the party line established by the clique. However, in addition, there is a pecking order within the system of class groups that should not be

---

[2] [A reference to the less formally structured groups stemming from the student and antiwar movements.]

overlooked. For example, a woman might not participate in the discussion in the presence of her counterclass, men, yet dominate a discussion in the Women's Movement.

It's important to keep in mind that the persons who speak influence the views of the others and, thus, determine the direction of the group. This is, of course, not altogether the case within formal hierarchies. Speaking, alone, does not determine direction. On the other hand, the officers do most of the speaking as part of the system of the structure.

We have struggled very hard with these problems in The Feminists. One technique we use is the "disc" system. Every member is given 15 to 20 chips at the beginning of the meeting. Each time someone speaks, she throws a disc in the middle of the room. When your chips are used up, you can no longer participate in the discussion for the remainder of that meeting.

In addition, we have refined the lot system into two major types: "routine" and "privileged." This division is based, in part, on my earlier discussion of equality and the nature of tasks. (Recall my use of the example of the automobile factory with the assembler and the designer.)

All shitwork is divided equally by lot. The privileged lot operates somewhat differently. We recognize that some women, like myself, have greater opportunities to speak, write, appear on television, et cetera. For this reason, all privileged activities are counted whether or not they come about through the group or through one's own efforts, such as my being here. By this method, we are assured equal experiences in amount and in category.

Aside from its just aspects, this privileged lot distinction builds a stronger group —a chain, all of whose links are strong, experienced, self-sufficient, thus reliable. The group is not dependent on a few of its parts. The opposition might be able to wipe the group out, but it couldn't knock the group off balance.

Now I will return to the question: how can the primary class of women be divided within itself. I think it is intuitively clear that the class system within the primary class of women is of a different nature than the class confrontation within the sex class system itself.

The class of women is in a sense *the* "sex" class, since its position is determined by that characteristic. In this sense, then, women are the *first* sex, not the second. The class of men floats free of the sex class and is then further subdivided on other pretexts.

Women cannot accurately be said to *belong* to any other political class. However, they do evidence certain expressions characteristic of the members of power classes in relation to subordinates.

The first idea that occurred to me was that some women were simply mimicking men, and this was grotesque but not fundamentally dangerous. But all oppression is dangerous—whatever its inspiration.

The analogy then occurred to me of a beggar with the delusion he was actually a king. The beggar is grotesque. He has acquired the accoutrements of royalty, and yet he is powerless. *However,* should the beggar exercise such royal prerogatives as lopping off heads, he would have to be dealt with as an exerciser in power.

The danger stems from just the fact that the beggar's act is not truly grounded in a primary, or "power," class. The street people might take out all the frustrations they are afraid to express against the true holders of power by savagely murdering the demented beggar.

Women, like the beggar, identify with other classes via the family to which they belong. That is, women identify first with their father's class (based on economics and education primarily) and, second, with their husband's class.

I call the primary classes "power" classes, and I call the classes within classes "identification" classes.

Power classes oppress all other power classes derived from them as well as oppressing all identification classes. Identification classes can only exercise oppressive acts within their own primary class or over under-classes within weaker class systems in the total power hierarchy.

A woman in the audience, particularly a feminist, might wonder why I appear to be washing our dirty linen in public. For several reasons. First, because it's the truth, and the one thing women cannot stand more of is lies. Second, while I cannot forgive men for all they have robbed of women's lives—of your lives as well as my own—when you understand that oppression is a human problem and that even *you* may have participated in it, this makes a solution possible. Yelling from a pedestal —whether that pedestal is built with "love" or with hate—forecloses any chance of dialogue. And dialogue, whether it be violent or nonviolent, can only be functional if it's based on understanding. I draw a line, however, between understanding and compassion.

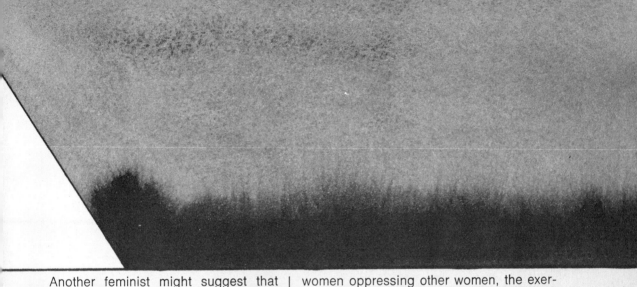

Another feminist might suggest that while some women may well oppress some other women, the system *within* the sex class is so far less significant than the class system defining women, that the instance of women oppressing other women should be ignored for the present. In fact, it might be suggested that all feminist efforts be concentrated on the oppression of women by men. My motives for opposing this position are in no way inspired by compassion for men. I have separated myself off from men more decisively than any woman I know of in the Movement.

Since the male/female system is the first and most fundamental instance of human oppression, all other class systems were built on top of it. Women will not be free until all oppressed classes are free. I am not suggesting that women work to free other classes. However, in the case of women oppressing other women, the exercise of class privilege by identification in effect locks the sex class into place. In identifying one's interests with those of any power class, one thereby maintains the position of that class. As long as any class system is left standing, it stands on the backs of women.

In addition to the logical proof, there is all too sufficient evidence for this theory. The first women's movement was not only racist but horrifically class structured as well. It was primarily upper-middle-class, as is the present movement. The Feminists are a glaring exception to this generalization. With the exception of myself, we are lower- or lower-middle-class and/or black. These people were drawn by the equality issue.

The last movement paid for its prejudices by struggling for over 70 years, selling out piece by piece, and finally driving itself over a cliff—popularly known as "the vote." Our heritage is their mistakes. Such a heritage can be a rich one if studied.

There is a tendency in the current movement to glorify the suffragettes. I'm not convinced yet that we are so weak we have to suppress the truth. I'm not concerned about deceiving men but very concerned about deceiving ourselves.

The Women's Movement has much against it:

(1) our oppression has been the longest
(2) our oppression is the most obscured and intricate because of interconnections and confusions with other class systems
(3) we are the most obviously dependent class on the liberation of other oppressed classes.

The feminist dilemma is that we have the most to do and the least to do it with. We have one asset but a sufficient one if cultivated. We have a potential membership of over half the population of the world.

The Women's Movement has never begun to tap its one resource. It will require almost superhuman efforts on the parts of women. They must relinquish the only self-respect, or "face," which they have been permitted within society.

Women must give up their identification with the oppressor class of other oppressed groups. Frankly, I have no reason to believe we can do it. But I *do* know that it's our only chance. The women's revolution must be *for,* thus, *by* all women.

Other oppressed groups are also dependent on *our* liberation. This is not as obvious as in our case since all men know and cling to the notion that all women are underneath them. But history has, I hope, illustrated the interdependency of liberation enough times now to be an evident proposition.

All other revolutions have ultimately failed because they left the seeds of oppression intact in some form. This was, and is, usually in the form of the oppression of women, although often, *in addition,* in the oppression of blacks or ethnic groups. You can find examples of this wherever you have or have had a revolution. Russia is a classic example, and Cuba's coming up.

You might ask why this discussion of equality should be of interest to men. Most men are oppressed—not by women but by their counterclasses higher up in the class hierarchy. Those women who perceive the germ of the oppressor role in themselves will be more willing and constructive in pointing out the oppressor in you. When you understand that, you'll have a chance against *your* oppressor. Maybe even *conceivably,* you might have the Women's Movement as an ally.

The white male in this country does not begin to have himself together politically. I have wondered what these frantic, blustery misinterpretations of Marx were really about. Does it reflect the white male's ambivalence as to whose side he's on?

This talk has been rather long. And I'm afraid it's been too tight and too packed for you to have gotten much from it.

I have literature lists here for those of you who might be interested in studying some of these ideas at your leisure.

I'll end this on a personal note.
Sisters, walk tall.
And brothers, sleep light. You never know when you may have just fucked the revolution.

METAPHYSICAL CANNIBALISM OR SELF-CREATIVITY³

Feminism is, of course, a political concept as well as a movement. However, there has been almost no effort, either in the last movement or the present one, to articulate a systematic political theory. This is not to say that there are no feminist ideologies. On the contrary, every feminist has one. But these ideologies are either internally inconsistent, irrelevant to a political analysis, or based on unexamined assumptions. These faults are due primarily to the lack of systematization. For the time being, I won't discuss possible motivations for this oversight. Suffice it to say that it is at the very least irresponsible.

Political theory is usually inspired by some collection of verifiable evidence, which I will call here "raw data." If the theorist is cool, she will collect the greatest quantity of evidence possible, preferably statistical, and then study this collection until some pattern seems to emerge. The theorist must proceed, of course, from an overview position. This overview, or these basic assumptions, are, unfortunately, usually arrived at emotionally. They comprise the foundation out of which the political theory is largely determined. All political theories contain basic assumptions, or metaphysics, either implicitly, or, more often, sketchily suggested. It is essential that the metaphysics are carefully spelled out and meticulously examined.

I think all feminists in their secret moments must cry out "why?"

"Why do men act like they hate us?"

"Why am I drawn to my enemy?"

"Why can I never hope to be free in my lifetime and, yet, free enough to *understand* I'll never *be* free?"

"Why does what I know to be the truth make me so sad?"

³ [February 20, 1970; Juniata College, Huntingdon, Pennsylvania.]

"Why is it that I don't realize myself to the small extent it *is* possible?"

It is in response to these questions that a metaphysics—or more accurately for me, an epistemology—is developed. Some feminists hold that the reason men act as they do is because they're inferior by nature. These feminists recommend either radical surgery on the society, that is, the elimination of men, or, more commonly, that an elaborate and rigid body of law be developed to curb men's sadistic inclinations. Proponents of this line are Valerie Solanas and adherents to the pro-woman line respectively. In addition, this theory holds that women are morally and aesthetically superior. Now, moral and aesthetic judgments are applied after the fact and hardly explain first causes. The question is *why* men do the things they do and have constructed the system they have. The question is one of intention. It must be psychologically grounded.[4]

Other theorists refuse to gather data from the loci of women's oppression, that is, from the institutions that enclose and define their positions in society. Unsurprisingly, these conservative feminists do not see the oppression of women as severe. Since it is not severe, larger questions are unnecessary. The discrimination against women can be treated as accidents that will correct themselves when understood. When this discrimination proves as resistant to correction as in the case of blacks, it remains to be seen if these women persist stubbornly in this approach. Probably some will, as did some blacks. But the "mistake" theory will probably be primarily supported by the oppressor class against the more radical feminist position.

But what questions must a metaphysi-

4 [But it must be empirically proven!]

cal theory, as the basis for feminist theory, answer? Some of the questions that seem legitimate and pressing to me are these:

(1) why does the human race have such an extreme and elaborate structure reinforcing the male/female distinction in comparison with the rest of the animal world?

(2) Why, given mankind's ability to construct alternatives with its mind, did men choose to oppress women? (It seems reasonable to me that the answers to these and many other related questions might turn on the characteristic which distinguishes men from animals: rationality.)

(3) What is the nature of rationality that might account for the oppression of women?

It seems that human beings can understand just enough to scare them to death. In an attempt to defend himself against an environment both vast and unknown, man used woman as a weapon, as an extension to, although really as an expression of, his own power. Man has also used woman as a defense or shield between himself and the rest of the world.

I think that it is a reasonable question to ask why women permitted this. It's at this point I think childbearing is relevant. This temporary incapacity, thus vulnerability, provided the opportunity for exploitation.

Okay. But now what. There is one thread that seems to run through all rationalizations for oppression: the proposition that life is not self-justifying. Oppression is

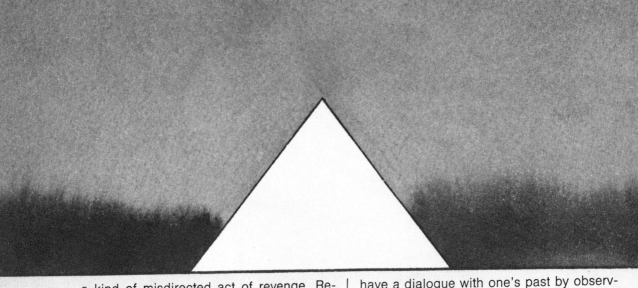

a kind of misdirected act of revenge. Removing oppression at this late date requires no less than an elaborate and intact theory restructuring life as self-justifying in and of itself.

It seems to me that aesthetic theory might be of help. Traditionally, ethical and aesthetic theory have been separate. But the structure of aesthetic theory, particularly that concerning the appreciation of a work of art, seems applicable here. If the act of creation and the act of appreciating are combined, we might have the circular, self-contained structure we need. At present, identity[5] is built from the outside. We are dependent for our very existence on recognition. But what if identity were built from the inside? What if one's life were like a work of art, created by a dialogue with one's surroundings, whether animate or inanimate. At the same time, one would have a dialogue with one's past by observing change. The work of art, one's life, would have the potential for completeness or incompleteness at all times depending upon one's existence. When the dialogue, that is life, stops, the work is complete.

Our society is based on dependency as a given, guaranteed by a rigid institutional structure. What would happen to the family if each individual life were independent and *self*-justifying? And what would happen to love?

It's a common belief that women can't do *real* philosophy, such as metaphysics. It's been my contention for some time that the reason this belief has some basis in fact is that the terms in which metaphysics are presented are irrelevant to women's experience. I'd like discussion now on some of

5 [See *Untitled: Some Notes Toward a Theory of Identity*, pp. 109–116.]

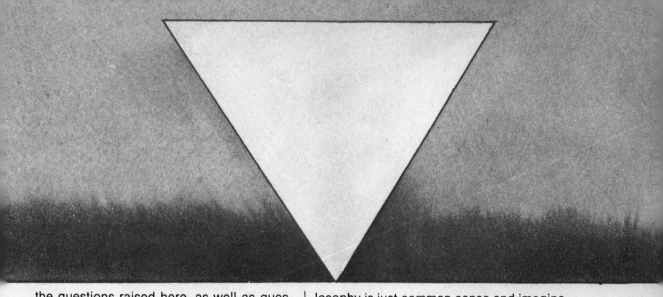

the questions raised here, as well as questions you consider relevant that I have perhaps not dealt with. Remember, good philosophy is just common sense and imagination, double-checked.

LESBIANISM AND FEMINISM[6]

It has seemed clear to me, for about two years, that there is some important connection between lesbianism and feminism. I wish I could claim that this idea came to me without outside assistance. However, this is not the case.

From the conservative beginnings of this movement, men have been countering all accusations of injustice toward women with the charge that these accusations were being made by "just a bunch of lesbians." For the first year, I couldn't understand the connection. The remark would be made (more often yelled). It would bounce off me, without comprehension, and fall to the ground.

But after a certain amount of repetition, I began to wonder what the connection was that men saw between lesbianism and feminism. By that time, I knew that any man understood what his class *had* been and *was* up to far better than any woman could ever decipher it. I decided that it was worth understanding what men were trying to say.

Another factor I should mention is that the charge seemed to have a threat in it. "I want the same pay for the same job as men get." "You must be a lesbian."

Let's try to figure out the meaning of this connection.

Lesbianism and feminism both have to do with women.

Both concepts are, in some sense, *exclusive* to women.

But, someone might suggest, there are more significant differences than similarities between these two concepts. Lesbianism is a "sexual" position, whereas feminism is a "political" position.

The beginning of this current move-

83

[6] [February 21, 1970; Juniata College, Huntingdon, Pennsylvania.

This paper was read to an exclusively female audience. I did not present it publicly for some time, because lesbianism was not recognized as a legitimate feminist issue. I believe it *is* recognized, as such, now. This paper raises a number of questions about feminist ideological difficulties concerning lesbianism. It should, however, be read in conjunction with *Lesbianism and Feminism: Justice for Women as "Unnatural,"* pp. 131–134, for an appreciation of the strategic and tactical significance of lesbianism for feminism.]

ment, and, still, its conservative wing, was and has been consistently terrified of so-called "sexual" issues. This was one of the primary reasons for the reluctance to come out on abortion.

It was not clear, early in the Movement, *what* sex had to do with women. However, if women are *defined* by this characteristic, what could be more relevant than sex?

As the movement has evolved, *some* connection between the concept of women and the concept of sex has become increasingly evident. But in what ways are these two concepts connected?

I think that lesbianism, to men, is the ultimate political position for women. This is not to say that lesbianism actually *is*. But consider how a man might view it.

If a woman really didn't like what men were doing to her, that woman would turn her back on men. And given that the male dynamic toward women is sex, he could hardly see any woman without it.[7]

Now "sex," for men, is genital contact. So, if women should rebel, it's clear to men, this rebellion would have to take the form of "woman." A "woman" is something to be screwed. Therefore, women together—feminists—must be women who screw each other.

I think we have some sketch of the connection *men* see between feminism and lesbianism. But, now, let's consider whether *we* can see a connection. If so, what is it?

Is lesbianism political? If so, what is its analysis and program?

Does feminism, intrinsically, have a position on sex? Is sex inherently political?[8]

---

[7] [See *Vaginal Orgasm as a Mass Hysterical Survival Response*, pp. 5–7; *The Institution of Sexual Intercourse*, pp. 13–23; *Radical Feminism: Declaration of War*, pp. 46–55, and *Metaphysical Cannibalism*, pp. 56–63; *University of Rhode Island: Movement Politics and Other Sleights of Hand*, pp. 95–108.]

[8] [See *The Institution of Sexual Intercourse*, pp. 13–23, for more questions along this line.]

Most lesbians deny that lesbianism has anything to do with rejecting men.[9] "Some of my best friends are men," they say.

On the face of this, one might claim that lesbians are simply lying when they say they don't hate men. After all, in a society which is militantly heterosexual, homosexuality must be, at some point, a conscious *choice.*

Keep in mind that both heterosexuality and homosexuality are exclusive in their class dynamic: men relating only to women, either toward or against; and vice versa. Sometimes I think that lesbianism is just about as apolitical as black nationalism.

It's true that the very concepts of lesbianism depend upon the positing *of* that counterclass, men. One *might* want to claim that there is a certain rejection operating here, and that for that reason alone, lesbi-anism qualifies as a political act.

Still, lesbianism is totally dependent, as a concept as well as an activity, on male supremacy. This fact, alone, should make a feminist nervous.

Certainly, all politically serious oppressed groups base the structure of their *resistance* on their counterclass. For example, guns are met with guns.

But lesbianism is based ideologically on the very premise of male oppression: the dynamic of sexual intercourse. Lesbians, by definition, accept that human beings are primarily sexual beings. If this is the case (that human beings are primarily sexual), one would have to grant that women *are,* in some sense, inferior.

"Sex" is based on the *differences between* the sexes.[10] Sexual intercourse is the interrelation between these two classes, and sexual intercourse, unsurprisingly, is

85

not in the interests of women.[11]

The institution of sexual intercourse is anti-feminist, first, because the source of woman's arousal and pleasure is in the clitoris, not in the vagina. And, second, it is anti-feminist, because sexual intercourse is the link between the wife and mother roles.

Lesbians and feminists are both members of the identification class[12] of women. Both are "political" in that they are both responses to oppression. But a case could be made that lesbianism, in fact *all* sex, is reactionary, and that feminism is revolutionary.

As I hope I got across yesterday, reaction and revolution, unfortunately, are not necessarily very far apart. There is certainly role-playing in lesbianism, whether as butch/femme or as mother/daughter.

A strong case could be made that *all*

sex is role-play, that is power politics, as long as sex is picked out as a special activity.

Because lesbianism involves role-playing and, more important, because it is based on the primary assumption of male oppression, that is, sex, lesbianism reinforces the sex class system.

Feminism, also, entails the rejection of men. Most feminists simply pay lip service to this; they don't act on it. This will be part of my topic for this afternoon.[13]

The *raison d'être* for feminism is the existence of class disparity between men and women.

The *raison d'être* of lesbianism is sex, which is an apparent evasion of class disparity.

It is at this point that we can locate the significant distinction between the two po-

86

[11] [See *The Institution of Sexual Intercourse*, pp. 13–23.]
[12] [See *Juniata II: The Equality Issue*, pp. 65–75.]
[13] [See *Juniata II: The Political Woman*, pp. 89–94.]

litical concepts of lesbianism and feminism, and the point at which there is the most political tension between the two.

There is no question that lesbians, like all homosexuals, have suffered a great deal of harassment in society. One can, thus, sympathize with their defensiveness at the challenge of feminism.[14] There is, also, the practical matter for lesbians of not drawing the government's attention to themselves by advocating radical political positions.

On the other hand, feminists must be honest with themselves about why lesbianism is so threatening to them. I don't believe it's just fear of being condemned. After all, we've all been called lesbians from the beginning anyway.

One of the central problems for all members of oppressed groups is self-hatred. To feminists, lesbianism represents a kind of self-identification. If any individual spends most of her time dealing with the ways in which members of her class are abused, it's unlikely that she will be able to maintain too much of a positive attitude either toward herself or toward other members of her class.

One of the more unfortunate consequences of a society based on sex ideology is that nearly every aspect of human contact is determined by class principles.

Women are dependent, for reinforcement of their individuality,[15] on their class enemy. Woman's identity must be sought in the eyes of her Oppressor. To turn to other women for ego support is like trying to catch a reflection of herself in a darkened mirror.

Definitely, lesbians have the mutual advantages of greater self-love over fem-

[14] [As of February 1973, many lesbians are embracing feminism.]

[15] [See *Untitled: Some Notes Toward a Theory of Identity*, pp. 109–116, for a few ideas on a positive identity construct.]

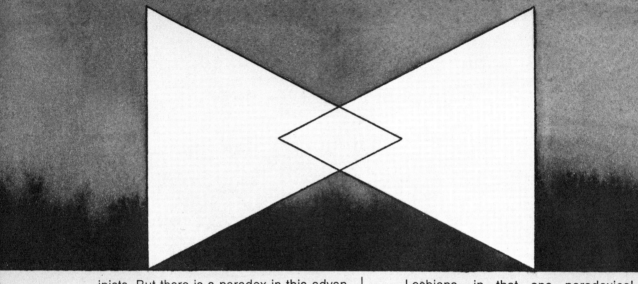

inists. But there is a paradox in this advantage. The price of self-respect for oppressed people is to adopt the role of the Oppressor, and, thus, ultimately, toward oneself.

Lesbians, in that one paradoxical sense, become their own Oppressors. But feminists, so far, have had to try to construct an identity out of negatives.

In other words, it's a tossup.

THE POLITICAL WOMAN[16]

Several women, this weekend, have suggested a certain reluctance to seeing men as the enemy. I would be the last person in the world to suggest that this reluctance is unnatural. It's the most natural thing in the world. I believe it's called the instinct for survival.

Other women, no doubt, admit the logic of men as our class enemy. But, by some happy accident, their present boyfriend is one of the rare exceptions to this rule.

Unless these women have verifiable evidence, of a political nature, for this claim, this second position is a cop-out.

And then, there was the man in North Dakota with the "scarcity" argument.

"The reason," said he, "for the rapid increase in the Women's Movement—and the apparent bitterness toward men—is *not* because men oppress women. No, the problem is that there is not enough of a good thing (that is, male supremacists) to go around."

There is nothing very complicated about being political.

A political person is some individual, who has a particular set of beliefs, and who acts in accordance with these beliefs. What has made being a political woman so complicated, are the elaborate evasions of the *second* part of this definition. The part about *acting in accordance* with a given set of political beliefs.

Men have been telling women about the battle of the sexes since the beginning of time. Of course, from our point of view, it's been a massacre.[17]

89

---

[16] [February 21, 1970; Juniata College, Huntingdon, Pennsylvania.

For the political woman, as individual, see *University of Rhode Island: Movement Politics and Other Sleights of Hand*, pp. 95–108 ("equality," "discipline," and "consistency" issues). See *Untitled: Some Notes Toward a Theory of Identity*, pp. 109–116, for problem of "identity."

See *Individual Responsibility and Human Oppression*, pp. 117–130, for "responsibility" issue.

For the political woman, as class, see *Strategy and Tactics: A Presentation of Political Lesbianism*, pp. 135–189.]

[17] [See *Radical Feminism: Declaration of War*, pp. 46–55.]

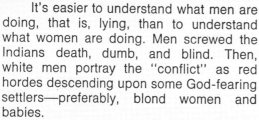

It's easier to understand what men are doing, that is, lying, than to understand what women are doing. Men screwed the Indians death, dumb, and blind. Then, white men portray the "conflict" as red hordes descending upon some God-fearing settlers—preferably, blond women and babies.

But the "pathology" of oppression, in this case, the male–female class division, exists in women denying what men themselves are spelling out.[18]

The price of clinging to the enemy is your life.

To enter into a relationship with a man who has divested himself as completely and publicly from the male role as possible would still be a risk.

But to relate to a man who has done any less is suicide.[19]

Women are still operating on a personal rather than on a political basis.

The proof of class consciousness will be when we separate off from men, from these one-to-one units. (For example, marriage and motherhood.)[20]

There can be no significant improvement in the situation of women until this happens.

So far, the feminist movement has, primarily, been women coming together to complain.

But this complaining is nothing new. Women have been complaining to each other for centuries and, then, daily, trudging back to their kitchens to cook supper for their husbands.

This practice, continued over many, many centuries, has developed in women a

[18] [See Radical Feminism and Love, pp. 41–45, and Radical Feminism: Metaphysical Cannibalism, pp. 56–63.]
[19] [See Strategy and Tactics: A Presentation of Political Lesbianism, pp. 135–189.]

[20] [See University of Rhode Island: Movement Politics and Other Sleights of Hand, pp. 95–108. See, especially, the "consistency" issue.]

kind of multiple personality,[21] each face of which is kept intact.

I can illustrate my points, just mentioned, right here and now. The majority of the women, here, no doubt, have some institutional alliance with men, either marriage or "love." If you don't have such an alliance, you're probably looking for one.

Now, how can you be looking for such an alliance, and, also, be here?

This contradiction is not present only here, but throughout the Movement. The most anti-male feminists, who hold—not just, as I do, that male *behavior* or role is unacceptable—that *all* men are the enemy, can, still, be seen walking down the street hand in hand with this very enemy!

I, personally, have taken the position that I will not appear with any man publicly, where it could possibly be interpreted that we were friends.

Since my position is that male *behavior* (yet to be defined) is the enemy, some distinguishing apparatus must be built in to my position.

Therefore, any exception to my rule would be something like "such a man as had publicly and tangibly, meaning he'd *done* something significant, disassociated himself from the male role and from the male class as much as possible."[22]

The papers claim that this rather politically modest act makes me a separatist.

A separatist, technically, is someone who advocates a separate state for a particular group of people. I have never done that—yet.

For myself, I believe I am only being consistent. And this seems the least that's

91

[21] [See *Radical Feminism and Love*, pp. 41–45, and *Untitled: Some Notes Toward a Theory of Identity*, pp. 109–116.]

[22] [See *On Violence in the Women's Movement": Collaborators and Self-Deception*, pp. 198–221. Following the events presented in this paper, I have been in the process of refining and redefining the position outlined in the three paragraphs above.]

necessary for any personal self-respect.

One of the striking features of this movement is that the government is not really worried about it. But why should it be?

It's true, we women say some pretty radical things. But we've given no evidence that there's any connection between what we say and what we intend to do.

At our present rate, we're ridiculous and funny. Contradiction is, after all, the "heart"[23] of comedy.

We must try to understand this anomaly. We women must ask ourselves why we pair off with men.

One begins to understand the political function of love. Consider how important "love" is in that political structure called "religion."

"Love your fellow man." Of course, it's just another "accident" that the most powerful religions, such as the Catholic, are primarily composed of the poor.[24]

What if the poor didn't love their brothers? Would they perhaps see their "brothers," then, as their class enemy, and revolt?

Have you ever considered the relationship between love and violence?

Violence is a transgression of someone else's person, or self.

Isn't love a transgression of the self? A giving over of what we know will be taken by violence if we don't?

Is "love" the answer of the slave to slavery? Did you ever wonder why they didn't have to chain second-generation slaves?

Did you ever wonder why so many

---

[23] [See *Radical Feminism and Love*, pp. 41–45.]

[24] [See *Catholic University*, pp. 190–197.]

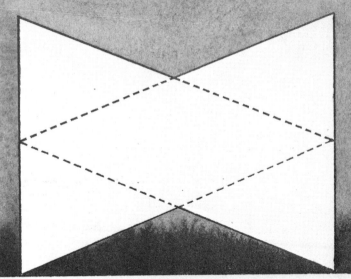

preachers preach nonviolence? And "love your enemy"?

Did you ever wonder why the churches are destroyed in all revolutions?

If we were free, would we *need* love?

93

UNIVERSITY OF RHODE ISLAND

MOVEMENT POLITICS AND OTHER SLEIGHTS OF HAND[1]

I have broken up the material I want to present to you this evening into five parts. First, I want to be sure you have some context, both historical and current, by which to properly understand my own position and to determine the positions you yourselves might take. Second, I want to present what I think to be the correct political analysis of women's oppression, out of which any program for overthrowing this oppression must issue. Third, I want to examine the question of alternatives for the individual woman to both oppression, at the one extreme, and near-total commitment to the Movement, at the other extreme. Fourth, I'll explore how the political analysis is relevant to you as university women. And fifth and last, although not intimately related to the other four points, I want to explain the poster on the front of this lectern. The story of the Amazons may shed some light on the possibility of a woman's culture and a tradition of resistance by women to oppression by men.

The last three years have come to be popularly known as the "second feminist wave."[2] The first "wave," or political move-

ment, covered some 70 years (1850-1920) and ended when women won the right to vote with the Nineteenth Amendment. While there were feminist reverberations in several concurrent movements, the feminist movement proper was divided into two camps. There were those women who placed women first at all times, known as the *National* Woman Suffrage Association and headed by Susan B. Anthony and Elizabeth Cady Stanton out of Washington, D.C. And then there were those women who did not always put women foremost, the *American* Woman Suffrage Association. This group operated out of Boston and was headed by Lucy Stone, with her husband Henry Blackwell close at hand and playing an important role in Lucy Stone's feminism.

These two associations joined forces as the National American Woman Suffrage Association at an opportune moment, in 1890, when there were no longer any other distracting political issues such as slavery, the vote for black men, or a war involving this country in any major way. A fact that has been considerably neglected, however, is that buried within these groups and on their fringes were a number of women

[1] [March 4, 1970; Kingston, Rhode Island.]
[2] [This was the title of the first major article on the current feminist movement. Martha Weinman Lear, "The Second Feminist Wave," *New York Times Magazine*, Vol. CXVII, No. 40,223 (March 10, 1968), pp. 24ff.]

who saw feminism as having far greater repercussions than getting any vote. (I would include Elizabeth Cady Stanton as among these women, in what I view as some of her better moments.) These women thought that the woman's revolution was not only challenging the major institutions on which this society is built, such as the family and its bulwark, religion, but challenging the still sacred notions of sex and love. (*Revolution,* by the way, was the name of Anthony and Stanton's weekly publication —this could hardly refer to just a vote.) What these women somehow missed was how these institutions and values interconnected through other concepts, such as equality, with all the movements for freedom in the world and in history.

Radical feminism in our time is the culmination of four centuries of women alone, and God knows oppressed, struggling to even *propose* a way out of the imprisonment of women. There was Anne Hutchinson in seventeenth-century Boston, Mary Wollstonecraft in eighteenth-century England and France, the early Lucy Stone in nineteenth-century New York. And there were many of these women, these precursors of radical feminism, in the *first* feminist wave, but they never exerted any influence with their radicalism. They were separated from each other—sometimes by organizations, more often by geography. There was never a radical *wing* in the last feminist movement.

As I mentioned earlier, the current movement is often called the *second* feminist wave and began over three years ago. It began when President Kennedy called a number of educated and powerful women from around the country in 1961 for his Commission on the Status of Women. (The report was issued in 1963.) Many of these women slowly pooled their political dissatisfactions and organized the National Organization for Women, in the fall of 1966. The central issue was employment; their chief remedy, Title VII in the 1964 Civil Rights Act outlawing discrimination in employment against women. (It may interest you that according to the United States Department of Labor the average working woman earns considerably less than half that of the average working man.)

The first regular meetings of N.O.W. were held in New York, and I began to attend these from the beginning. These monthly meetings in 1967 used to draw as few as 13 people. During the three years that have passed, it is conservatively estimated that now some 500,000 women are meeting in various groups and organizations in the United States. There is not a country in the world today without some sort of feminist organization.

The first rift in the Movement came over the abortion issue in 1967, but the split was not formalized into radical feminism versus moderate feminism until the fall of 1968. During this first rift (in 1967) the moderates and radicals stuck together, and the right wing of the Movement was formed in response to this. N.O.W. lost some of its nuns and Catholic labor, although "labor" left primarily over the Equal Rights Amendment. Some other women organized W.E.A.L., the Women's Equity Action League, in the professed belief that taking stands on such controversial issues as abortion would alienate a significant proportion of women otherwise attracted by feminism. (You must be wary of this argument in the Movement. It is a common one. Women don't admit to backing off issues because it threatens their personal lives. Instead, it's only because those poor slobs "out there" aren't "ready" for it.)

It was not pointed out at the time that the women supporting this conservative position, W.E.A.L., also happened to be at least token members of the Establishment, that is, for example, corporate lawyers. Some women maintained membership in both W.E.A.L. and N.O.W. This double membership is a familiar phenomenon in the Movement by this time. I call it double-treachery. A person, by this means, manages to be personally covered as more radical, while at the same time maintaining an organization which in effect undercuts the other's efforts. For this personal gratification, the Movement as a whole is held back.

The moderate-radical alliance in 1967 was a spurious one. The two factions *had* differed on the abortion issue. They had not differed on whether abortion law repeal was the correct position, but rather on whether abortion law repeal should be *fought* for. In other words, the moderate-radical alliance differed on whether or not the movement should be a vanguard or a rear-guard action vis-à-vis women outside the movement.

This disagreement—belief versus action—is still very much alive in the Movement and still divides the radicals from the moderates. To the radicals, to be feminist *means* to be vanguard. To the moderates, to be feminist means to respond to the *voiced* needs of women—that is, to be a rear-guard action.[3]

I should clarify one point. The feminist political spectrum does not follow the lines of any other political issue. For example, a woman in the Resistance or even a Communist woman might well be a moderate or even a right-wing feminist. Feminism has its own issues.

In the fall of 1967—to be exact, over Labor Day weekend—the Conference on New Politics was held in Chicago. As you may or may not know, this conference focused on the war and the black issues. But over half of the conference representatives were women. Several women's caucuses were scheduled and then canceled. Finally, Florynce Kennedy and I issued a two-page statement protesting the omission of the oppression of women as a conference concern. I was amazed at the enthusiastic response from women. A resolution was brought to the floor demanding appropriate representation on committees, etc., that is,

97

---

[3] [I use "rear-guard action" here in the traditional sense. See *Strategy and Tactics: A Presentation of Political Lesbianism* for a development of such terminology. Specifically, see pp. 150–159 and 169–186, for a *creative* use of the concept of "rear-guard action."]

51 percent representation. And the Women's Caucus *was* finally held on the last day.

Out of this caucus came Women's Liberation. Jo Freeman stayed in Chicago and began the first newsletter, *Voice of the Women's Liberation Movement.* Chicago was, for a long time, the heart of Women's Liberation. One of these early founders, Shulamith Firestone, moved to New York and with several other women began the New York Radical Women. The formation of Women's Liberation marked the beginning of the end of N.O.W.'s hope to be an umbrella group for the Women's Movement.

In all fairness, it should be pointed out that, through 1968, there was no significant difference on *feminism* between N.O.W. and Women's Liberation. The difference lay in the politics of the men to whom these women were attached. To some degree, this affected the organizational forms—parliamentary hierarchy versus participatory democracy demagoguery respectively—but these issues were not of any particular assistance to women *qua* women.

In October, 1968, there was a left-wing split-off from N.O.W. in which I was very active. The issue was a two-pronged attack on what has come to be known as the "equality" issue. The first prong was that all institutions and practices that are founded on inequitable principles, the short ends of which fall to women, must be destroyed. Some of these institutions are marriage, motherhood, sex, love, prostitution, religion.

The second prong was that the inequities among women, both outside the Movement and more particularly within, must be faced and eliminated. These inequities are expressed by some women dominating the rest of the group. These women make the decisions, and it falls to the rest of the group to carry these decisions out. In other words, the Women's Movement, still, on the whole, has internalized in their organizations, as well as personally, a traditional class structure in attitude and in practice.

Looking back on the situation, it seems incredible that any person, much less group of persons, could have possibly believed that N.O.W. could have incorporated such changes. In effect these changes—based on the equality principle—would have destroyed the rigid hierarchical structure of the organization, with authority, in the main, stemming from the president. In addition, these changes would have put N.O.W. up front on the firing line, simply because these changes would have made N.O.W. more efficient—more activist. The vote by the membership was 2 to 1 against these changes. Some of us split away to form our own organization, the October 17th Movement, named in honor of the day both of our departure from the rest of the Movement and our inception. That organization is now known as The Feminists.

In November, 1968, just outside Chicago, Women's Liberation held its first national conference. Radical women in New York had already had a right-wing split off, W.I.T.C.H. These women in W.I.T.C.H. were not as feminist as those in Radical Women. After this conference, Radical Women split up into separate groups, ostensibly to organize in more manageable numbers. But these divisions quickly assumed a political character. Several groups became "study" groups. Redstockings emerged, temporarily, as an action group. The most radical feminists came to The Feminists.

In the fall of 1969, The Feminists had a split-off, on the discipline and consistency issues, to form The New York Radical Feminists under which are formed Brigades. The discipline issue concerns equal participation. This may sound like a repetition of why The Feminists was founded. But it is not. The first instance of this principle concerned equal *opportunity*—the *right*—to participate, guaranteeing everyone an equal chance on every level of the organization. This second instance concerned the *requirement*—the *responsibility*—that every member participate in equal amounts. Thus, the first instance was directed toward the lower class[4] being guaranteed a repertoire of experiences. The second instance was to stop the exploitation by the upper class of the lower class.

The consistency issue[5] is that there must be some consistency between a political person's beliefs and its actions. Thus, since The Feminists is against marriage,

we instituted a quota that no more than one third of our membership could be married. The consistency issue is at the heart of the failures of the last and of the current women's movement. There was and still is enormous resistance to the consistency issue in the Movement. But I believe it will be one of the key issues in the next couple of years.[6]

I have been pushing for the last couple of years for feminists to develop a political analysis. A political theory is somewhat akin to a map of the enemy's territory. One can hardly develop a battle strategy without it. Perhaps a less controversial analogy would be this: a doctor must have a diagnosis before he can prescribe a treatment.

A rough outline of an analysis was developed a year ago. (Keep in mind that it took Marx over twenty years to perfect his analysis and, in the end, it was still far from perfect.) Instead of simply going over the analysis, I want to dwell on certain points which, in my lecturing, I have found are key to the women in the audience in maintaining an identification with the analysis.

Every feminist group I know of agrees to at least one point: that women are (at the very least) discriminated against. My contention is that from that one subject and passive verb structure, a radical analysis necessarily follows.

I have come to realize that many peo-

99

---

[4] [See *Juniata II: The Equality Issue,* pp. 65–75, for my use of "class" here.]
[5] [See *Juniata II: The Political Woman,* pp. 89–94.]

[6] [Lesbianism became a full-blown facet of the consistency issue in 1972.]

ple, especially women, do not know what a political theory is. First of all, politics is about groups and their relationships. Political theory is an analysis of these relationships, of how these groups affect each other.

The first important point in feminist theory, and one of the ones I find women in a group such as this resist the most, is the proposition that women are a class, more precisely, that women are a *political* class. Somehow, women usually let this point pass by, secreting the belief at the same time that all the theory later built upon this point does not, in fact, apply to them. At least some women hang onto the belief that they, as individual women, are exceptions to the proposition that women, *all* women, are members of a political class.

I'd like to take this from the beginning. A "class" is a group of individuals all of whose members share a common characteristic. A "political class" is a group of individuals *all* of whose members are treated differently on the ground that they belong to class A. It is part of the nature of class theory that *every* individual in the universe which has characteristic "A" as one of its components *necessarily* belongs to class A.

There is extensive evidence that women are a political class. Women as a class are paid less than *half* of what men are paid. Sometimes people say in response to this that money isn't everything. But money *is* the means of exchange in our so-

ciety. Having it or not determines our survival and freedom of movement.

There are so many laws on the books that discriminate against women that this country is unable to sign the United Nations Convention on the Political Rights of Women.

We are the largest single political class in this country. And what kind of representation do we have in either the legislative or judicial branches? How many Senators and legislators from Rhode Island are women? On either the federal or state levels.

These questions and their concerns are apart from all the institutional laws strapping women into the sex institutions. For example, the domestic relations laws denying women freedom of movement, compelling unpaid domestic labor, legalizing rape in marriage. And what about all those laws made by men determining the use of women's bodies, such as birth control laws and abortion laws?

The evidence is all around us. Why, for example, do you have a segregated student organization? Why does the "Association for Women Students" exist? Be careful how you answer that. You may reveal too much to yourself.

A few weeks ago I spoke at a college I had spoken at last year also. When I arrived on campus, there was a long letter waiting for me from a faculty wife I had met the year before. She told me that she wanted very much to see me, since due to recent events she now understood everything I had been talking about last year. She added that the year before, feminism, certainly radical feminism, had not seemed relevant to her.

Now this woman had been in philosophy. She should have known better than that. And yet, to me, it is just such moments of hideous realization, such moments when one realizes that one has molded one's life on false beliefs[7] and that one's life is in a very real sense unrecuperable, that gives the Women's Movement its strength and force. If we have time this evening, I will read one of the letters I've received from such a woman.

Mar. 10, 1968

I am forty-five now and have four children from twenty years old to eleven years.

I came from a poor family of thirteen (the oldest girl) and I too was told or learned the lesson, men are to be given a hot meal at night they are the breadwinner, and that was that—

There were good and bad people and the women must "always be there" meaning the home—

I have put in twenty-three years now, and having little schooling, I have just com-pleted my high school equivalency, and passed.

I had taken a test at the state employment and they told me (it was an I. Q.), "You are best working with your hands, you would do well to be a meat-packer in a supermarket, or a presser, better still factory work."

I have always read and learned a great deal about art, and I told the man, for you to put me in a factory would kill me, I have nothing to talk about to these people—

He didn't know that I wanted to be proud of what I might do, I wanted dignity more than $1.75 an hour.

The colleges told me you're too old, why bother, you ought to stay home now & enjoy yourself.

I have done volunteer work, for free, it was like a bunch of kids playing house—there was nothing real about it.

I don't want this letter to sound like an Ann Landers thing—but my husband no longer wants hot meals, and he has his own life apart from me, which hurts terrible, he was all I knew, I don't know anything else—

I have an older girl in College & she says that I must find my own life. It's like working for a company for 30 years & you go to work one morning & your name is off the door—and someone else is sitting in your desk—

There must be an awful lot of women like me—

I am going to take a course in typing

101

[7] [I, personally, experienced one of these "moments" after the attempted assassination of Joseph Colombo. See *On "Violence in the Women's Movement": Collaborators and Self-Deception*, pp. 198–221.]

& shorthand—my heart is not in it—

Would you be kind enough to answer my letter? you can not tell me what to do—but could you suggest some direction for me. I must be of use in the world—

I do not think I am going to set the world on fire—and I am rather poor in math—

The usual reply is get a salesgirl's job, or join some clubs.

I have been to women's fashion shows & luncheons. There is something tragic and wasteful when you look around at all these women not using any of their resources—

I was not prepared for being 40, and my home was a very safe place for me—

I would look forward to hearing from you—

Sincerely,
Phyllis M. Kennedy
51 Kings Highway
Middletown, N. J.
07748

Now, while I was very moved by this woman's situation, and while I have done whatever little I could do to help her, and while I have brooded over her situation, still the question nags me—how could she have believed that she was *not* one of "them"?

If my political analysis is correct, we should have the answer to that question. But the focus of the analysis does not turn so much on the fact that women are treated, as a matter of *fact*, as a class. Instead, the focus of the analysis turns on the second part of my original proposition: women *are discriminated against*. The oppression of women, and the way in which all the various fragments we now have of this oppression fit together, can be understood, I believe, only by understanding the nature of oppression itself.

There is a question, the answer to which I am not yet sure of, about the generally agreed upon fact that women were the first oppressed group in history. Does this fact indicate, then, that the class of women is the *model* for all other class systems of oppression? Or does it mean that all other class systems are intended as the *means* of shoring up the original class of oppressed people, women.

I don't believe that too much turns upon this question, for our immediate purposes. But it would have to be resolved, before any class theory of society as a whole could be complete.

What does the class of women tell us about the nature of oppression? And would these insights hold for other class systems?

One of the unique features of the class of women is that there has been no essential change in its material conditions from the time of recorded history. This absence of qualitative change seriously challenges the most prevalent revolutionary theory of dialectical materialism begun by Marx and Engels. The only possible alteration over time, and I'm not sure if even that really happened, seems to be in the perception of the Oppressed of its own oppression.

Our original proposition, if you recall, had an inverted word order. Interestingly enough, there is no subject. There is no other class doing the oppressing. (However, as Stokely Carmichael and Charles Hamilton pointed out in *Black Power,* the Oppressor makes up the definitions.)

Oppression is an activity initiated, elaborated upon, and maintained by the Oppressor. The class of women is determined by some sexual characteristic. It is, let's call it, a "sex" class.

Now, part of the nature of political classes is their dichotomized aspect: white/black, rich/poor, and male/female. There is only one other class in the oppressed class's domain—its contrary. It is, then, *necessarily,* the contrary of the female class which is the Oppressor. The male class is the oppressor class of the female class. Or, in political terms, men oppress women. That means *all* men, and that also means *all* women. Is that point clear?

The activity of oppressing seems to involve several rapidly performed sleights of hand.

The Oppressor, first, fosters and develops his own class consciousness in response to some perceived common characteristic in the class he later oppresses. The oppressor class is, thus, in a sense, determined by negation. In the case of women, the characteristic perceived by the Oppressor is obviously the childbearing capacity and, by extension, the secondary sex characteristics.

There are several anthropological accounts of this historical phenomenon, this first sleight of hand. One account is that the capacity for childbearing was perceived by men as a source of political power, whether or not it was actually realized—for example, in matriarchies. A second theory is that childbearing represents at least a temporary incapacity undergone for the sake of the community and exploited by men. My argument, however, does not depend upon the motivation of the Oppressor.

The determining characteristic of the oppressor class is the direct opposite of the determining characteristic of the counterclass it posits. The determining characteristic of the class of men is their sex characteristic. But, primarily, it is that sex characteristic, the penis, which is closest in nature to the primary reproductive characteristic of the Oppressed. This could account for the male obsession with sex. Sex acts as a reassuring reminder of his class supremacy. In addition, given the context of her class oppression, sex acts as a convenient reminder to the female of her class inferiority.

This first stage in oppression is more or less covert. It is in the context of the second stage that the Oppressor can afford to show his hand. The Oppressor must conceal his act of political class formation in order to preclude resistance. It is necessary to the consolidation, hence the maintenance of oppression, that the onus for the oppression be transferred to the Oppressed so as to justify the oppression as part of the necessary and natural order of the universe. The Oppressed is transformed from a group of individuals into a unified or single function of society.[8] This function is then a tool or extension of society.[9]

I think it's clear that the capacity to bear children, as a *capacity possessed by certain individuals* in society, was transformed into a *function necessary for society.* It's also clear that this individual capacity was politically, that is, artificially, transformed into a *class incapacity.*

Having jockeyed women into this false position, men were able to consolidate the activity of oppression into societal patterns, known presently as "institutions."

Because of these prior sleights of hand, these institutions could be presented as "protections." Marriage is the most obvious of these. And the laws read clearly. A wife is an extension of her husband. Given this principle, the structure of the institution is hardly surprising: no freedom of

movement, unpaid domestic labor, and sexual intercourse at the will and determination of the husband.

Since "normal" intercourse within marriage is defined as "without contraception," if the husband so desires, the man controls the woman's reproductive process.

One of the famous "achievements" of the last feminist movement was the "Married Woman's Property Act." How about a Slave's Property Act? How much sense would that make? Would you want to claim this as a qualitative change in the institution of marriage? On what possible basis can the institution of marriage be saved?

I mentioned earlier that the only possible alteration in the past within the oppression of women would have to have been in the consciousness of the Oppressed of their oppression. Many first generation slaves had to be kept in chains. By the second generation, few slaves needed chains or overt coercion. If the Oppressed are isolated from each other, and if from birth they see other members of their class in certain roles, and if the conditions of freedom represent only a modification of their immediate situation, the slave may accept its political definition as Oppressed or inferior.

But no human being can "accept" oppression as such. The dilemma, psychologically, is either to resist the Oppressor or to accept that one is indeed inferior and that one's circumstances are appropriate to this fact. The alternative to this dilemma

104

[8] [I am indebted for much of the analysis within this paragraph to Linda Feldman.]
[9] [See *Abortion: Paper Number II*, pp.1–3; *The Institution of Sexual Intercourse*, pp. 13–23; *Radical Feminism and Love*, pp. 41–45; *Radical Feminism: Declaration of War*, pp. 46–55, for fuller developments of the political significance of the concept of functionalism.]

is to accept the notion of being an extension of another as one's identity. A woman's very life as a human being depends upon her attachment to, her identification with, her counterclass—men.

It is argued by some people in the Movement that the phenomenon of "love," particularly "romantic love," is a relatively recent development. But before I enter into that controversy here, I should point out the significance of the issue of love itself. Perhaps the most damning characteristic of the class of women is that, in the face of horrifying evidence of their situation, they stubbornly claim that, in spite of everything, they "love" their Oppressor. Now, some feminists advocate that until fairly recently women *did* resist their oppression, and that only recently their hatred for their Oppressor was perverted into its inverse—love.

This mental state, so desperately searched for by women, does not seem to me difficult to explain. It seems that "love" has a tradition as a response to overwhelming oppression.[10] In addition, it's part of the process of identifying with "the Man." In loving, there is a giving up of self. You could look at it as the only way for an oppressed individual to escape her oppression. She flips out.

Prostitution would seem to be the Oppressor's false alternative to marriage—keeping, by object lesson, the average woman locked into marriage and depend-

ent upon her Oppressor.

Rape would seem to be a terroristic activity.

Roles, as distinguished from function, are the expressions of aspects of class character within institutions.

As for what the Movement labels "civil rights" activities, such as fighting job discrimination, it should be evident by now that these are facets of women's oppression, are in that sense secondary, and reflect the roles assigned to women within the major sex institutions. Fighting job discrimination, as a primary attack on the oppression of women, is somewhat analogous to the blacks fighting "job discrimination" as a primary attack on the oppression of blacks in the 1850's. Tactical suicide!

Religion would seem to be some kind of governmental arm in charge of adjusting the consciousness of women to oppression.[11]

Keep in mind that any theory of women's oppression must account for every instance, construct and institution within that oppression.

Briefly, I want to suggest a rectifying program for the oppression of women. Clearly, women must first—as many as possible—cut themselves out of these sex institutions so that by organizing together, women can create a counter power block to that of men. So for God's sake, don't get married, for your own sake as well as for the Movement's. At the same time that the

---

[10] [See *Radical Feminism and Love*, pp. 41–45; *Radical Feminism: Metaphysical Cannibalism*, pp. 56–63; *Juniata II: The Political Woman*, pp. 89–94, for some thoughts on the politics of love. Note, especially, the interdependencies of religion, violence, and love.]

[11] [See *Catholic University*, pp. 190–197, for a development of the role of the Church in the oppression of women.]

major institutions are under attack, some means of crossing from oppression to freedom must be fought for.

The Feminists has proposed a reparations program modeled on the Veterans' Administration programs. This could be done by Executive Order. The program could be divided, as is the Veterans' Administration, into three categories of recipients: single women, married women, women with dependents. This would be a national commitment on such a scale that the expenditures might well approximate what we now appropriate for "defense." It would be naive to think that *any* government, much less ours, could be persuaded to such a commitment without, shall we say, gigantic pressure.

As for tactics,[12] what I found works the best is to separate out your goal and batter it from every possible angle, until it falls. For example, in the case of marriage. We'll need a massive educational campaign. And then we might bring a case against marriage under the Thirteenth Amendment, United States Constitution, which outlaws slavery and *involuntary* servitude.

Our government, as well as all others I know of, claim marriage to be *voluntary* servitude. But since women are not apprised of the terms of the contract, and since this ignorance invalidates every other kind of labor contract, the marriage contract should also be judged invalid.

Even the United Nations, hardly in the habit of radical viewpoints, claims that servitude is unnatural to the human condition. So unless someone wants to claim that women are inhuman, which would not be a *novel* claim, "voluntary" servitude is a contradiction in terms.

At the beginning, I said I wanted to speak about the possible alternatives for the individual woman. I think the answer to this is implicit in what I've said already. There is no such possibility as an "individual" woman. By class definition, women are not individual or free but rather extensions of other human beings.

Our society is constructed in such a way as to close off any alternatives to you except those set up by your Oppressor. You can't survive within marriage, and you can barely subsist outside of it. In fact, you have no choice at all, a fact which more and more women daily are acting upon.

You can only organize, and I mean *seriously* organize. This means nearly full-time commitment with other women to overthrow your oppression.

I also want to mention some of the instances of extensions of women's oppression in your own situation.

Most campus dispensaries do not prescribe birth control methods. Again, this becomes a kind of reproductive coercion.

The vast majority of your professors are men, so women have no role models.

106

[12] [See *Strategy and Tactics: A Presentation of Political Lesbianism*, pp. 135–189, for a fuller development of both defensive and offensive tactical warfare.]

The ratio at the University of Rhode Island is four males to one female.

There is a quota on the number of women students admissible. Here, it's two males to one female. Because of this asymmetrical quota system, colleges require a much higher grade average from women than from men. Tuitions are sometimes higher for women. Scholarships are fewer for women. Academic programs for men and women are different: colleges claim we have a different future. You'd better believe it!

The highest academic ratings are given to the all male, top colleges. The average academic ratings for the top five, female colleges are well over 250 points *lower* than those for the top five, all-male colleges. For example, Princeton's rating is 789, Barnard's is 520. Coeducational colleges fall someplace between.

The average college man can earn $6,000 to $8,000 per year on the strength of his B.A. The average college woman— $4,000 annually.

Compare the number of pages in your history books devoted to how white men (44 percent of our population) and black men (5 percent of our population) and women—black *and* white—51 percent of our population) won the right to vote.

And what about the University's segregation policies? Male and female student associations? Male and female dormitories? Male and female bathrooms? And, then,

when I prefer to speak to all women, the colleges and universities charge *me* with discrimination. They've got to be kidding. That's not discrimination, that's self-defense. It's wonderful how self-righteous men can become in the face of women getting their thing together.

I'd like to make an announcement before I tell you about the Amazons. For any women who want to stay after the coffee hour, I'll be glad to discuss whatever you like—particularly organizing.

I first came to know the Amazon legend in any detail in an attempt to find a precedent for Valerie Solanas' theories. It was at the time of her arrest.[13] Perhaps the strongest argument offered in support of the accusation that Miss Solanas was simply a kook was that women could never separate off from men. I thought I had recalled something to the effect that some group of women *had* formulated some sort of female nationalism.

I began to trace the story back. While it has many variations and these groups have been reported in several areas, these histories have some common components.

One of the most persistent legends in all of Greek mythology is that of the Amazons. A group of women, without men, lived on Phrygia. These women were agricultural and peaceful, except in self-defense of their homeland. They worshiped the Goddess

[13] [Valerie Solanas wrote *The Scum Manifesto,* the most important feminist statement written to date in the English language. She also shot pop-artist Andy Warhol and was arrested for this in June of 1968.]

Athena, the Goddess of wisdom, skills and warfare. Athena was said to have been an Amazon herself in past history.

At the same time, Theseus was on the Greek mainland trying to unify the Greek city-states into one nation. He had conquered all the other states, thus attaching them to the rest of his spoils. Theseus and all his people worshiped the God Dionysus, the God of wine and intemperance.

The Amazons were the last holdout to the Greek nation. Theseus and his warriors invaded Phrygia and abducted their queen, Antiope. The historians report that Theseus, in order to subdue and enslave Antiope, married her and knocked her up. All the historians agree that the greatest violation to the Amazons was marriage, not intercourse.

The Amazons prepared to make war on the Greeks. Since heretofore, all their wars had been defensive, thus fought on land, they had little skill with crossing the sea. And they arrived on the mainland much weakened by their voyage.

The Amazons laid seige to Athens for months. Antiope, corrupted by her enslavement, fought by the side of her husband and son. Accidentally, an arrow from one of her own people killed Antiope at her husband's side.

The Amazons retreated. But the Greeks commemorated this battle in verse, sculpture, architecture—in all their culture. Some historians claim that the Amazons really existed. I don't know if they did or not, but it seems reasonable to me that the legend is an indication of some historical resistance by women to men's oppression. Or it could represent some kind of ambivalence or guilt on the part of men because of their oppression of women.

In any case, it is a haunting legend and certainly has several morals.

UNTITLED

SOME NOTES TOWARD A THEORY OF IDENTITY[1]

Moral philosophy is an attempt to reconcile the claims of the individual and the claims of society. No political theory that disregards either of these claims can be successfully implemented.

There are many theoretical traps members of oppressed groups in revolt can fall into. One is the inability to see the forest for the trees. Since it is precisely that, the denial of individuality, which motivates class revolt, it is especially easy to overlook the necessary balance between the individual and society. This point, as well as many other difficulties, are avoided by name-calling: "individualism," "cult of the personality," "star," and so forth.

Any adequate account of the oppression of women must include or have implications for nearly every philosophical concept. The Women's Movement has barely grazed the surface of these issues, partly because this would be such a mammoth undertaking. But some issues, such as this one of the interrelationship between the nature of the individual and the nature of society, seem to continuously present themselves and demand resolution.

Since every individual is born and dies alone, as well as being one's own most constant companion, it seems reasonable to propose that the fulfillment of one's human potential would be of primary concern to each individual. The definition of "human potential" is obviously critical.

I suggested in *Radical Feminism: Metaphysical Cannibalism* that the distinctive capacity of Mankind is constructive imagination. A definition of "human potential" might be the exploration of and experimentation with all one's capacities, which are then realized as the sum and order of these activities. Perhaps it would be clearer in imagery: imagine an individual as the fusion of both the artist and the work of art, in mixed media. The individual is both the connoisseur, the conscious or objective, and the artistic process itself, the unconscious or most personal and unique aspect of the individual.

In terms of the artistic process, the artist has literally an infinite and necessarily unique number of materials to select from: the perception of objects alone or in combination from memory, of objects (animate and inanimate) outside itself, of relationships (e.g., cause and effect, orderings),

109

[1] [May 2, 1970.]

and so forth. The fulfillment of human potential would be the sense of completeness through a discrete temporal ordering. Every moment of one's life would have the characteristic of intactness, therefore, of completion. There would be, in theories of consciousness, therefore, some significance to the notions of past, but not of future.

The above is a sketch of the direction I think a humanistic metaphysics and epistemology must go in. Insofar as we are individuals, that is, human beings, we are discrete units—self-contained—and are primarily dependent upon ourselves for our humanity, or human "life."

One way of defining oppressed people is just this—that we are so violated by another group/groups as to deprive us of our humanity. Our mental processes are absorbed, so that choice and evolution are denied us. We are not discrete. We are not unique. Our time and activities are used, not to the end of each of our unique constructions, but as parts and additions to other individual's ends. It *is* consistent with freedom for all if individuals "use" each other as perceptions or phenomena. It is *not* consistent with freedom for all when some individuals, "Oppressors," violate the discretion of other individuals by appropriating their, the "Oppressed," time and capacities to the fulfillment of the Oppressor.

As soon as two or more persons cooperate in some activity, there is an "association," a "community," a "society." If one considers "human" life from the point at which it is conceived, that is, the mind, then the activities in which an individual engages with another individual must be secondary from the point of view of consciousness, the reality of the individual.

For whatever the original reasons, human beings collect in groups. Judging from present-day society, there are certain conveniences developed through specializations that no individual could produce or create alone. The same model I used for the individual human being can be used for any individual community, and again for any culture, era, or any other spatial or spatial/temporal unit. Every society has its own unique parts and orderings which interact to construct its particular character. This may be a more mechanistic process, or one might try to defend some notion of societal consciousness. The answer to that dilemma is not central here.

If the primary desire of the individual is to "live," then it seems reasonable that the individual with these values (I do not pretend these theories are current, just the opposite!) would take care that its human interrelationships would constitute an exact exchange of "services."[2] Any unequal exchange would jeopardize the evolution of individual identity. I'm assuming Kant's categorical imperative here, that human intellect understands the introduction of precedent as principle. If I induce some individual to work *for me,* then I accept a principle

110

[2] [See *The Institution of Sexual Intercourse*, pp. 13–23, and *Radical Feminism and Love*, pp. 41–45, for two key reciprocity issues within the oppression of women.]

that could theoretically result in my working *for him.*

A community, as an entity, entails certain activities peculiar to societies: community work (e.g., collecting garbage, farming, child care), and community legislation and commitment priorities (e.g., regulation of exchange, community investment). The community as a whole (one individual, one vote) determines what the community requires in terms of goods and services. The production of the items from these categories would be divided into the significantly creative and those items not considered by the community as creative. (Each member must vote on the basis of whether *it* would choose to be employed in its spare time at that task.) All noncreative tasks would fall into the category of "community work."

The equality issue[3] is common to all political theory. Most political theorists claim some version of it. It is generally agreed that it refers to equal *treatment* or just distribution of goods. The arguments turn on the criteria used to determine what is "just" or equal treatment. But in reference to what? Would you be prepared to accept that an individual who did not contribute an equal share of labor would still be entitled to an equal share of the goods produced by everyone else's labor? Or would you say that such a person would not qualify as a "citizen." And how might one distinguish between an individual who *could* not participate, because of some alleged incapacity, and someone who *would* not participate. This last distinction is an important one, since an individual who contributes unequally through no will or fault of its own could hardly be denied the privileges of society. In fact, such an individual would need the services and goods of society more than some others, since it could hardly provide for itself if it couldn't participate in the minimal work divided among many.

All I have said so far is "theory" in the worst sense. It assumes numerous concepts as fact, any one of which, if false, would challenge what followed. I "assume" that it is "natural" to human nature to desire satisfaction (but what about the death wish and *angst?*). I "assume" that such a major cultural reversal is possible as to radically change the source of identity from outer-directed to inner-directed.[4] (What kind of evolutionary theory would be consistent with that?) I "assume" that human nature could function so as to fuse one's self-interest with the interests of others in a categorical imperative. (Where is the evidence for any of this?) It is one of the many nightmares of feminism, that to even conceive of what could count as significant changes for women, one must begin by jumping off one cliff after another. And I haven't even considered, here, how such changes could possibly be implemented!

Now that I have made the barest sug-

111

---

[3] [See *Juniata II: The Equality Issue*, pp. 65–75.]

[4] [See *Juniata II: Metaphysical Cannibalism or Self-Creativity*, pp. 76–81.]

gestion of a possible nature of the individual and the barest suggestion of a possibly reasonable society in which such an individual might live in justice, how do our present circumstances compare to this ideal? How discrete are our human individuals? Is every one realizing the fulfillment of their own unique identities? Is *anyone* realizing their potential? Are some people doing so more than others? Are there degrees of fulfillment? of humanity? of oppression?

We, as feminists,[5] have banded together in an association. But there is a difference between the "association" described earlier and a *political* association. A political association has several additional characteristics:

(1) it is formed for some external purpose or function, and
(2) because of this purpose, more of the needs of individuals are subsumed in terms of time and standards than in an ordinary community.

If a political association is formed around oppression, the implication is that not only is the association such that the nature of the individual is temporarily subsumed, but that, in addition, the nature of these particular individuals is already in a state of deprivation. So that to say that oppressed people must give up part of their identity in order to organize against their oppression is to claim, in some sense, that the *cause* of their oppression and the *effect* of their oppression are synonymous.[6] Thus, "x" must move from "A" to "B," in order to remain at "A."

It seems much more reasonable to suggest that, given the desirability of personal identity, properly based, those persons deprived of this would join together as individuals in a confederation to struggle together as individuals against whatever relevant political association is depriving them of their individual identities.

The direction the Women's Movement is going in is just the opposite. False identity, identity imposed from the outside,[7] is apparently being confused with individual identity of any kind whether established from without, from within, from some combination of these two, or identity resulting from some other process altogether. The trend is toward collective identity, which is a contradiction if applied to individuals. How can an individual who is being denied its individual identity by being classified and restricted through this classification achieve a *greater* sense of individuality by further subsuming itself within that very classification depriving it?

The concept and function of resistance groups seems to be very tangled at this point in the Movement. It seems reasonable

---

[5] [This paper was originally written, as were so many of my pieces, as an intra-Movement statement.]

[6] [In other words, the *cause* of an individual instance of class oppression is the identity-building process of the Oppressor. The *effect* of that same individual instance of class oppression is the identity casualty: the Oppressed. Ergo, "identity," or "individuality," is the enemy.]
[7] [The "identity" resulting from the process I describe as "metaphysical cannibalism."]

that individuals come together on the basis of certain shared beliefs and intentions. On these beliefs and intentions, they act in concert. It also seems reasonable that such an association should operate on the same principles as a just society described above: equal participation, equal decision-making powers, equal distribution of the goods produced by the equal participation. These principles are very easily and simply implemented. Every associate must contribute equal labor, and any other pledge the association may determine, in equal amounts; every associate must participate equally in discussing and determining (by majority vote or consensus) the policies and activities of the association; every associate is entitled to an equal share in any benefits accruing to the association (e.g., money, participation as association representative at conferences, spokeswoman for the association in interviews, programming).

The issue of equality has generally been understood, in political theory, as referring to the equal treatment of all individuals. It has never, to my knowledge, meant that any two individuals are the same. "Equality" means that, insofar as any individual is a participant in some association, the same rights accrue to each member as individuals within that association. There is a great difference between saying that

(1) each individual in association "A" is entitled to a vote, and
(2) each individual's definition, or identity, is synonymous with the definition of either a "pro" or "con" vote, except under the *most* restricted interpretation.

It might seem incredible to someone outside such a movement that such a confusion could occur. However, it's consistent with a deeper psychological understanding of oppression and of some of the binds in which oppressed people find themselves.

First of all, there is a distinction between, on the one hand, characteristics of *class* "A," and, on the other hand, all the characteristics held by the *members of class* "A." This is especially the case in political classification. A "class" is some group, that is, object, that is posited. A "class" has no psychology or motives.[8] "Members" of that class, especially when they were the initiators of their own class conception, *could,* or perhaps even *should,* have motives ascribed to them.

In the case of the oppressor class, a class is organized *around* some characteristic unique to some group of members picked out of society at large. The Oppressor then claims this identifying characteristic as the rationale for privileges. This characteristic, then, by association, comes

113

[8] [Whenever I use the term "motive" or "motivation," I am referring to some pattern of behavior sufficiently strong to prove intent.]

to have positive connotations. Members flock to this group, because it offers benefits, both material and psychological, to all qualified persons *regardless* of whatever other class characteristics they may have. Subsumption into this class, even in many cases to the point of anonymity, is a characteristic of at least some members of the Oppressor. For example, a construction worker may belong to only one positive class, the male, so that he clings to that class almost exclusively—not as an individual, but as a member of that Oppressor class.

Anonymity,[9] or "class facelessness," is advantageous *to class solidarity* only if one intends to oppress.[10] Responsibility for oppressive acts can then fall on no *one;* responsibility for group acts can then be shifted from one member to another; irresponsibility and immoral acts are concealed behind a fortress (but only people in power have fortresses) of "class" identity. *Any* actions by such a group are, simply by virtue of anonymity, impregnable. "I do 'X' because I am a male. Don't blame me for it. It is a characteristic of my class. My *class* won't

114

surrender the characteristic of power." That quotation, in some variation, should be familiar to all feminists.

The advantage of class facelessness for individual members of the oppressor class is obvious. The individual male (or white, or rich, et cetera) cannot be held to account for his behavior. He reinforces the behavior (thus, the rights or privileges) of his class, and, thus, only *accidentally* derives benefits, while ostentatiously displaying clean hands. That's not a bad bargain; privilege *sans* penalty. The *motive* behind class solidarity for individual members of the oppressor class are clear: profit for himself, at the expense of his counterclass.

Anonymity is, then, one of the artificial and crucial characteristics that maintain the oppressor class as stable. The class, and classification itself, is, of course, also manmade or artificial. But that's what political theory should be about. It must answer these questions. "*What* is the structure of oppression?" And, then, "*Why* does the structure of oppression exist?"

Oppressed people in revolt (my model

---

[9] [Anonymity for individuals within the Weatherpeople (a militant antiwar group), for a given act, may have a tactical value. But this is not the sense of "anonymity," or anti-individuality, at issue here. Rather, this paper concerns such disputes within the Movement as over whether or not a writer should sign her name to her work, et cetera.]

[10] [*Within* oppressed groups, the term "exploitation" is probably more appropriate than the term "oppression." The exception to this would be when a highly formalized structure exists, such as the hierarchy of offices in formally structured organizations.

The point of "exploitation" within oppressed groups is made in *University of Rhode Island: Movement Politics and Other Sleights of Hand,* p. 99, in a reference to and brief discussion of the "discipline" issue. The "discipline" issue concerns the exploitation of some members of a group, who contribute their agreed upon share

of group work, by other members, who contribute less than their agreed upon share.

The "identity" issue is an extension of the "discipline" issue. The "identity" issue concerns work done by individuals over and above the mutually agreed upon work for the group. "Identity" acts have a cumulative effect.

Perhaps one of my greatest regrets from my period in The Feminists (October, 1968 to March, 1970), is that I let the Creative Workshop die out. This workshop, formed in the winter of 1969-1970, was to encourage and support individual members in seeking out and developing their creative potentialities. This development is crucial to the formation of individual identity.

The Creative Workshop met only a few times. Its purpose, as well as its topic, was shifted. The Creative Workshop was changed to the Class Workshop.]

here is "women") classically engage in *"folie à deux."*[11]

Folie à deux is known as a psychological phenomenon, or, more technically, as a "functional psychosis." It is found among pairs of individuals in prolonged personal contact. *Folie à deux* is the *transference of abnormal reaction patterns from one person to another.*

In an extensive analysis[12] of 103 cases, this is the breakdown in terms of relationships:

sisters:	40 cases
husband-wife:	28 cases
mother-child:	24 cases
brothers:	11 cases

What was *not* noted, however, was the sex pattern: three times the number of females to males.

Almost no feminist work has been done on "mental health": on the relationship or lack of it between sex and types of mental disorders. The literature claims there is no significant correlation. However, in the types known as "hysteria" and *"folie à deux,"* there are very strong patterns. I believe this is yet another fruitful area for feminist (i.e., political) investigation.

Folie à deux occurs when adjustive capacity is reduced and stress occurs. (Up against the wall, against a gun.)

My suggestion is that the oppressed class falls prey to *folie à deux*. The evidence is overwhelming and varied.

The first Women's Movement, and the initiators of the second one, insisted on "equality" between men and women. While the sense of equality here is "equal rights," the *meaning* could not be that. The class "men" is artificial politically. The rights they now have are clearly Oppressor rights. It is contradictory, i.e., impossible, for the Oppressor and the Oppressed to *ever* have "equal" rights. *Folie à deux.*

Marriage, if one examines the laws which define it, is as much if not more in the interests of men than slavery was in the interests of the master. And yet, the aims of the Movement are to get rid of the abuses *within* marriage, *equalize* the roles, but, for *God's* sake, keep the institution. How can you equalize the roles when the essential *nature* of these roles is to be *contrasting*? Could you maintain slavery if you "equalized" the roles of master-slave to master-master? *Folie à deux!*

115

---

[11] [The following work on *folie à deux* was originally done in connection with *Radical Feminism and Love,* see pp. 41–45. My reason for transferring the work to this paper was to project another facet of "identity" confusion by the female class with the male class. This is yet another dimension to the problem of identity as it relates to oppressed people.]

[12] [Alexander Gralnick, *"Folie à Deux—The Psychosis of Association: A Review of 103 Cases and the Entire English Literature, with Case Presentations," Psychiatric Quarterly,* (April 1942) pp. 230–263.]

It's true that both "men" and "women" are classes. But their separate functions within their class system, the male-female class system, make any further analogy untenable.

The oppressor class is defined by its own members, that is, by the recipients of the benefits deriving from that definition.

The oppressed class is just the opposite. The members of this class are not so as a matter of choice, but by default. They do not define themselves, they are defined by their counterclass.

It is in the interests of the Oppressor to claim *class* identity, because this identity insures him guaranteed expansion of his privilege and, thus, his identity as an individual.

Membership in the Oppressed, however, is just the opposite. It represents a guaranteed restriction of that member's identity as an individual.

The oppressor class must be a power class to maintain its position.

Members of the Oppressed have traditionally tried to escape their class definition by attaching themselves, individually, to a member of the oppressor class. This is usually referred to in the Movement as a "personal" solution. There is no personal solution to a political problem.

Men often threaten feminists that, if we're not careful, *men* will organize. They already are. It's called the Establishment.

As women have recognized that we are treated in certain ways because of this class identity, we have tried to organize in groups as a counterforce or power to counteract our counterclass: i.e., men.

INDIVIDUAL RESPONSIBILITY AND HUMAN OPPRESSION

(INCLUDING SOME NOTES ON PROSTITUTION AND PORNOGRAPHY)[1]

Before the Women's Movement re-grouped in 1966-67, my field was aesthetics. Among other things, I was a staff critic for *Art News.* I recall an incident in the early 1960's that seems relevant here today.

John Canaday, an avowed enemy of the contemporary abstract art, reviewed a collection of "old masters" with consider-able warmth. It was later discovered that roughly a quarter to a third of these paint-ings were fakes—and not particularly good fakes even at that. To make matters worse, the fakes were within the range of Cana-day's specialty ("late impressionism", as I recall).

Now you might ask, what's so special about that? Can't a man make a mistake? As one wag pointed out to me at the time: "Of course, but FIFTY-NINE???" The up-shot of the debate surrounding this incident was that Canaday, simply by virtue of being a critic, presented himself as some sort of expert on his subject. He had, because of this, certain standards he must meet—over and above honesty. His special responsi-bility as an authority was more than simple belief but, in fact, knowledge. Good faith, when one separates oneself out from the rest of humanity to address a topic, requires the *"truth."* This is especially the case when one's opinion carries consequences for others.

Canaday could make or break many artists, at least until their next exhibition. If he liked a show, thousands flocked to it. The artist was guaranteed, thereby, enough sales to continue his work.

No one could expect a critic to lie. However, given the stakes, the critic would certainly seem to have an absolute obliga-tion to take every conceivable measure to make certain his judgments were correct and precise *and* carefully documented. And the public certainly should, as it in fact did, judge and listen to Canaday in the future on the basis of his past performance.

In aesthetics, as well as in almost all other fields, individuals are judged and re-spected in accordance with their behavior. In politics, however, this standard criteria is not applied. This is interesting, since from a reasonable point of view, politics would seem the most important point at

117

[1] [May 28, 1970; presented at the Women's Conference co-sponsored by the National Conference of Christians and Jews, and by the Women's Unit, Office of the Governor; New York City.]

which such criteria *should* apply. After all,

(1) everybody should be an expert on right and wrong.
(2) A society is no more nor less than the individuals who are in it: *every* individual makes it a little better or a little worse.
(3) The consequences of the decisions made by a society can be overwhelming for the members within that society.

Politics would seem the paradigm case for individual responsibility. The fact that it is not treated as such merits examination.

In a democracy (for our present purposes to be defined as "a society wherein the majority of individuals vote"), the individual is up against the wall. There are only two possibilities: to be an accomplice or to be a revolutionary. The "choice" is from a stacked deck. There is almost no room in which the individual can maneuver. Thus, the "maneuver" that most of us make, in order to avoid either having blood on our hands or blood on our heads, is to deny that we as individuals *can,* much less *ought,* to do anything at all. This evasion, of course, leaves us with blood on our hands.

The reason I began with the critic incident is that I think it parallels the position of the feminist. To be a feminist is in itself to make a kind of critique. One sets oneself up in opposition to what is now a monolith—society.[2] What should be the norm—that is, dialogue and consensus—is, instead, personally dangerous.

To speak out and try to persuade other people to the *truth* is the work of revolutionaries. It is not enough to *believe;* a citizen has the obligation to *know.* The work of the revolutionary is simply that: to be, in whatever society it may find itself in, a good citizen of the world. The definition of a "good citizen" must be found in the conscience of each person, and that person must be held accountable for it.

The definition of a revolutionary seems to me, from a moral point of view, to be obvious: one whose behavior is determined by what *should* be. The first step in changing bad conditions is to reject them. One must wash the blood off one's own hands before suggesting, with much credibility, that others do likewise. For example, the abortion laws were immoral and, thus, from my view, illegal. I ignored them by what appeared to be open violation of them.

Only when all people, *each* of us, refuse to submit, will oppression disappear. Each of us *is* the revolution. The revolution will have occurred when *each* and *all* of us have gotten off our knees—whether *within* the church or *to* the government.[3]

No one has, or should have, power over anyone else. But each of us *is* responsible for ourselves. When I get off my knees,

---

[2] [This is, to say the least, not safe. But the price of safety is total submission. Being one of the living dead is not my idea of a solution.]

[3] [This paper was "sponsored" by the National Conference of Christians and Jews, and by the Governor's Office.]

I've done all I can, and the revolution is complete for me.

You may wonder what these abstractions concerning individual responsibility and human oppression have to do with Women's Liberation. At the moment, a proper understanding of these "abstractions" is the pivot upon which any hopes for us turn. There has never been a true revolution in history. There have been many incidents which have been *called* revolutions, which would, more properly, be called "shake-ups." The oppression of women has never even been seriously challenged by these so-called revolutions.[4]

The male-female class division is generally agreed to be the first class division in society. Some group of individuals were assigned some artificial set of tasks—later to be designated as a "role." This assumption, that the male-female division was the first major class division, also suggests that the male-female division is the *model* for human oppression. Thus, the fact that our oppression has never been fundamentally changed is significant for *all* people. History bears this out.

Women themselves, however, for better or for worse, have no temptations for minor changes. It's all or nothing.[5]

This current women's movement has been going on for four years. This movement, as was the last, is a mess. On the one hand, we have revisionist groups (revisionist for women? you've got to be kidding!) working feverishly on irrelevancies. On the other hand, we have revolutionary groups chasing themselves in circles and not moving out. The conservatives claim women "out there" aren't ready for radical change (see what I mean? no blood on their hands!). The "radicals" take the offensive: individual responsibility[6] is not only unwise, it's treasonable. Everyone must move at once. Everybody must wait for everybody else. Anyone who moves out according to their individual conscience is a "leader," unless, of course, they are "leading" to the rear.

All of this hysteria is understandable. The problem is that it is self-defeating. Again, the revolutionary is one who acts as it thinks everyone must act in a good and just society.[7]

The truth is, fortunately, quite simple. The obfuscations of it, on the other hand, require ingenuity—ingenuity inspired by fear and self-deception.[8] My point is that a feminist gives up the privilege of self-deception at that moment she claims the role of social critic.

A good illustration of all that I've said is the economics issue. First of all, since

119

---

[4] [A reference to my paper delivered on Bastille Day (July 14), 1970; *Radical Feminism, Revolution, and Truth (A Critique of "Revolutionary" History)*; Sacramento State College. Unpublished.]
[5] [See *Juniata II: The Equality Issue*, pp. 65–75.]
[6] [The issue of "individual responsibility" is clearly tied to the questions concerning "identity" raised in *Untitled: Some Notes Toward a Theory of Identity*, pp. 109–116.

"Individual responsibility" also encompasses the "equality," "discipline," and "consistency" issues. See *University of Rhode Island: Movement Politics and Other Sleights of Hand*, especially pp. 98 and 99.]
[7] [See *Untitled: Notes Toward a Theory of Identity* for my use of Kant's categorical imperative, pp. 110 and 111.]
[8] [See *On "Violence in the Women's Movement": Self-Deception*, pp. 212–221.]

economics as a major social institution developed *after* the oppression of women, there's some question whether we should attack that as a primary target. But leaving that question aside, the feminist economic strategies have been employment discrimination and socialism. Now if, as all feminist groups hold, women are oppressed as a *class,* then this class oppression can only be *broken* in class terms.

What follows from the assumption that women are a class, and that they are oppressed, is that some other class is doing the oppressing. Since there is only one other class in that universe of discourse,[9] namely men, men must be oppressing women. This is not to say that men are intrinsically the enemies of women, anymore than when the Germans invaded France it was generally held that Germans were the *natural* enemies of the French. It does mean, however, that when the public policy of one group is to abridge the rights of another, it is prudent of the victim to take certain precautionary measures, such as keeping tabs on the agents and wearing bulletproof vests while in their company. The alternative is death.

Now, if men as a class are systematically oppressing women as a class economically, is it reasonable to believe that men would allow any significant number of women *out* of that class oppression? Anything more than a token number would challenge the class definition of women.

Moreover, and even more important, positions taken by women would deprive men of those same positions, which would challenge the class definition of *men*! Not only does history give evidence against the efficacy of this approach, it doesn't make sense.

Socialists come in as many varieties as do egalitarians. No one, however, has focused on the primacy of the housewife to economic systems. At this moment, housewives account for an unemployment rate of 23 percent which never appears on the Labor Department's reports. And we are currently in a panic over 4.8 percent![10] When I have suggested the relevancy of this point to Marxist women, the basic reply is "housewives are irrelevant, politically, since they're unproductive labor." Now, I can understand why Marxists are not interested in an economic base of unpaid housewives, but this is hardly an appropriate attitude for a feminist! The result is that there is no radical feminist economic analysis. Thus, the feminist economic position seems to be revisionist.

A current variation of the economics issue combines both positions mentioned earlier, in that it does not challenge the class definition of women, and it depends methodologically on a Marxist position—which necessarily does not include a solution applicable to women.

---

[9] [The universe of sex classes.]

[10] [Since the writing of this piece, our unemployment figures have reached 6.5 percent.]

The argument goes like this (I will try to represent it at its best):

(1) every woman, because she is oppressed, *understands* this oppression as well as every other woman

(2) since every woman *knows* the same things, every woman has essentially the same things to *say*

(3) since every woman has the same things to *say,* every woman should be *listened* to equally

(4) therefore, the opportunities to be heard should be divided equally among all women *in the Movement* (sic)[11]

(5) in addition:
   (a) since the condition and the knowledge of it are synonymous
      (1) to accept any benefit (e.g., money) from a negative source (oppression) would be immoral
      (2) therefore, any monies, earned from work connected with the Movement for women, must be turned over to the Movement.

To begin with, to *be* or *have* something does not necessarily entail understanding it in great detail. For example, the individual possessing a pain knows best what that pain *feels* like. (And all women may *be* unhappy—whether they admit to it or not.) But to claim that to *feel* a pain is synonymous *with,* or even necessary *to,* understanding its cause and, thus, its cure, is not self-evident. Evidence of knowledge would depend on past performance. (We're back to the critic.) The challenge to (1), if it holds, undercuts (2), (3), and (4).

The second part of the argument, starting with (5) is still, however, of some political interest. If women working for the cause are not able to sustain themselves from their work (no one gets rich pushing a true revolution), what will be their source of income? There's only one other possibility: the employ of the opposition. The Oppressor pays far better; however, he *never* employs people except to work in his interests. If the choice is between working for the revolution and subsisting on that, or working for the enemy and living on *that,* the choice seems clear.

My personal view, which I have presented many times in the Movement, is that we should fix some minimum wage (e.g., $5,000 @ year) per individual, and that whatever anyone earns over that, through any means, should be contributed to the Movement or some part of it, so that as many persons as possible could devote all their time to the cause. That, however, is only part of my reason for this suggestion. Even

121

more important is that I believe that in the good society, the societal product should be equally divided; I think the consistency issue[12] is of primary importance. Most objections I've heard to this, within the Movement, turn on not being willing to accept a survival level of subsistence.

I have come increasingly to realize that all the apparent contradictions and inconsistencies, which perforate Movement ideology, form such a persistent pattern that it is this *pattern,* at the moment, which it is *crucial* to understand and to which it is necessary to find the key.[13] It is with the intention of understanding this pattern and attempting to devise a resolution to it, that I will not, at present, participate in any one group.

Another example of this pattern[14]—the pattern of contradiction and inconsistency —is to be found around the issue of marriage. This issue has been less developed, within the Movement, than have been some others.[15]

It would seem that if a feminist has a class analysis of the oppression of women, that the obvious place to look for its loci would be in those institutions peculiar to the male-female relationship: marriage, motherhood, prostitution, rape, lesbianism (as a reaction formation). Since the highest incidence of the male-female relationship is in marriage, it should be a primary target. An examination of the domestic relations laws

bears out this elementary deduction. Marriage contracts the woman's unpaid labor for life. In addition, the woman loses freedom of movement, and the authority for initiative and control of sexual intercourse (a necessary deprivation for the entailment *within* marriage of motherhood, thus, the family). Love and affection are judicially held to be irrelevant to the essence of the marriage contract and its fulfillment.

There are two basic responses to these facts in the Women's Movement:

.   (1) we must abolish these abuses and keep the institution; or
    (2) marriage must be abolished but. not until there is an alternative for women.

To suggest that we abolish the abuses and keep the institution is something like suggesting to a woman that she remodel a house by removing, without replacement,

(1) the roof
(2) the floor, and
(3) all four walls.

To suggest that we all sit tight until there's an alternative begs the question. For, from whence might we look for this miracle? Is there anyone, not a member of the Oppressed, from whom it's reasonable

[12] [See *University of Rhode Island: Movement Politics and Other Sleights of Hand,* p. 99, for a reference to and brief explanation of the "consistency" issue.]
[13] [See *On "Violence in the Women's Movement: Collaborators and Self-Deception,* pp. 198–221.]
[14] [What Florynce Kennedy calls part of the "pathology" of oppression.]

[15] [As of February, 1973, a general interest has begun to be developed around the institution of marriage. The Feminists pioneered this issue, in 1969, when we brought charges against the Marriage License Bureau for "fraud with malicious intent," and against Mayor Lindsay for "conspiracy to enslave, imprison, and rape the women of New York City."]

to look to for a solution? A happy thought. But is it reasonable?

The thread that runs through all of this is that just about everyone knows, in varying degrees of consciousness, where women are at present. Considerably fewer know, in varying degrees of detail, where we want to go. But that yawning *gap* in between—in fact, the Revolution—only a miniscule number even seem to see. On the one hand, solutions are acted upon that seem staggeringly inadequate. On the other hand, we wait as if expecting the revolution to descend from above. If we have learned nothing else in the last years, it should be that SHIT comes from above, not Liberation.

You might wonder why I came here to speak if I had nothing, in a sense, to say. I believe that's a legitimate question. Quite frankly, I came because I committed myself to it some time ago. However, the truth, or an attempt at it, is perhaps the best we can do at the moment. Perhaps liberation is, in part, the self-respect to say whatever that truth seems to be.

I have the main question. I have a very few answers. I have no solution. I hope that by working out the rest of the answers, a solution will suggest itself.

A few of these questions are:

what is the structure and behavior of the oppressor role;

what is the structure and behavior of the oppressed role;

what is a method of effecting internal change;

what is the nature of class—of institution—of role—of value;

what ethic and motivation would the good and just society require;

how would the concept and source of identity change, and to what?

As I mentioned before: we women do not have the temptation of mediocrity. It's all or nothing. Can we do it? I don't know. That I am a feminist commits me to the belief that we can create a revolution. But since I don't believe one can recommend an act of faith, I leave you in the quandary of doing nothing, or adopting some position I have, at best, only raised questions about.

123

I have two last issues to raise: one for action, and one to close. The first is prostitution.

The significance of prostitution for the Women's Movement should be apparent. It's the oldest profession in the world. Until the last Movement, it was the only possibility for a dependent woman to be self-supporting. It is, still, the best paid profession for women. It is the necessary function, in some degree or variation, for "women" as defined in our past and present society. Appropriately enough, for today, prostitution began as a practice within the institution of religion.[16] Prostitution is the false alternative posed by men for women to the female role.

---

[16] [This Conference was sponsored, in part, by the National Conference of Christians and Jews.]

One of the more interesting features of prostitution is that, while it is still in some form the only means by which women can achieve social success (make lots of money), its concomitant is that prostitutes are set outside the market place. In other words, the price of success is ostracism.

It has been particularly important to segregate prostitutes from "good" women. The purpose of this appears to be to mystify the political function of and to, thereby, magnify the fear in "good" women of prostitutes themselves. A "peripheral" benefit of this segregation is the prevention of contact between the "good" women, and the only street fighters we've got.

I tried to begin to rectify this division today. As I write this, I still am not sure how successful that attempt will be.

I had wanted my friends, the prostitutes, to come and speak for themselves. They were being badly hassled, at the time, in the Times Square area—arrested for vagrancy, entrapped, and so forth.

I had wanted the "bad" women to confront the "good" women and to appeal to these good women to come out into the streets and help them.

The prostitutes seemed willing. The conference sponsors were upset at the prospect of my sharing my platform time with such outlaws. I won them over with my ultimatum: "Either the street comes inside, or I go out to the street."

In the end, the prostitutes decided not to participate, because they feared they would be singled out for retaliatory measures by the City.

Since I had no way of being sure, until the conference was under way, whether or not my friends were coming, I had to ad-lib when they didn't show. Thus, I am compensating here for what I actually said at the conference but did not have written down in my original paper.

I include a proposal I made to Human Rights for Women, Inc.,[17] at approximately the same time as this conference, for a Preliminary Survey to a Comprehensive Study on Prostitution.

Considering its importance in society, prostitution has received only the most cursory of sociological study. There has been no significant political analysis of it. There are several reasons for this seemingly inexplicable neglect.

Prostitution serves a complex political function. It is a symbol, or totem, to women of the alternative to the traditional female role. Mystery is essential to symbolic potency.

Prostitution is the specter of economic success for women: institutionalized rape in its most public, brutal form. To "good" women, prostitutes are the corpses of lynched victims. (Rape would be comparable to the

124

---

[17] [Proposal submitted in June of 1970.]

terroristic device of the "lynching" process.)

Men wish the realities of prostitution concealed because of what such a study would reveal about them. Women fear it, because they fear some revelation about the true nature of the political position of *all* women.

Men and women seem to have reached a tacit agreement to conceal prostitution out of sight, but not out of mind. Thus, prostitution is in all countries either illegal, in which case it must operate underground, or it is legal and segregated, which serves the same political purpose.

Thus, prostitution has not been studied, first, because no one has wanted to know about it, and, second, because its concealment makes such a study by standard methods extremely difficult.

It seems clear, however, that to all women concerned with improving their situation as women, an understanding of prostitution is essential. It is the "oldest profession" for women in the world. Until the end of the last century, prostitution was virtually the *only* occupation open to dependent and unattached women.

Prostitution has generally been viewed by the "experts" as the natural form of anti-social regression for women, instead of being viewed as a crime (with all of those *political* implications), as would be the case with men.

According to Kinsey, 69 percent of U. S. white males have visited prostitutes at least once.

Prostitution is key to any economic analysis of women. It is key to any political analysis of the class of women. And, finally, and most important, prostitution is key to any adequate analysis of the structure of the male-female class relationship.

I propose a preliminary survey to any major project on this subject for two reasons. My first reason is that there has been no important work done on the subject before. My second reason is that it is necessary to permit the structure of the project to suggest itself through the nature of the institution. One of the chief dangers of a study of prostitution is that we all have strong, preconceived notions of it from our culture, without any substantial body of facts.

I met four prostitutes, while I was in jail[18] two months ago. They, in turn, have introduced me to twenty other prostitutes, near whom they work. The study would cover four boroughs—Manhattan, the Bronx, Brooklyn, Queens—and, Westchester.

I will prepare a questionnaire based on the interviews I've had so far.

[18] [April, 1970.]

I shall ask the women I know now to prepare lists of relevant questions. I shall, then, prepare my final initial questionnaire and interview a sample of five hundred prostitutes.

Based on my present information, the survey will eventually be divided into these areas: the history of prostitution; its political significance; legal approaches to it; international and cultural variations; an economic interpretation and comparison with other female occupational alternatives; hierarchical structure within prostitution; social breakdown of sample (by education, parental status, personal history); sociological description of clients by class, race, religion, marital status; significance of prostitution to feminist movement.

SAMPLE QUESTIONS

1. How long have you been a prostitute?
2. What would you guess to be the average length of time of a prostitute's career? What determines this?
3. What is the duration of average boyfriend?
4. Do you have a pet? What kind?
5. How would you describe the options open to women in our society? Wife? Mother? Secretary?
6. What ten areas in this country would you think heaviest in prostitution? In what order?
7. Do you know much about the situation in other countries?
8. Are you ever denied your civil rights if someone knows your occupation? How?
9. Are you charged more for services, e.g., cleaning, food, taxis, etc.?
10. If other women condemn prostitution, why do you think they feel so threatened by it?
11. What do you think of marriage?
12. Do you think most women are too dependent on men?
13. Do you think prostitutes held in jail are political prisoners? Why?
14. Do you think prostitution is political in nature? Why?
15. Why do you think so few women buy men as prostitutes? Because women don't have enough money?
16. How does being a prostitute affect your attitude toward sex?
17. Do you think sex is a natural need? Do you think sex is, in some way, more natural for men? If so, how do you explain this?
18. Why do you think prostitutes are ostracized socially? To discourage more women from going into the profession?

The second, and last issue is pornography. I define pornography as political propaganda to distinguish it from erotic literature. Roughly one-third of pulp literature is pornography. More is designed for male consumption than female.

To maintain oppression as stable, the key is the Oppressor. The key to revolution is the Oppressed.

I list, briefly, some current pornography, with title headings, under male and female subdivisions.

MALE PORNOGRAPHY

1. *Man's Life: the Action Magazine for Men* (June 1970)
   —"One Night of Hell in the House of Naked Pain"
   —"Exposed: the Truth about Nymphomaniacs"

2. *New Man*
   —"Soul Mates of Torment for France's Monster King"
   —"Revealed: the Strange Sorority of Women who want to be Murdered"
   —"Smash the Latins' Jungle Combine of Sin and Slavery"

3. *World of Men* (July 1970)
   —"I fought the Maiden-Butchering Fiend of Hell Village"
   —"The Devil's Fangs to Strip her Flesh"
   —"Exposé: the Sex Perils of Coed Nymphs"

4. *Battle Cry* (July 1970)
   —"You can buy a Woman's Body —but the Price is your Life"
   —"Special Feature: Men Wanted —for Women who can't get enough Sex"
   —"The Girl who gambled for Blood"

5. *True Mystery Detective* (July 1970)
   —"Joy Girl and the Jail Bird; she was a Night Club Hostess with *Red Hot Passions!*"
   —"Who strangled the Stripteaser?—We made love and then she bit me!"
   —"Hot Flames and a Cold Corpse!—She was a Luscious Beauty and he was a Desperate Killer!"

6. *Thrilling Adventure* (July 1970)
   —"Sex on the Moon!—All Female Passengers on a Space Voyage shall enter Apollo unclad!"
   —"The insatiable Nympho!—She beheaded 26 lovers!—Until she was caught by a French detective!"
   —"The Night Hitler murdered his Mistress!—two trusted Storm Troopers entered Hitler's bedroom and carried away a grisly Bundle!"

7. *Detective Files*
   —"Held Captive for seven Days by a sex Maniac!"
   —"What is a Man to do when his own Wife is pregnant? Some Girl in this Town is gonna get raped!"
   —"The Mad Dog marked his Trail with bloody Corpses!"
8. *Man's Conquest* (June 1970)
   —"Operation Sofia: Bring out Bulgaria's prize Beauty"
   —"Latest terror Craze—Cycle Queens of Violence"
9. *True Police Cases* (June 1970)
   —"He committed 4 'perfect' Murders—the 5th was fashioned by the Hand of God"
   —"Was it illicit Love which drove the Engineer to concoct One of the cleverest and most cunning multiple Murder Plots in Criminal History?"

FEMALE PORNOGRAPHY
1. *True Experience: for today's young woman* (May 1970)
   —" 'Good Morning, Sex Fiend!' my wife says each day"
   —"Husband-Hating Town: they made their women suffer"
2. *Modern Confessions* (June 1970)
   —"My Husband needs 12 Women to keep him Happy"

—"Pregnant and I'm only 13 years old!"
3. *My Story* (1970)
   —"Tired of waiting for My Frigid Wife to thaw out!"
   —"Terror in a T-Shirt"
   —"Because I looked sexy Boys Got The Wrong Ideas"
4. *Exciting Confessions: the magazine that turns you on* (July 1970)
   —"I asked him to rape me—just so I could slap him down"
   —"The bra-less marcher—I led a women's revolt—without knowing it"
   —"I offered my virginity to save his life"
5. *Daring Romances: the magazine for women who love* (July 1970)
   —"Ashamed to be a Virgin—being good made me a loser"
   —"Talked into a Sex Spree: boys wanted one thing from me"
   —"Nice Girl or Vice Girl?—she preyed on his innocence"
6. *Intimate Story* (published by *Ideal* magazine) (June 1970)
   —"Forced to Submit to Him and I loved it!"
   —"When he whistles I run to his bed"

I illustrate two examples of "image" products sold in "His" and "Hers" categories.

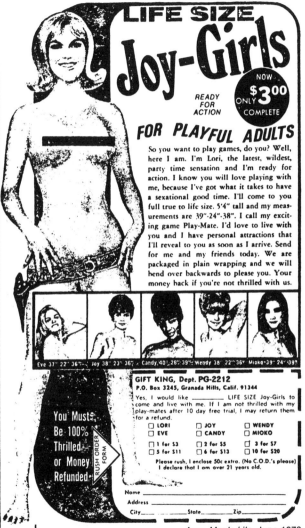

About a month ago, nine feminists were arrested for seizing the executive offices of Grove Press. Our demands were that Grove Press stop publishing pornography (Grove is a major producer of chic pornography), and that they turn over the profits of their past production of pornography to begin to undo some of the damage they and their ilk have done to women. "Justice" included free birth control/abortion clinics, child care, funds for recently divorced or widowed women, et cetera.

Of course, *we* were arrested as the criminals and brutalized by the police. In short, pornography in action.

The police required us to strip and squat. I refused. They punished me by spread-eagling me on the front of the cell block and, *then,* stripping me. I'm skipping the gruesome details to make the point appropriate here.

As soon as I had decided not to cooperate, I started to shake and sob spasmodically. These convulsions continued, with occasional respites, for at least an hour. What interests me here is that my psychological response was shame! I felt *ashamed* that I was afraid.

The most sadistic of our guards was astounded. He said: "If she's so afraid, then why is she doing it?"

I have asked myself that question many times since. There was never any question that I must refuse to cooperate with what I knew to be wrong. At the same time, I could not deny the terror my body expressed in spite of my will. Then, why? Isn't that question really about the gap between where we are, at present, and where we know we must go?

For today, I will try to answer my question. I did it, because it had to be done. If I did not oppose something wrong when presented with it—in this case, something *very* wrong, it would have been to say to myself that the revolution was not possible. Not because I thought I was special among women. But just because I am not.

I was and am my own act of faith. I can only believe the revolution is possible if I do it. The revolution is me.

I suspect that it is a prejudice, but I believe, still, that I should not have come here empty-handed. My gift is simply this: there is no revolution without each of us.

LESBIANISM AND FEMINISM

JUSTICE FOR WOMEN AS "UNNATURAL"[1]

When I heard about and then saw the recent *Time* "exposé" on Kate Millett's bisexuality, I called her for the first time in years. I wanted to congratulate her on her redemption within the Movement. That picture in *Life* (August, 1970) of Kate kissing her husband, Fumio, made a farce out of feminism (see, everybody? in spite of anything I may have said, I'm a *good* nigger).

It was decided by some members of the Women's Movement to seize this attack on Kate as an opportunity for the Movement to take a stand on lesbianism. A press conference was scheduled for December 17th, and I was asked to attend by two women who had helped plan it—Ruth Simpson and Barbara Love.

I was disturbed by the evasions in the statement to be presented. The unique political and tactical significance of lesbianism to feminism was either not understood (stupidity pays in "politics") or was ignored. The fact that the announcement was to be made in a church also made me very nervous. It is too short a step from respectability to collaboration.

If this press conference had been on any other aspect of feminism, I should not have attended. But I feared my absence would be misinterpreted either as a condemnation of lesbianism and/or as a denial of its importance, as an issue, to feminism.

Since the beginning of this current movement, feminist activity has been labeled lesbianism. The first time I was called a lesbian was on my first picket line in front of the *New York Times*—a picket line to desegregate the Help-Wanted Ads.

Generally speaking, the Movement has reacted defensively to the charge of lesbianism: "No, I'm not!" "Yes, you are!" "No, I'm not!" "Prove it." For myself, I was so puzzled by the connection that I became curious.

Whenever the enemy keeps lobbing bombs into some area you consider unrelated to your defense, it's always worth investigating.[2] The Oppressor never has "mechanical failures." This is a malaise suffered only by the Oppressed, and, even then, only at strategic and convenient moments.

Why is lesbianism significant for feminism? Since the beginning of the Movement, lesbianism has been a kind of code word for female resistance. Lesbianism is, in

---

[1] [December 21, 1970; prepared at the request of the *New York Times,* Op-Ed Page. This piece was rejected by them; it was later published, in part, by Jill Johnston in her *Village Voice* column, March 30, 1972.]

[2] [See *Strategy and Tactics: A Presentation of Political Lesbianism,* pp. 135–189. See especially my discussion of the political "buffer" zone, pp. 138–160.]

many ways, symbolic of feminism as a political movement. While the charge of lesbianism has generally been made by anti-feminists, that fact does not disqualify the relevancy of lesbianism to feminism. The paranoia of one's enemy is, frequently, both educative and inspirational.

Lesbianism, for feminism, is not just "another" issue or "another" example of human oppression, as the church-release[3] indicates. Nor is lesbianism about "autonomy," as the church-release suggests at the end. Lesbianism is pretty clearly about "association," not about aloneness. *If* lesbianism were about aloneness, it could hardly be relevant to anything in a political sense. "Political" concepts, by definition, are about society. These concepts must concern at least two or more persons in relationship to one another.

It is the association by choice of individual members of any oppressed group—the massing of power—which is essential to resistance. It is the commitment of individuals to common goals, and to the death if necessary, that determines the strength of an army. In war, even political warfare, there is no distinction between the political and the personal. (Can you imagine a Frenchman, serving in the French army from 9 A.M. to 5 P.M., then trotting "home" to Germany for supper and overnight? That's called game-playing, or collaboration, not political commitment.)

It is this commitment, by choice, full-time, of one woman to others of her class, that is called lesbianism. It is this full commitment, against any and all personal considerations, if necessary, that constitutes the political significance of lesbianism.

There are women in the Movement who engage in sexual relations with other women, but who are married to men. These women are not lesbians in the political sense. These women claim the right to "private" lives. They are collaborators.[4]

There are other women who have never had sexual relations with other women, but who have made, and live, a total commitment to this movement. These women are "lesbians" in the political sense.

Lesbianism contains the key principle to a successful feminist revolution—"guilt" by association. This mark of resistance divides the feminists from the anti-feminists, whether within or outside the Movement. The church-conference[5] was not relevant to the issues of feminism and lesbianism, because this political essence of lesbianism as synonymous with feminism was suppressed.

The crucial features of lesbianism, that were not addressed at the church-conference, were the political and tactical significances of lesbianism to feminism. This involves both analysis and strategy.[6]

Oppression, as a phenomenon, includes two parties (or classes)—the Oppressor and the Oppressed. These parties

132

---

[3] [Press release issued at the December 17, 1970, press conference at Washington Square United Methodist Church, New York City.]

[4] [See *On "Violence in the Women's Movement": Collaborators and Self-Deception*, pp. 198–221.]
[5] [December 17, 1970, press conference held at Washington Square United Methodist Church, New York City.]
[6] [See *Strategy and Tactics: A Presentation of Political Lesbianism*, pp. 135–189.]

are artificially created and are, then, combined into systems by dichotomizing the human race sequentially on the basis of various pretexts—sex, race, religion, et cetera. Any given class system, or the phenomenon of oppression, is stabilized by institutions (all of which are, by definition, "political"): in the case of women, marriage, motherhood, prostitution, rape, pornography.

But no system is absolutely perfect. There is always at least a tiny minority within the Oppressed who simply *will* not (later coopted by the Oppressor as *can* not) play out its proper political function in society. This minority is labeled, by those in power (the Oppressor), as the "criminal" element.[7]

The "criminal" element, when contained—that is, not politicized—serves several functions for the Oppressor. This element is permitted to exist by being bought off by the Oppressor and paid out of the pockets of the Oppressed—crime *does* pay. But the Oppressor keeps check enough, on this element, so that there is always sufficient risk (deterrent) to discourage too large a number of the Oppressed from becoming "criminal." (The distinction between "criminal" and "revolutionary" is partly quantitative.) The criminal element is the "buffer" between the Oppressor and the remainder of the Oppressed. "Criminality" is both a safety valve and an object lesson.

The "criminal" element is, however, seriously dangerous to the Oppressor in only one instance. It can be the source of revolutionary leadership.[8] If the oppressed class begins to get restless, this buffer zone must be removed—annihilated. This removes both the potential leadership for a revolt and serves as a scapegoat, or sacrifice, to coopt the rage of the Oppressed. The "criminal" element is presented, by all the propaganda machines, as the *primary* exploiter of the Oppressed. Since most people who've been shit on for thousands of years tend to stink, the Oppressed will usually accept this explanation and help turn over their own people.

Lesbianism is clearly the buffer between the male and female classes. The "benefits" are, primarily, a relative degree of independence from the institutional alternatives available to women: marriage, motherhood, prostitution.

The strategic importance of lesbianism to feminism can probably best be understood by analogy. It is still extremely difficult for people to understand feminism, *per se,* in political terms.

The trade-union movement originated as a response to desperate working conditions. As this movement grew, an understanding of the *causes* of these conditions evolved. The principle goal of this movement became a reduction of the discrepancy between the incomes of economic classes.

Numerous and varied socialist theories

133

---

[7] [See *Strategy and Tactics: A Presentation of Political Lesbianism,* especially pp. 138 and 139, for my theory of the political buffer zone.]
[8] [See *On "Violence in the Women's Movement": Collaborators and Self-Deception,* pp. 198–221, for my reference to parts of the Mafia as examples of this.

I distinguish between "political" Mafiosi and counterrevolutionary Mafiosi. The distinction is based not on tactics but on the focus of activity. For example, counter-revolutionary Mafiosi might be into drugs, prostitution, pornography; "political" Mafiosi might be into hijacking, ripping off Wall Street, possibly gambling, et cetera.]

developed. But the government made a primary distinction between socialist *theory,* with its relatively uncoordinated actions, and the Communist *Party.* The Party was "political," in the sense of directly and publicly attacking the class structure. It was "militant" socialism.

The witch-hunt that followed, on the Communist Party ostensibly, was government terrorism aimed at the socialist principle. And the witch-hunt worked. Many people's lives were destroyed by this. Many more people fled from socialist thinking. And, in addition, there was a metamorphosis within the trade-union movement.

Our government *now* has the nerve to talk about labor racketeering. The labor bosses are just small-time entrepreneurs. The government destroyed the principle of unionism, then permits a "criminal" element to run the government's capitalist show, and *then* proceeds to keep checks on the "criminals" by timely exposés. Criminality is a relative thing, at this time and especially in this country, and our government is in the most embarrassing position to be making accusations.

Lesbianism is to feminism what the Communist Party was to the trade-union movement. Tactically, any feminist should fight to the death for lesbianism because of its strategic importance. If the government witch-hunts lesbianism (and all feminists have always been aware of this possibility), and if the government *succeeds* in isolating lesbianism to *any* degree from feminism, feminism is lost. Feminism, like unionism, will be a complete racket. Feminism will be coopted and subsumed by its Oppressor.

STRATEGY AND TACTICS

A PRESENTATION OF POLITICAL LESBIANISM[1]

Today, I want to put on a little demonstration of something. Something I've been harping about for over three years in the Women's Movement.

FIRST, we need a "map" of our oppression. This map must include maps of the enemy's strategy.

SECOND, we must develop our tactics as feminists. Our tactics, today, will be designed to fight

    (1) in opposition *to* the enemy's system of stasis (strategy), and
    (2) *on* the enemy's territory.

Our tactics must satisfy two necessities. We must mount immediate holding actions to freeze our current position. (We must create a temporary stalemate of the enemy's position.) And, we must mount an offensive designed to wipe out the imbalance of power between the male and female classes.

This paper is, also, an attempt to analyze the ideological and tactical significance of lesbianism to feminism itself. It is an attempt to analyze the role of lesbianism within the struggle to achieve a virtually sexless society. A society in which sex is pivotal neither personally, nor politically.

Most people, now, accept feminism as a political movement. Certainly, its *raison d'être* is to change the conditions under which women must live. However, I believe the Movement itself, so far, has neither demonstrated itself as political nor organized itself to effect major change.

It was within the context of feminism that lesbianism first began to interest me. This was in the early part of 1968. Lesbianism was not, then, regarded as "political" and was seen as anathema to the Women's Movement. Lesbianism was seen as counterfeminism. And in some respects it may be.[2] More probably, both feminists and lesbians can benefit and learn much from each other.

My own interest in lesbianism stemmed from two weak and indirect motives. Nevertheless, I'll list them:

    (1) from the outset of the Movement, most men automatically called all feminists "lesbians." This connection was so widespread and

135

---

[1] [January 4, 1971; prepared for and presented at dedication of first Lesbian Center in America, *Daughters of Bilitis,* New York City.]

[2] [See *Juniata II: Lesbianism and Feminism,* pp. 82–88, for some of my feminist questions concerning lesbianism.]

consistent that I began to wonder myself if maybe men didn't perceive some connection the Movement was overlooking,

(2) a feminist analysis seemed to be leading to a male/female class confrontation. I tried to maintain the distinction between *men* (as biological entities) being the enemy, and the *behavior* of men being the enemy. The loss of this distinction has led to serious strategic errors on the part of the Movement. Among other ideological blunders, this collapsing of (1) agent, and (2) *act* of agent, put us off our guard in recognizing the nature of acts, when these acts—oppressive in character—were performed by women against women.[3] And, increasingly now, there is a sexual variable involved here as well. However, this blurring between *men* as the enemy and the *behavior of men* as the enemy also increased my interest in lesbianism as a potential political factor within feminism itself.

My reasoning, at the time, went something like this:

If men, as biological entities, were the enemy, then any women who rejected men as a class might be potential allies. I was very lonely as a feminist radical, and iso-

lated, and I, now, admit I jumped too eagerly. Lesbianism was *not* political at that time. And the female homophile community rejected my attempts at a coalition with the feminists as firmly as did the feminists reject a coalition with the lesbians.

I would now say that, in 1968, lesbianism was a "personal," not a "political," solution—much in the same way marriage to a man, for a feminist, is a "personal" solution.

I see earlier lesbianism as a kind of pre-revolutionary feminism. Lesbians are women who perceived early in life the role that would be assigned to them as women. Lesbianism is a rejection of this female role in the world at large.

As individuals, women cannot "take on" the male world. Lesbians turn their backs on *all males,* but they cannot turn their backs on the *male world.* Men impose the female role and lesbianism is an attempt to assimilate into an existent culture. The personal solution of lesbianism is an attempt to salvage as much of the human as possible.

But lesbianism overlooks that the female role can still be imposed on lesbians as a group.[4] In addition, because of their particularly unique attempt at revolt, the lesbian role within the male/female class system becomes critical. Lesbianism is the "criminal" zone, what I call the "buffer" zone, between the two major classes comprising the sex class system. The "buffer"

136

[3] [See *Juniata II: The Equality Issue,* pp. 65–75.]

[4] [A reference to my theory of the political buffer zone developed later in this paper.]

has both a unique nature *and* function within the system. And it is crucial that both lesbians and feminists understand the strategical significance of lesbianism to feminism.

Is lesbianism, in itself, "political" in any sense?

Some lesbians have challenged my right to hold any opinion on this question, since by their definition I am not "lesbian." However, since I believe that there are at least greater and lesser approximations to the truth, and since I also believe in some methodology and rules of evidence, I also believe that every individual has a right to express an opinion on all questions. By my own standards, however, one should only express this opinion after the given question has been considered carefully.

As I understand the homophile definition of "lesbian," it is this: "a woman who has engaged or would prefer to engage in sexual relations exclusively with women." Most "lesbians" have either drawn a blank on the question "is lesbianism political?" or vehemently denied that lesbianism was, is, or should be "political."

A more recent development, by some younger women, is to claim that lesbians are super-feminists. This, however, remains to be seen. Lesbians have, heretofore, been conspicuously absent from the vanguard of the Women's Movement.

It could be argued that this question,

of lesbianism being "political," is in fact two questions:

(1) is lesbianism political on the homophile front? and/or
(2) is lesbianism political on the feminist front?

Most lesbians would probably answer "yes" to the first question. But it is imperative that women participating in both the homophile and feminist movements work out (at least for the enlightenment of the Women's Movement) some satisfactory answers on the political position and/or potential positions of male homophiles on feminism. Most feminists are as suspicious of male homophiles, without feminist positions and life styles, as are most lesbians suspicious of feminists without homophile positions and life styles.

There is far more disagreement among lesbians on the second question: is lesbianism political on the feminist front. Two to three years ago, the answer was an almost uniform "no." But the Women's Movement has forced lesbians onto the front line (as distinct from the "vanguard") of feminism. The Movement has unwittingly forced lesbianism from a personal *solution* to a political *position*. How and why this occurred is the concern of this paper.

This center is being sponsored by the oldest lesbian organization in this country, the Daughters of Bilitis. I see it as an expression of the realization of the lesbian's present political situation. This center is not a "defensive" action. Rather, it says— "don't just 'come out'—'come out *front!*'"

There has already been a split over lesbianism as personal versus political within D.O.B. But political moves always generate splits.

And I want to respond, here and now, to the complaint that I am trying to put women on a war footing. Any group being shot at is immediately confronted with a "dilemma." It can die. Or it can confront and, possibly, at the very least, take some of the opposition with it. People who turn their backs on aggression tend to lose wars.

Feminists, those dumb bitches who've taken up fiddling with the Man's supremacy, have forced the issue.

For the moment, until I've laid out my general political analysis relevant to feminism and lesbianism, consider this proposition: I'm enormously less interested in whom you sleep with than I am in with whom you're prepared to die.

I propose that lesbianism is the "buffer," or "criminal," zone between the male and female classes within the sex-class system. My comments on this "zone," and its strategic function, apply to the structure of other class systems as well.[5]

The nature and function of the buffer,

or "criminal," zone is varied and complex. I don't pretend, here, to have a proper analysis of all its parts, or of how these parts integrate.

The nature of the buffer is that it is small in size and is composed of individuals who refuse to function in their "appropriate" identity (oppressed) class. They cannot be allowed into their contrary class (oppressor), in the interests of maintaining the balance of that particular class *system.*

While these individuals cannot fully escape their native class, their rebellion segregates them into an area, neither fully outside one class (the Oppressed), nor quite within its counterclass (the Oppressor). These individuals insist on violating the "law" of their class system (they insist on living *outside* that law), and, thereby, become "criminals" *within* it. Thus, the nature of this subgroup or class is "criminal." That is as far as "self-determination" can carry the Oppressed *within* its system.

The *function* of this group, *within* the system, is that of "buffer." Even the "outlaws" can be so strategically placed that they become important factors in *maintaining* that very system they are outlaws for rejecting!

Individuals within the "criminal" element are permitted a certain edge of power above the individuals within its original class (the Oppressed). This "edge" takes the form of greater freedom of movement, money, general independence. However,

138

[5] [Black "criminals," Italian-American "criminals," et cetera.]

what might appear to be a concession, or advance, is negated by the conditions, or "riders," on any extra benefits. Any additional benefits are extralegal, by virtue of their recipients' political status and, as such, can be withdrawn at any time. Further complicating the situation of the buffer zone into a "squeeze play," is that any extra benefits which accrue to this criminal element are derived at the expense of their native class, the Oppressed.[6]

The "criminal" element becomes the buffer between the opposing classes. The buffer takes the shocks from both sides. The "criminals" are the fall guy for the Oppressor, when it is necessary to obscure especially oppressive measures. The "criminal" element is, also, the sacrifice accepted and torn apart by its own class.

The "criminal" element is supported against the interests of the Oppressed, but it is the Oppressor who determines that. The political relationship between the two major classes is not altered by the buffer—only obscured. The "criminals" are primed scapegoats whenever necessary, so that they serve the double function of safety valve and object lesson. These two conflicting possibilities, along with the slim pickings for *anyone* after the Oppressor has taken His share, restricts and stabilizes the criminal element to tiny manageable numbers.

THE BUFFER IS, ABOVE ALL, THE KEY *MANIPULATIVE* MARGIN WITHIN ANY GIVEN CLASS SYSTEM.

The distinction between the criminal and the revolutionary is in one rather nebulous sense qualitative, but for the most part this distinction is quantitative. This buffer sub-class is the primary source of revolutionary leadership. But special conditions are necessary for this transformation to occur: gains must be reduced and risks maximized. Either the entire criminal element is virtually crushed, or, some part of it must (1) metamorphose itself into an understanding of its political position, and (2) transform the Oppressed's cowardice into effective resistance to the Oppressor.

139

The *function* of the criminal element is that of "buffer." The functions of a class system overlap with the *strategy* of the oppressor class. The distinction I am making, for the moment, is that the *function* accounts for organic stability over time for a given system. *Strategy* is the design or plan for maintaining the stability of class relationships in those rare instances of internal shiftings within the class of the oppressed.

Strategy is a long-range plan, developed prior to any given incident of rebellion. Its elements are built in to the system, as in the case of the buffer. Strategy is a kind of second line of defense to the class functions.

---

[6] [See *Juniata II: Lesbianism and Feminism*, pp. 82–88.]

We must understand the strategy of the Oppressor before we make our offensive moves. If we overlook His strategy, we risk falling into His traps. We must understand and block His defense system, if our own attack on His class nature, and the system itself, is to be effective.

I have three sets of charts here. One series lays out the function of the buffer in the Oppressor's strategy against the Oppressed. The second set proposes tactics designed for the Oppressed to effectively block the Oppressor's strategy. The third set proposes an offensive strategy for the Oppressed against the Oppressor.

Strategy Chart #1 shows the relationship between the oppressor class, and the buffer sub-class, and the oppressed class. Strategy Chart #1 is a class system in a "pre-revolutionary" state.

Strategy Chart #2 lays out, in visual terms, those conditions under which the Buffer is shifted from the *functional* (class system in stasis) to the *strategic* (the maneuverability factor *within* the Oppressed, at the command of the Oppressor). The condition shown is that of an incipient revolt among a portion of the Oppressed (that zone labeled "Pro-Rebellion"), and a general consciousness of oppression in the remainder of the Oppressed (those zones labeled, in contradistinction to "Pro-Rebellion," "Neutral" and "Anti-Rebellion"). Strategy Chart #2 shows the preliminary stages of an attempt by the Oppressed to shift class relationships vis-à-vis the Oppressor. As opposed to Strategy Chart #1, which I called "Pre-Revolutionary," I call Strategy Chart #2 "Prelude to a Revolution."

The Oppressor, insofar as He wishes to oppress and be true to His nature, naturally enough wants to put down the Rebellion. He, first, brings collective pressure against the Oppressed. (See Strategy Chart #3.) The "Buffer" becomes the "front line," and is hardest hit politically. (This, I believe, explains the initial hostility of lesbians to the Women's Movement. Lesbians perceived what feminists didn't: that feminism put lesbians' bodies under the first fire.)

The re-action from the Oppressed, to this pressure from the Oppressor, depends for its effectiveness on how soon this pressure is employed by the Oppressor. My thesis is that this pressure[7] *was* employed very early against the Women's Movement. And it was, and remains, effective.[8]

Strategy Chart #4 shows the intended results of the Oppressor's first move. Individuals within the Buffer, still within the oppressed class and, thus, with "passing" credentials, put pressure on individuals within the rebel class. This throws the Rebels, as well as those neutral to the rebellion, into confusion. This initial strategy of the Oppressor is designed to reduce the rebellion.

(We usually think of a reduction in a rebellious movement as being quantitative.

---

[7] ["All feminists are lesbians" is one of its telling slogans.]
[8] [This is less true in February, 1973, than it was in January of 1971.]

STRATEGY CHART #1
PRE-REVOLUTIONARY

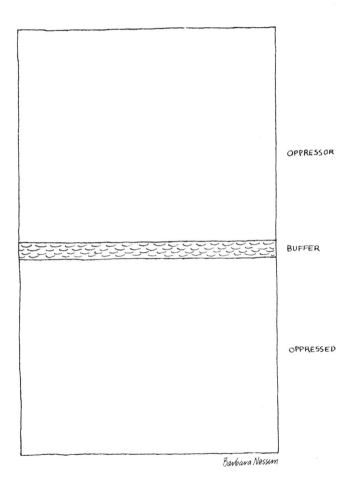

OPPRESSOR

BUFFER

OPPRESSED

Barbara Nessim

 BUFFER
(lesbianism
[within class system])

STRATEGY CHART #2
PRELUDE TO A REVOLUTION

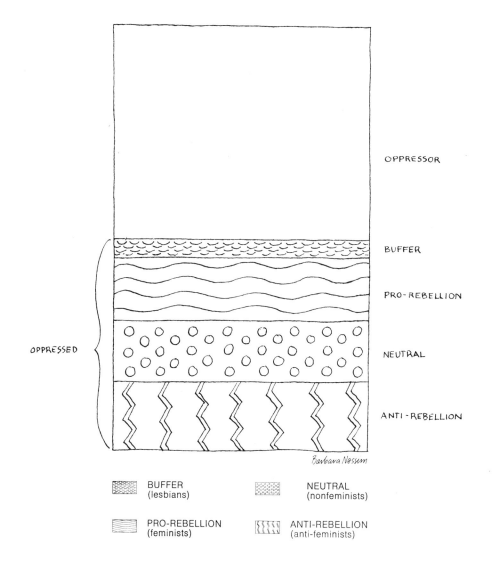

OPPRESSOR

BUFFER

PRO-REBELLION

OPPRESSED

NEUTRAL

ANTI-REBELLION

Barbara Nessim

BUFFER
(lesbians)

NEUTRAL
(nonfeminists)

PRO-REBELLION
(feminists)

ANTI-REBELLION
(anti-feminists)

STRATEGY CHART #3
RE-ACTION TO PRELUDE

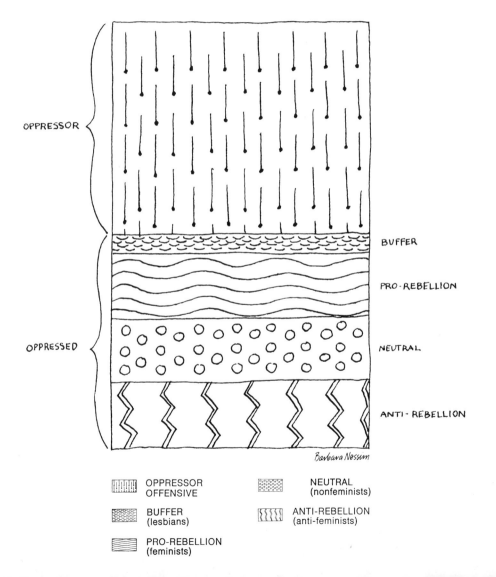

OPPRESSOR

BUFFER

PRO-REBELLION

OPPRESSED

NEUTRAL

ANTI-REBELLION

Barbara Nessim

	OPPRESSOR OFFENSIVE		NEUTRAL (nonfeminists)
	BUFFER (lesbians)		ANTI-REBELLION (anti-feminists)
	PRO-REBELLION (feminists)		

STRATEGY CHART #4
RE-RE-ACTION ("BUFFER ACTION")

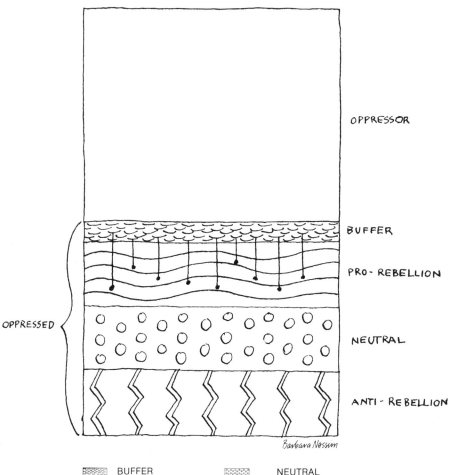

OPPRESSOR

BUFFER

PRO-REBELLION

OPPRESSED

NEUTRAL

ANTI-REBELLION

Barbara Nessim

 BUFFER
(lesbians)

 NEUTRAL
(nonfeminists)

OPPRESSOR
OFFENSIVE

ANTI-REBELLION
(anti-feminists)

 PRO-REBELLION
(feminists)

The Movement has fewer members. But if one has a proper understanding of the nature of class as identity,[9] the Oppressed does not identify *with* its own class.)

Individual members are set up for individual attack. A Movement can grow numerically while under attack, especially when the Buffer is still functional within the class system. But the *quality* of the rebellion can be crushed. The *quality* of feminism within the Women's Movement started running scared very fast. The most virulent expression of this was "consciousness-raising."

As an early witness in the Women's Movement, I know and must now say things, here,[10] that I know will be hated. I now know that the greatest counterrevolutionary force *within* this early women's movement were the lesbians within it. These women did not identify themselves, then, as lesbians, but they have since. And I can't tell you how astounded I was to find that, instead of being *for* women, they were the most reactionary on feminism. And in inter-movement struggles, they fought—quite literally—*alongside* the men and for their interests.

I have been called "lesbian" far more often than any lesbian I know of in this Movement. And it is for my feminist politics.

(I am not saying lesbians *cannot* become good feminists. But I *am* saying that we'd better understand the past.)

The rebellion *was* reduced by this strategy. And the Rebels are the least likely to reveal this. And why should the Oppressor expose what is in His interests? The radicalness, the degree of rebellion, of the Women's Movement has become harmless —negotiable.

Strategy Chart #5 shows this damage, in a qualitative sense. In terms of action—rebellion—at least half of the existing women's movement was neutralized by politically neutral activities, such as consciousness-raising. The Anti-Rebellion zone within the Oppressed also decreased as the danger from the Oppressor decreased. The teeth of the Movement are pulled. It's immaterial how many toothless gums may still be smacking away.

Good strategists make several plans to allow for any one plan not working out as expected. As it happened, the Oppressor's first move worked, because the Women's Movement was ideologically unprepared. But if this move hadn't worked, let's try to imagine at least one alternative to which the Oppressor might have turned.

Let's imagine that the Buffer did not respond uniformly to the Oppressor's pressure. And that this division within the Buffer is more than just pro-Oppressor versus neutral-to-Oppressor.

Let's imagine that at least a few individuals within the Buffer begin to identify with the Rebels. And, let's say, that this identification with the Rebels is at least equally as strong as the identification with

145

[9] [See *Untitled: Notes Toward a Theory of Identity,* pp. 109–116.]
[10] [Now that some lesbians seem to think they are the *only* feminists, it's time these things were said publicly. In the interests of a little balance.]

the original "criminal" Buffer zone. Strategy Chart #6 illustrates the sort of proportional division I'm proposing. A small minority is Pro-Rebellion, and the overwhelming majority is neutral to the rebellion.

Strategy Chart #6 does not change the riskiness of the Buffer zone: possible instant front line. And Chart #6 implies open identification of class group. In other words, the "Buffer" individuals could not be Rebels and "secret" members of the Buffer, but would necessarily be open members of both.

(It is not difficult to understand why this duo-membership was absent early in the Movement—although the Movement has paid dearly because it *was* absent.)

There are no "Neutrals" on the front line. Individuals within the Buffer zone are forced to choose sides in the sex class struggle, and these individuals, plainly, have more to fear from the Oppressor than from the Oppressed. The Buffer individuals have even more to fear from the Oppressor than does the rest of the Oppressed. The Buffer is a prime target; it is a "criminal" zone by definition. The Buffer stands outside the law of the system; individuals within it are especially vulnerable.

Individuals within the Buffer zone are a special category in a special strategic sense. The Buffer is, in fact, a sort of no man's land. The Oppressed must decide whether to take these individuals under their "protection" (weak as that "protec-

tion" might be), or whether to suffer the consequences of the Buffer individuals functioning as agents within the ranks of the Oppressed. Buffer individuals, because of their "criminal" character, are necessarily hostages in the hands of the enemy. It is a question of "ransom."

Strategy Chart #7 suggests what such a coalition, of some of the Buffer with the Pro-Rebellion faction, might look like from an overall systematic viewpoint. It obviously strengthens the Pro-Rebellion forces.

One could hardly expect the Oppressor to take such an open alliance lying down. He would have to hit hard, *very* hard. But to expect the Oppressor to respond only in terms of force would be naïve. This more complicated maneuver from the Oppressed is likely to draw a response in *kind,* as well as in increased force, from the Oppressor.

The most obvious move for the Oppressor would be to de-neutralize the remainder of the Buffer zone.

Those individuals within the Buffer zone, who did not align with the Pro-Rebellion forces, would now be numerically even weaker. That part of the Buffer zone which has surfaced and is prepared to fight its "unlawful" definition, by so doing necessarily exposes in varying degrees the other individuals within the Buffer. This renders the entire Buffer zone more vulnerable. And those individuals, without even that minimal protection of political alignment with the

STRATEGY CHART #5
EFFECTS OF BUFFER "ACTION"
qualitative damage to incipient revolt

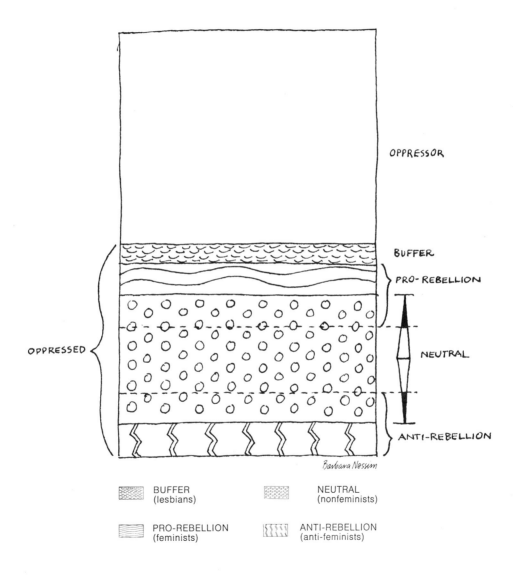

OPPRESSOR

BUFFER

PRO-REBELLION

OPPRESSED

NEUTRAL

ANTI-REBELLION

Barbara Nessim

BUFFER (lesbians)		NEUTRAL (nonfeminists)	
PRO-REBELLION (feminists)		ANTI-REBELLION (anti-feminists)	

STRATEGY CHART #6
ALTERNATE OPPRESSOR STRATEGY TO CHARTS #1-#5

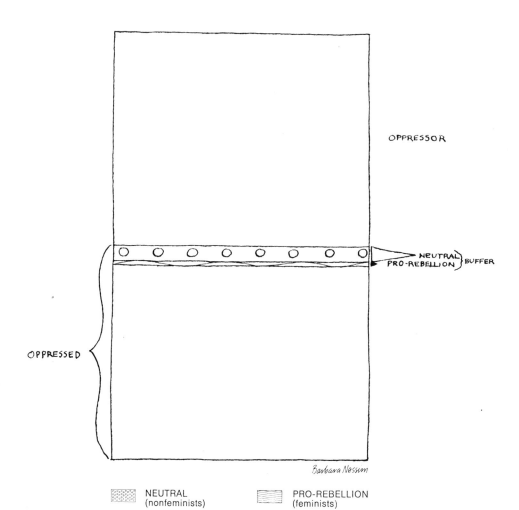

Barbara Nessim

| | NEUTRAL
(nonfeminists) | | PRO-REBELLION
(feminists) |

STRATEGY CHART #7
"BUFFER" AND PRO-REBELLION COALITION

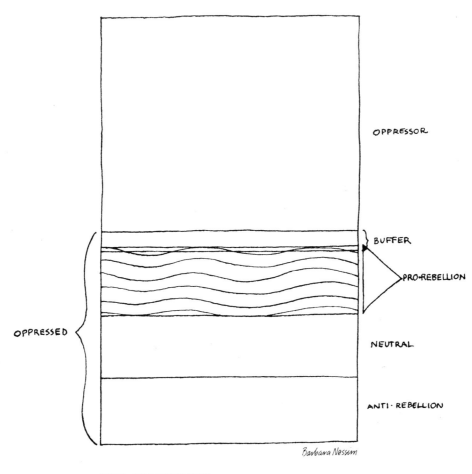

OPPRESSOR

BUFFER

PRO-REBELLION

OPPRESSED

NEUTRAL

ANTI-REBELLION

Barbara Nessim

PRO-REBELLION
(feminists)

Oppressed, should be expected to be forced into particularly vicious service by the Oppressor against the Oppressed. (See Strategy Chart #8.)

It is most likely that these individuals would be utilized in some sort of rear-guard[11] action—since their front line function has been stalemated and, thus, obviated. This rear-guard offensive would have to occur *behind* the Pro-Rebellion forces and *in front of* the Neutral zone. So, again, the Buffer has retained its nature and function as maneuverable margin.

Strategy Chart #9 demonstrates the shift of the Buffer to a rear-guard function. In a sense, a "two-front" war has been established. The Oppressor moves openly against the Pro-Rebellion forces. But He also attempts to isolate these forces, through inserting the Buffer between the Rebels and the nonaligned within the Oppressed. That is *one* function of this rear-guard Buffer.

But there is yet another, more important function here. The effect of "Buffer" pressure on Rebels must be less effective than when similar force is applied to non-rebels. Such a confrontation with non-rebels would predictably inspire fear in those who have little at stake, in terms of the rebellion. And what would operate as

fear on the "Neutral," could be expected to threaten and enrage that faction within the Oppressed who had been unsympathetic to the rebellion all along.

The Neutrals would, here, be caught in the squeeze play between the Buffer and the enraged Anti-Rebels.

In turn, then, the Neutrals might well turn on the Pro-Rebellion forces. The Oppressor would have achieved the original goal sought: to crush the Rebels. The Rebels would be caught between the Oppressor and the bulk of the Oppressed. (See Strategy Chart #10.)

From this situation, the Rebels could well evolve into the new "Buffer" zone between the Oppressor and the Oppressed. The "Rebels," too, could become "criminals." They, too, could function in the interests of the Oppressor (for a price, of course), by obscuring from the Oppressed, at least partially, the oppressive character of the Oppressor's activities. This, then, becomes a contribution to maintaining the oppressive system.

All that the rear-guard Buffer, as seen in Strategy Chart #9, must accomplish, is to create a wall of immobile hostility behind the Rebel faction. The Oppressor can, then, batter the Rebels to death against this wall from above, and annihilate the incipient re-

150

[11] [I use the term "rear-guard here in terms of military science.

Classically, a "rear-guard" strategy is one in which some faction of troops is detached from the main body of an army to protect that army's rear. Often, this strategy is used in a retreat.

However, everything changes in a Civil War. I speak, here, of a "rear-guard offensive" (apparently, a contradiction in terms). But if the Buffer is a criminal zone, and, thus, certain of its members can be pressured into

infiltrating for the Oppressor within the ranks of the Oppressed, then, such a faction of—in effect—the Oppressor's army is serving as a different kind of "rear-guard." It is "guarding" the rear of the Rebels *for* the Oppressor, to prevent any increment of the Rebel forces. This rear-guard serves to isolate the Rebels. And because, on whatever level of effectiveness, this rear-guard is an active adjunct of the Oppressor against the Oppressed, in an essential strategic function, I define this particular potential maneuver as a "rear-guard offensive."]

STRATEGY CHART #8
CHANGED BUFFER

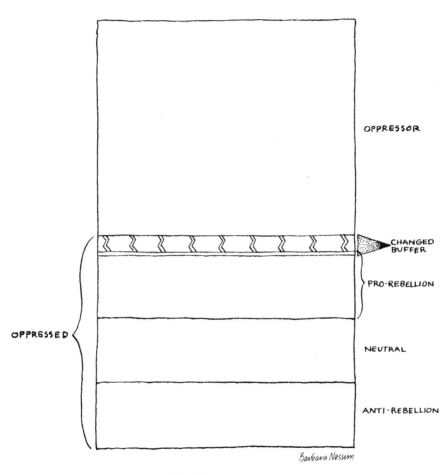

OPPRESSOR

CHANGED BUFFER

PRO-REBELLION

OPPRESSED

NEUTRAL

ANTI-REBELLION

Barbara Nessim

[SSSSS] ANTI-REBELLION
(anti-feminists)

STRATEGY CHART #9
TWO-FRONT WAR
re-located buffer as rear-guard offensive

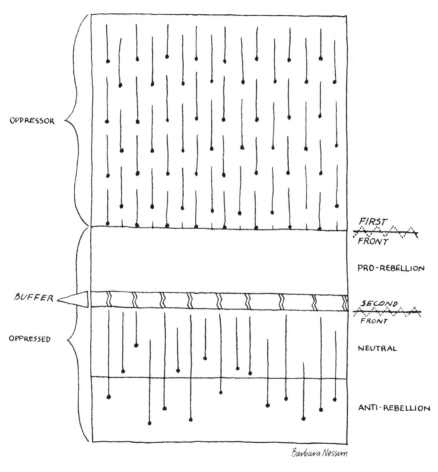

OPPRESSOR

FIRST
FRONT

PRO-REBELLION

BUFFER

SECOND
FRONT

OPPRESSED

NEUTRAL

ANTI-REBELLION

Barbara Nessim

| | OPPRESSOR OFFENSIVE | | ANTI-REBELLION (anti-feminists) |

STRATEGY CHART #10
SQUEEZE PLAY ANNIHILATION OF
INCIPIENT REBELLION

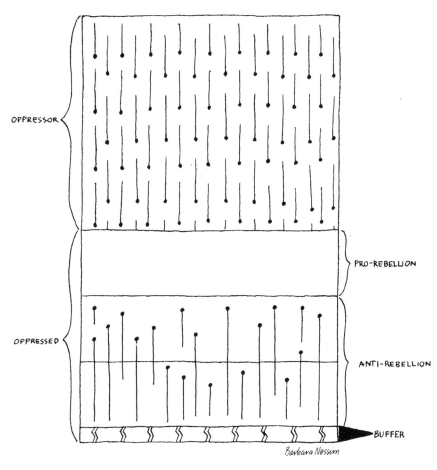

OPPRESSOR

PRO-REBELLION

OPPRESSED

ANTI-REBELLION

BUFFER

Barbara Nessim

| | OPPRESSOR OFFENSIVE | | ANTI-REBELLION (anti-feminists) |

bellion. *This* much is unquestionably within the power of such a rear-guard Buffer. (See Strategy Chart #10).

Traditionally, there is a distinction between "strategy" and "tactics." "Strategy" is a long-range offensive, designed to achieve certain conditions not presently in effect. "Tactics" include short-range activities, which are supportive to, but not necessarily part of, the main thrust of attack.

Armies are generally moved on the basis of strategy. Strategy determines the breakup of forces, where they are landed on enemy-held territory, etc. Tactics are the methods used to introduce troops into a given territory. For example, the decision to "soften up" the opposition, by several days of preliminary shelling (not necessarily with armaments) before landing troops to clean up, would be "tactical."

In this paper, I am making an even further distinction between "strategy" and "tactics." I must first point out certain negative aspects of even the ordinary distinction between "strategy" and "tactics." Every "side" needs *both* strategy and tactics. At this moment, the Oppressor has the strategy without much need for supplemental tactics. On the other hand, the Oppressed has, at best, "tactics"—without overall strategy.

The Oppressed *must* have a complete map of the enemy's territory. We must design an overall strategy based on His territory. And we must, then, relegate tactics to their proper *supplemental* place. But, for the moment, "tactics" *are* the strategy of the Oppressed.

Tactics, because they are short-range, are very limited in their usefulness or potential for long-range goals. "Tactics" are presently synonymous with "guerrilla warfare"—the hit-and-run strategy.

The *conditions* necessitating "tactics" are always the same. The strength of the opposition, in the given situation, is overwhelming, and cannot be attacked frontally. *Some* form of attack is necessary, either to check the enemy's advances, or to draw His attention off the *true* strategy of one's own "side."

The tactician's primary resources are information, guts, and surprise. Successful tactical forays require, from their troops, loyalty, secrecy, and imagination. The tactician's chief object is to throw the enemy off balance, and to maintain Him in that position for whatever period is necessary for the "strategy" to be implemented.

Tactics, as guerrilla warfare, are something like karate. It's an emergency measure that can't win the war, but *can* perhaps buy time. Within military strategy, tactics—like karate—are a "personal" solution.

I want to try a similar experiment, with my charts, in terms of tactics. Please try to

154

keep in mind that I consider this analysis and these illustrations the crudest and most minimal suggestion of the degree to which we must develop "war games."

The first necessary step I see for feminists is that we move from a position of retreat to one of stalemate. We are presently losing ground.

Our first move would have to be mounting some holding action to at least freeze our present position. Assuming Strategy Charts #1 and #2, and anticipating Strategy Chart #3, the Oppressed must shore up the Buffer zone from behind.

One miniscule suggestion, as a contribution in this direction, would be if all feminists began wearing buttons reading "I am a lesbian."[12] This could be a way of coopting the enemy's strategy. It's not unlike the tactic of the Danish king against the Germans during World War II. When the King rode out one morning wearing the Star of David, and most Danes followed suit, the effect was to frustrate the Nazi identification of Jews in that area.

If feminists would attempt to absorb the Buffer, this could dissolve the effectiveness of the earlier front-line pressure. It would also permit greater fluidity among the Rebels and, thereby, confusion to the Oppressor. Ultimately, in effect, such an absorption would shore up that front line.

Tactical Chart #1 illustrates something of the effect of such a maneuver. Of course,

not all individuals within the Buffer would join the Rebels. But, I believe, we could predict that the proportionate division, seen in Strategy Chart #6, could easily be reversed.

The minority, within the Buffer, would then comprise a rear-guard offensive. But the initial tactical offensive, mounted by the Oppressed, could shift the *numbers* to such an extent, that any rear-guard offensive could not be as qualitatively effective as in Strategy Charts #6–#10.

Through an elaborate tactical offensive (another small contribution: repeal of all "criminal" laws against homosexuality), the Rebels could dissolve the Buffer. The rear-guard maneuver—still to be expected in some form—could be weakened to something like Tactical Chart #2.

While it is true that the conditions seen in Strategy Chart #9 and those in Tactical Chart #2 appear essentially the same, there is one crucial difference: the rear-guard displaced Buffer is politically neutral. And while it is still true that the displacement occurred at the behest of the Oppressor, the *impetus* to the dissolution of the Buffer was initiated by an Oppressed offensive. The pressure from the Oppressor *follows* this dissolution, and, thus, falls primarily on the Rebels. The individuals within the displaced Buffer have missed the crucial political education through fear and confrontation with their own. While distinct from the main body of Neutrals, this Buffer

155

---

[12] [It is interesting (or discouraging, depending on one's point of view) that this "button" suggestion appeared to be the most striking point taken of my entire speech. It really seemed to strike women's "consciousness." Many were shocked into an awareness of their own fear of any identification with lesbianism, by their revulsion at the idea of such a button. For some reason, there was no hesitation over a button reading "I am a prostitute."

By the summer of 1972, in the August 26th Women's March, feminists were seen wearing lesbian solidarity buttons.]

TACTICAL CHART #1
COOPTING THE ENEMY'S STRATEGY
dissolving the front-line buffer zone

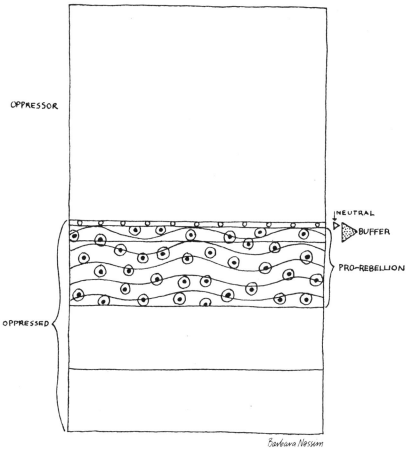

OPPRESSOR

NEUTRAL

BUFFER

PRO-REBELLION

OPPRESSED

Barbara Nessum

 NEUTRAL
(nonfeminists)

 COOPTATION

 PRO-REBELLION
(feminists)

TACTICAL CHART #2
"TWO-FRONT" DEFENSIVE WAR
re-located buffer as rear-guard defensive

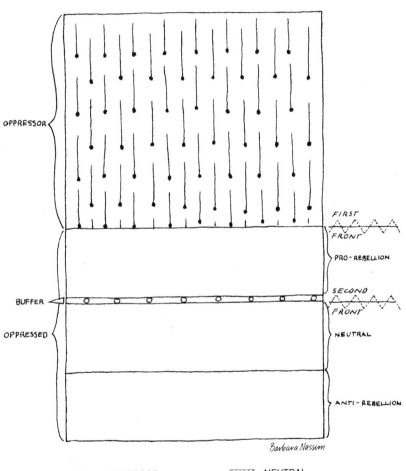

Barbara Nessim

OPPRESSOR
OFFENSIVE

NEUTRAL
(nonfeminists)

TACTICAL CHART #3
RESULT OF "TWO-FRONT" DEFENSIVE CAMPAIGN
inroads via cushion

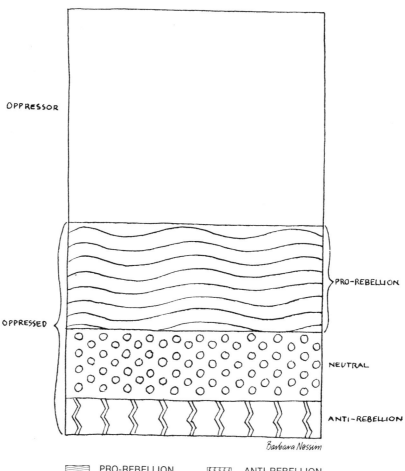

OPPRESSOR

OPPRESSED

PRO-REBELLION

NEUTRAL

ANTI-REBELLION

Barbara Nessim

 PRO-REBELLION (feminists)

ANTI-REBELLION (anti-feminists)

 NEUTRAL (nonfeminists)

cannot effectively hold their own as soldiers of the enemy.

This displaced Buffer, in short, lacks character as a rear-guard offensive. It cannot constitute such an offensive, but can, at best, mount a defensive holding action. Such a maneuver *can*not hold within one's own territory. It must be absorbed.

Essentially, the rear-guard becomes a cushion, against which the Rebels can bounce back at the Oppressor. And each bounce makes serious inroads against the Anti-Rebels within the Oppressed. (Compare the difference this one initial offensive maneuver can make in results: compare Strategy Chart #10 and Tactical Chart #3.)

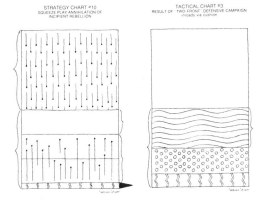

STRATEGY CHART #10
SQUEEZE PLAY ANNIHILATION OF INCIPIENT REBELLION

TACTICAL CHART #3
RESULT OF TWO-FRONT DEFENSIVE CAMPAIGN inroads via cushion

Instead of the Buffer acting as a wall against which the Oppressor can crush the rebellion, this Buffer becomes an indirect recruiter for the Rebels. (A small example of tactical karate.)

Former Buffer individuals, within the Rebel group, must conflict with the rear-guard Buffer. Without Oppressor muscle, directly behind, to support the Buffer, this conflict must win over many Neutrals to the Rebel side. At least half the rear-guard Buffer could be predicted to join the Neutrals— at the very least—as a result of this conflict.

These inroads would be sure to have reverberations within the Anti-Rebels as well. At least half of these would be neutralized. And whatever remained of the individuals from the rear-guard Buffer, now crushed by the squeeze play within the Oppressed, could be expected to join the Anti-Rebels.

Perhaps Tactical Chart #3 could be painted even more optimistically, but one should always resist being greedy.

But all of the above is worthless, unless the Oppressed mounts an offensive. And not just in the sense of forays.

Major offensives—that is, strategic ones—always involve moving into enemy strongholds. In short, we must invade the enemy's territory.

Tactical Charts #1–#3 cannot be regarded as more than holding actions. A *map* of the enemy's territory must be meticulously reconstructed. Exactly how is the sex class system constructed? What holds it in place? What keeps it going? Such a map should reveal the strongholds from within which oppressive power is generated. It is these strongholds which must be attacked.

The ways in which the Oppressor relates to various factions within the Oppressed depend upon the particular function of each of these factions within the system. The various *expressions* the oppression takes may vary, but the *sources* remain the same. For example, the Buffer faction is part of the oppressed general class, regardless of how the Buffer individuals may fantasize about their escape *from* the oppressed class.

Just as this paper attempts to suggest the beginnings of a strategic map of our own territory as Oppressed, we must begin to try to map out and understand the factions within the Oppressor.

If this paper establishes nothing else substantively, it should at least be clear that Buffer individuals have divided class loyalties, and that these "loyalties" are reasonable from a pre-revolutionary point of view.

In reference to Tactical Chart #1, I suggested that the Oppressed coopt the loyalties held by the Buffer for the Oppressor. This cooptation, in its offensive character, threw the Oppressor's strategy off sufficiently to prevent at least one method of crushing the rebellion.

Perhaps warfare on one's own ground is always "tactical," since it assumes occupation, thus control, by the opposition. We must survey the *enemy's* territory for any *real* gains. We must look within the oppressor class (in the sex class system, this means the "male" class) for factions with divided loyalties, somewhat similar to the Oppressed Buffer zone. Cooptation within the oppressor class, from the Oppressed, should be predictably more difficult than

that outlined in Tactical Charts #1–#3.

We must first look for factions within the oppressor class being denied certain rights by other factions within the oppressor class. These denied rights, for example, freedom of movement, economic freedom, life-style freedom, should, in some cases, coincide with crucial denied rights to members of the Oppressed in the sex class system. While the exact problem *style* may differ, it could be that similar solutions are required to meet all these, otherwise, varied, problems. For example, where economic deprivation is the problem—whether it stems from *under*- or *un*-employment— free housing, free food, the nationalization of Con Edison and telephone service, free transportation, and other minimal living prerequisites, *could* be a common solution.

If one even glances at Tactical-Strategy Chart #1, which assumes the tactical gains by the Oppressed (seen in Tactical Charts #1–#3), it isn't difficult to understand the need for the Oppressed to strengthen its forces. At least two-thirds of the sex class system is openly hostile to the rebellion. Of those not hostile to the rebellion, another third are neutral. Add to this, that those hostile to the rebellion have nearly all the material assets in the society within their control. Obviously, the Oppressed must attempt inroads into the Oppressor's strength. And this move is necessary for two reasons, as I believe the following charts will show. Not only can such an offensive win territory within the

TACTICAL-STRATEGY CHART #1
PRE-STRATEGICAL OFFENSIVE AGAINST OPPRESSOR

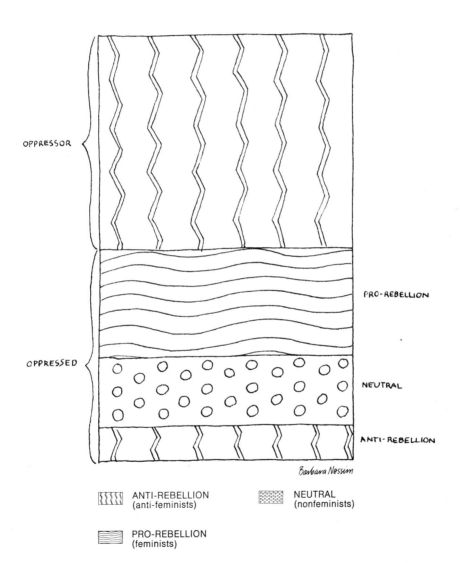

ANTI-REBELLION
(anti-feminists)

NEUTRAL
(nonfeminists)

PRO-REBELLION
(feminists)

Oppressor, but such an offensive—if even modestly successful—would have positive reverberations within the Oppressed.

In Tactical-Strategy Chart #1, the Oppressor is solidly Anti-Rebellion. Any initial major first offensive, into the Oppressor via factions, should at least neutralize nearly a third of the Oppressor. This takes into consideration that, in some comparable Buffer zone within the oppressor class, some individuals would become openly Pro-Rebellion. Others of this third would be supportive to a degree. Others would simply no longer *oppose* the rebellion.

Tactical-Strategy Chart #2 illustrates the conditions preceding such a shift within the Oppressor.

Tactical-Strategy Chart #3 shows the results of the infiltration shown in Chart #2.

Tactical-Strategy Chart #4 gives an overall systematic account of the new conditions prevailing, after the first stage of the first major offensive of the Oppressed against the Oppressor.

The *second* stage of the first offensive was referred to earlier, as the reverberations within the Oppressed of the positive power shifts within the oppressor class. The Oppressor is weakened. The fear within the nonaligned Oppressed *of* that Oppressor is, thus, reduced as well. I think the re-action, *within* the Oppressed to the offensive *against* the Oppressor, would be the elimination of fence-sitting. Nonparticipation would cease, among sympathizers within the Oppressed, to the rebellion itself.

The character of the Anti-Rebels, within the Oppressed, also, might *seem* to be transformed. But this would be a misinterpretation of a change in verbiage.

Tactical-Strategy Chart #5 shows the process of reverberation referred to above. I call it, here, "operation boomerang." Again, as in "rear-guard," "boomerang" has a negative connotation for those in power. But in tactical karate, "boomerang" can be used to positive advantage. In Tactical-Strategy Chart #5, the initiative for the offensive comes from within the Rebel forces. The Neutral zone within the Oppressor acts as a "conductor" from the Oppressed, against the Anti-Rebel forces in the Oppressor. This momentum, in conjunction with whatever counteroffensive the Oppressor-Anti-Rebels can improvise, causes the original attack to make the initial inroads into the Oppressor sought for via the attack. It also causes a "bouncing-off" effect of the Rebels back against their own Neutral zone within the Oppressor.

The establishment of a Neutral "base" within the Oppressor eliminates the *raison d'être* for neutrality within the Oppressed. (Tactical-Strategy Chart #7 shows a general expansion of borders in favor of the Oppressed-Rebels.)

Part of the Oppressor has been neutralized. The majority of the Oppressed-Neutrals have been "politicized" into open rebellion. Some of the Oppressed-Neutrals are alienated by the offensive, into alliance with the Oppressed-Anti-Rebels. Tactical-Strategy Chart #6 shows this realignment within the Oppressed.

TACTICAL-STRATEGY CHART #2
FIRST STAGE OF FIRST MAJOR OFFENSIVE
infiltration by oppressed of buffer-like
factions within oppressor

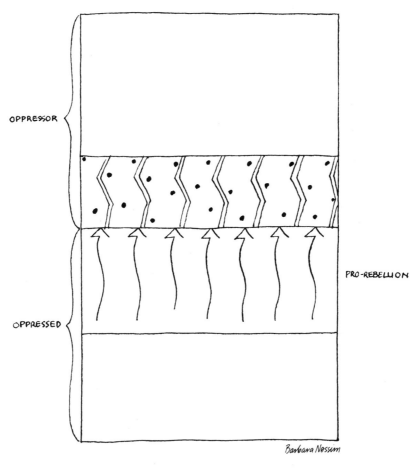

OPPRESSOR

PRO-REBELLION

OPPRESSED

Barbara Nessim

 ANTI-REBELLION
(anti-feminists)

INFILTRATION

OPPRESSED OFFENSIVE I

TACTICAL-STRATEGY CHART #3
RESULTS OF INFILTRATION WITHIN OPPRESSOR

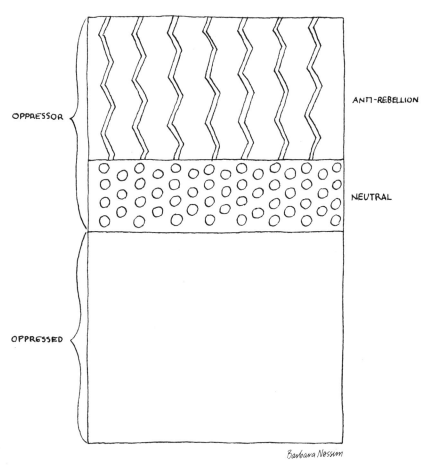

OPPRESSOR {

ANTI-REBELLION

NEUTRAL

OPPRESSED {

Barbara Nessim

§§§§§ ANTI-REBELLION
(anti-feminists)

▒▒▒ NEUTRAL
(nonaligned)

TACTICAL-STRATEGY CHART #4
OVERVIEW FOLLOWING FIRST STAGE OF FIRST STRATEGIC OFFENSIVE AGAINST OPPRESSOR

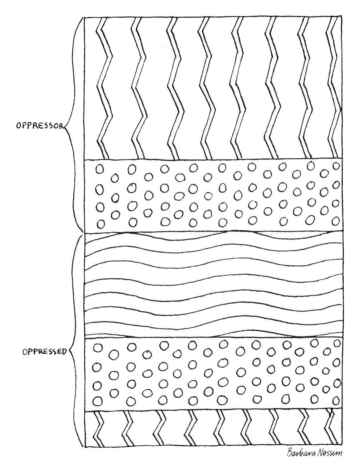

OPPRESSOR

OPPRESSED

ANTI-REBELLION
(anti-feminists)

PRO-REBELLION
(feminists)

NEUTRAL
(nonfeminists
[in Oppressed instance]
or nonaligned
[in Oppressor instance])

TACTICAL-STRATEGY CHART #5
SECOND STAGE OF FIRST OFFENSIVE
operation boomerang

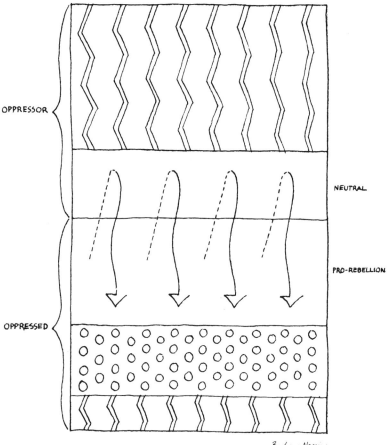

OPPRESSOR

NEUTRAL

PRO-REBELLION

OPPRESSED

Barbara Nessim

{{{{{	ANTI-REBELLION (anti-feminists)	::::: NEUTRAL (nonfeminists)
))))	BOOMERANG	

TACTICAL-STRATEGY CHART #6
EFFECTS OF OPERATION BOOMERANG WITHIN
OPPRESSED-NEUTRAL ZONE

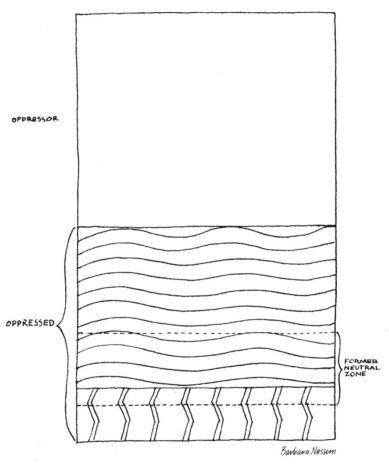

OPPRESSOR

OPPRESSED

FORMER NEUTRAL ZONE

Barbara Nessim

 PRO-REBELLION
(feminists)

 ANTI-REBELLION
(anti-feminists)

TACTICAL-STRATEGY CHART #7
EXPANSION OF OPPRESSED-REBELS' BORDERS

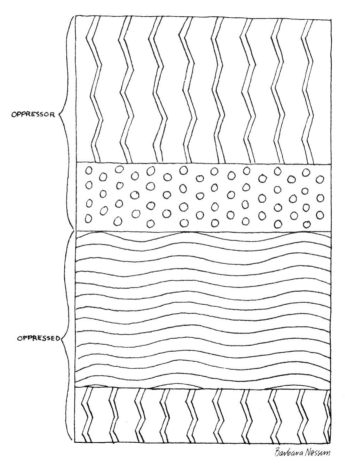

OPPRESSOR

OPPRESSED

Barbara Nessim

 ANTI-REBELLION
(anti-feminists)

 PRO-REBELLION
(feminists)

NEUTRAL
(nonaligned)

Tactical-Strategy Chart #7 demonstrates the overall situation. (Compare with Tactical-Strategy Chart #4.) It should be remembered that Neutral zones are always havens for agents, both for "contacts" and to build credentials. Part of our major first offensive would be to create conditions conducive to infiltration *within* the enemy's borders, and to eliminate such dangers within the Oppressed.

TACTICAL-STRATEGY CHART #7
EXPANSION OF OPPRESSED-REBELS' BORDERS

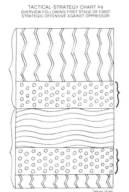
TACTICAL-STRATEGY CHART #4
OVERVIEW FOLLOWING FIRST STAGE OF FIRST
STRATEGIC OFFENSIVE AGAINST OPPRESSOR

Tactical-Strategy Chart #8 shows a two-front war again, only this one is initiated by the Oppressed. On the first front, the Oppressed can attack the Oppressor with the Oppressor-Neutrals as Buffers. These Buffer individuals are potential agents to infiltrate further into Oppressor territory.

The second front is against the Oppressed-Anti-Rebels. At present, these are, at least, isolated and identified.

The advantageous conditions illus-trated in Tactical-Strategy Chart #8 would have to be exploited into a major second offensive, if our gains were to be held.

Ideological offensives should, properly, precede Oppressed offensives. In the case of the Oppressor, this is not necessary, since He has the muscle to back up His "surprises." However, in the case of the Oppressed, ideological bombardments soften up the new enemy territory to be gained.

If the Oppressed wished to build on the work of the first Oppressed offensive, then the next ideological move seems obvious. But this would depend somewhat on the "field" findings of the first offensive.

Did the coalition on disparate points (free housing, nationalizing Con Edison, et cetera) work? Did the various factions appear, through their contributions, to be equally motivated?

If the overall experience of working together was positive during the first phase of the first offensive, then a further solidification of this coalition is reasonable. At this point, rather than concentrate on disparate issues, we might coalesce them into one, such as a base guaranteed annual income. This income would be over and above the minimal living prerequisites established in the first offensive.

If steps were taken in this direction, the *battle,* within the sex class system as a whole, would shift in our favor at this point.

In Tactical-Strategy Chart #9, the up-

TACTICAL-STRATEGY CHART #8
TWO-FRONT DÉTENTE INITIATED BY OPPRESSED

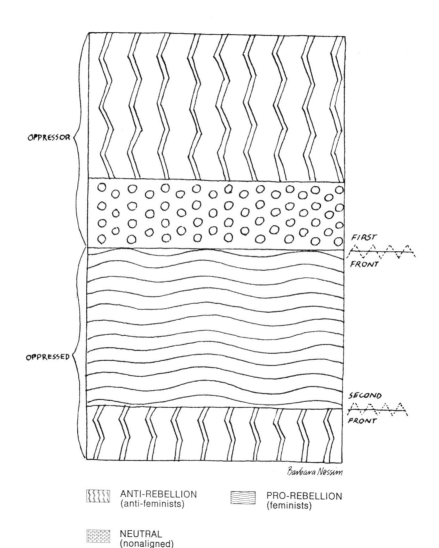

OPPRESSOR

FIRST
FRONT

OPPRESSED

SECOND
FRONT

Barbara Nessim

ANTI-REBELLION
(anti-feminists)

PRO-REBELLION
(feminists)

NEUTRAL
(nonaligned)

TACTICAL-STRATEGY CHART #9
"SOFTENING-UP" BOMBARDMENT PRIOR TO SECOND OFFENSIVE

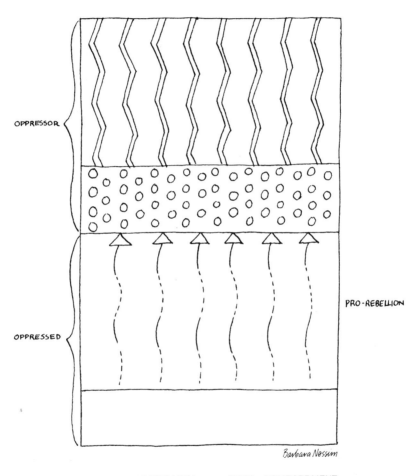

Barbara Nessim

	ANTI-REBELLION (anti-feminists)		BOMBARDMENT
	NEUTRAL (nonaligned)		

to-date holding conditions shown in Tactical-Strategy Chart #7 are shown again. But in Chart #9, they are shown as the *background* of the *second* offensive.

The purpose of strategic offensives always involves invasions of enemy territory, and attempts to hold this previously unoccupied (at least by you!) territory. As seen in Chart #9, the lower third of the Oppressor is already neutral. Neutral territory is not as "good" as "home" territory for Rebels. But it's the next best thing, when it exists within the enemy camp.

In Tactical Chart #2, Neutral territory within the Oppressed functioned in the role of a "cushion." *That* "Neutral" territory was a rear-guard Buffer, *designed* to act as a dike, shoring up the nonaligned Oppressed from the Oppressed-Rebels. In the end, that Buffer became not unlike the "conductor" of the Oppressor-Neutral territory seen in Tactical-Strategy Chart #5.

In Tactical-Strategy Chart #9, pressure is brought from the Oppressed-Rebels on the Oppressor-Neutrals. This represents the ideological bombardment prior to the physical assault. Chart #9 represents the "softening up" process.

Tactical-Strategy Chart #10 follows the pressure from the Oppressed-Rebels on the Oppressor-Neutrals. This process is somewhat like a reverse of the Oppressor use of the Oppressed-Buffer zone, seen in Strategy Charts #3 and #4.

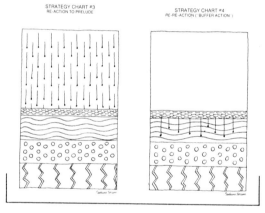

STRATEGY CHART #3
RE-ACTION TO PRELUDE

STRATEGY CHART #4
RE-RE-ACTION (BUFFER ACTION)

172

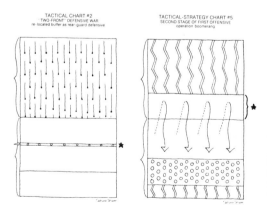

TACTICAL CHART #2
TWO-FRONT DEFENSIVE WAR
re-located buffer as rear-guard defensive

TACTICAL-STRATEGY CHART #5
SECOND STAGE OF FIRST OFFENSIVE
operation boomerang

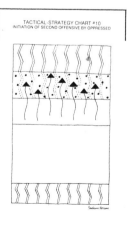

TACTICAL-STRATEGY CHART #10
INITIATION OF SECOND OFFENSIVE BY OPPRESSED

TACTICAL-STRATEGY CHART #10
INITIATION OF SECOND OFFENSIVE BY OPPRESSED

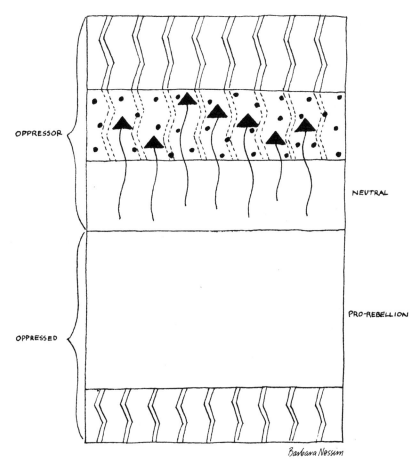

Barbara Nessim

ANTI-REBELLION
(anti-feminists)

INFILTRATION

OPPRESSED
OFFENSIVE II

This active participation by the Oppressor-Neutrals has two important consequences. First, the Oppressor-Neutrals are now openly aligned with the Oppressed-Rebels. And, secondly, this offensive should neutralize the second third of the oppressor class.

Tactical-Strategy Chart #11 indicates the first consequence: the open alliance between the Oppressed-Rebels and the Oppressor-Rebels. The first obvious danger, apparent from this pictograph, is that the sex class war could become somewhat blurred. But the demands, chosen as coalition "tests," should obviate this danger. This pictograph illustrates, however, the extreme intelligence that women would have to employ to pick out these issues to do battle for and with others.

Tactical-Strategy Chart #12 illustrates the second consequence to the Oppressor. The shifting of this Oppressor-Neutral zone, the dominant quality now held by the Rebels, pictures clearly that the battle has shifted in our favor.

The second offensive would also have repercussions within the Oppressed. My intuition is (and it's difficult to pin down such a long-range projection much further) that the second offensive would neutralize part of the Anti-Rebels, say, about one-third. This last group of anti-feminists, within the Oppressed, must be assumed to identify, in considerable depth, with the values maintained to oppress them. The one-third of this group that I posit as neutralizing, would

do so only from prudence, not conviction. This would be simply the result of the power shift.

Tactical-Strategy Chart #13 shows the above in terms of the source of initial pressure. The "pressure" comes from the recently neutralized men of the Oppressor. Only men could modify these women, because the women's identification with men runs so very deeply throughout their personality.

Tactical-Strategy Chart #14 shows the results of this pressure.

Tactical-Strategy Chart #15 illustrates an up-to-date reading of the sex class confrontation, and the new alliances within both camps. The Rebels, now, hold the advantage.

The third offensive would be an extension and formalization of the first two offensives. The Rebels would fuse into a common Party, with some vision of humanity, and how society should support the full realization of the equal humanity of each individual, within that society. A full program would have to be detailed of rights and responsibilities. This would, again, be the ideological pre-offensive.

The pressure would come, initially, from the Rebels on to the Oppressor-Neutrals. (See Tactical-Strategy Chart #16.) This, then, motivates pressure from the Oppressor-Neutrals on the Oppressor-Anti-Rebels. (See Tactical-Strategy Chart #17.) The first consequence within the Op-

TACTICAL-STRATEGY CHART #11
FIRST CONSEQUENCE WITHIN OPPRESSOR OF
SECOND OFFENSIVE BY OPPRESSED

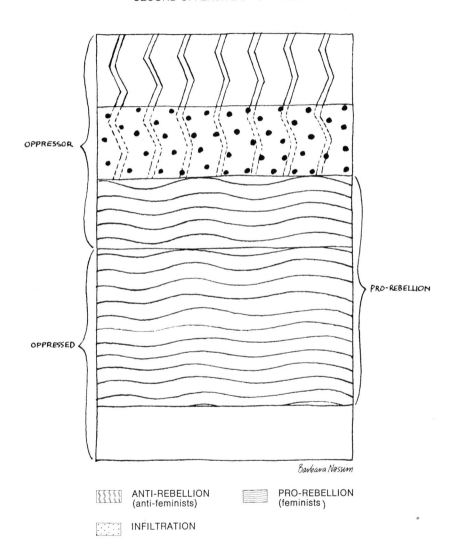

Barbara Nessim

ANTI-REBELLION (anti-feminists)	PRO-REBELLION (feminists)
INFILTRATION	

TACTICAL-STRATEGY CHART #12
SECOND CONSEQUENCE WITHIN OPPRESSOR OF
SECOND OFFENSIVE BY OPPRESSED

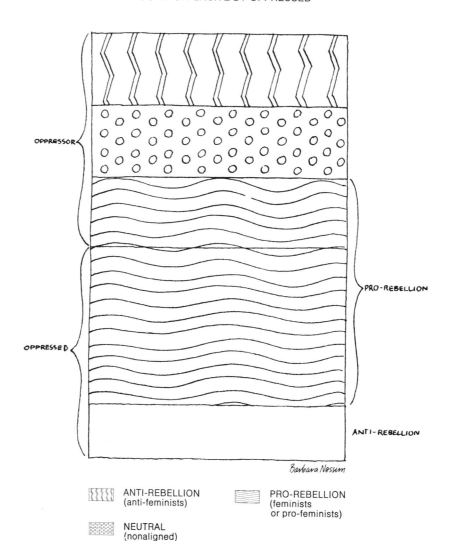

Barbara Nessim

ANTI-REBELLION (anti-feminists)	PRO-REBELLION (feminists or pro-feminists)
NEUTRAL (nonaligned)	

TACTICAL-STRATEGY CHART #13
INITIATION OF REPERCUSSIONS WITHIN OPPRESSED
OF SECOND OFFENSIVE

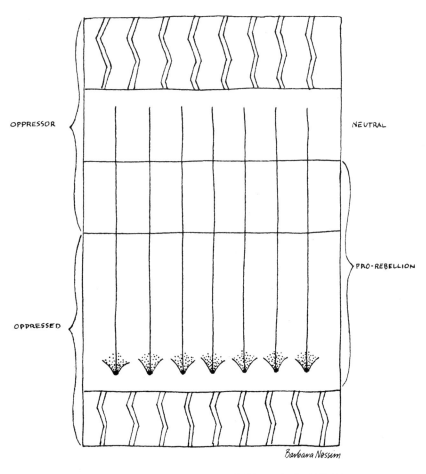

OPPRESSOR

NEUTRAL

PRO-REBELLION

OPPRESSED

Barbara Nessim

〧〧〧〧〧 ANTI-REBELLION
(anti-feminists)

⃒⃒⃒⃒ REPERCUSSION I

TACTICAL-STRATEGY CHART #14
RESULTS OF SECOND OFFENSIVE WITHIN OPPRESSED

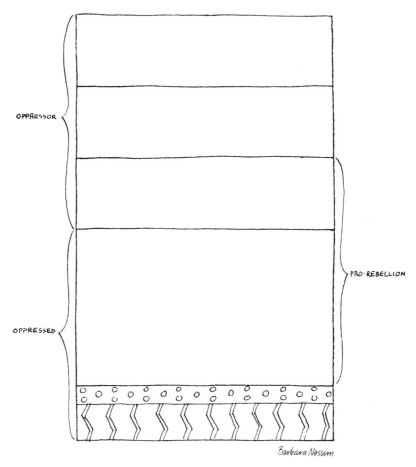

Barbara Nessim

| | NEUTRAL (nonfeminists) | | ANTI-REBELLION (anti-feminists) |

TACTICAL-STRATEGY CHART #15
CURRENT SEX CLASS CONFRONTATION
AND SUPPLEMENTAL POLITICAL ALLIANCES
AND/OR SIMILARITIES

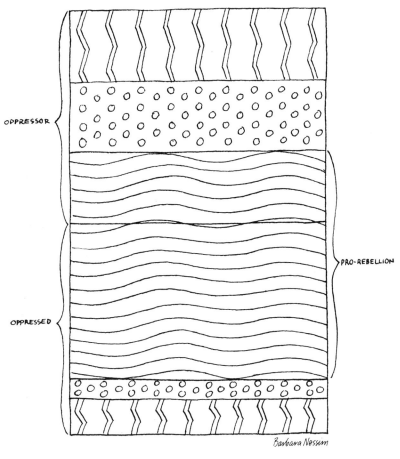

OPPRESSOR

OPPRESSED

PRO-REBELLION

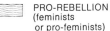

Barbara Nessim

	ANTI-REBELLION (anti-feminists)		PRO-REBELLION (feminists or pro-feminists)
	NEUTRAL (nonfeminists or nonaligned)		

TACTICAL-STRATEGY CHART #16
"SOFTENING-UP" BOMBARDMENT PRIOR TO THIRD OFFENSIVE

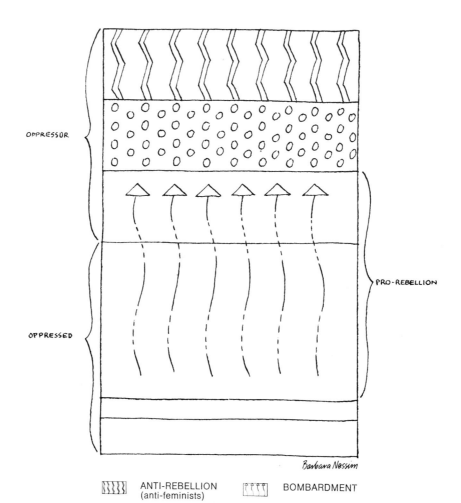

OPPRESSOR

OPPRESSED

PRO-REBELLION

Barbara Nessim

ANTI-REBELLION (anti-feminists)	BOMBARDMENT
NEUTRAL (nonfeminists or nonaligned)	

TACTICAL-STRATEGY CHART #17
INITIATION OF THIRD OFFENSIVE BY OPPRESSED

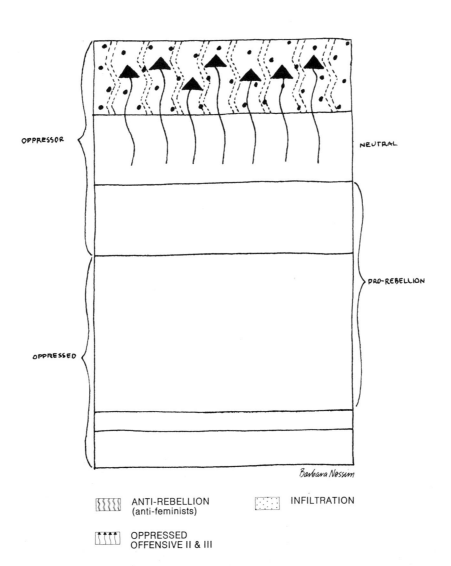

Barbara Nessim

ANTI-REBELLION
(anti-feminists)

INFILTRATION

OPPRESSED
OFFENSIVE II & III

pressor is the transformation of the Neutrals into Rebels, because of their participation within the offensive. (See Tactical-Strategy Chart #18.)

The second consequence within the Oppressor would be the neutralization of the remaining anti-feminists among the Oppressor (see Tactical-Strategy Chart #19).

The final consequences of the third offensive concern the Oppressed. The process causing the changes in the Oppressed are not dissimilar to that process already sketched in the second offensive.

TACTICAL-STRATEGY CHART #13
INITIATION OF REPERCUSSIONS WITHIN OPPRESSED
OF SECOND OFFENSIVE

TACTICAL-STRATEGY CHART #20
INITIATION OF REPERCUSSIONS WITHIN
OPPRESSED OF THIRD OFFENSIVE

The success of the third offensive, initiated by the Oppressed within the Oppressor, has repercussions within the Oppressed. As a result of the second offensive, about one-third of the Oppressed is, still, alienated from the Rebels. One-third of those alienated are Neutral, and two-thirds are Anti-Rebel. (See Tactical-Strategy Chart #14.)

The initiation of the repercussions within the Oppressed of the third offensive is, again, a kind of backfire, or bouncing-off, from the main thrust of the offensive: the attack on the Oppressor. This initiation, within the third offensive, would look something like this (see Tactical-Strategy Chart #20) under prevailing conditions.

The effect of this second front of the third offensive would be to incorporate the Neutrals into the Pro-Rebellion faction, and to neutralize the former Anti-Rebels. Because of the nature and dependency of the Anti-Rebels within the Oppressed, if the Oppressor faction of Anti-Rebels collapsed, the Oppressed co-relative would never stand.

I think it's possible that even half of the former Oppressed-Anti-Rebels would join the Rebels, but, for the moment, I'll stick with the more conservative estimate. Tactical-Strategy Chart #21 indicates the projected results of the third offensive, within the Oppressed.

Tactical-Strategy Chart #22 represents the overall strategic picture, of the sex class confrontation, and the supplemental political alliances and/or similarities. The Neutrals are strong enough, within both the Oppressor and the Oppressed, that it would be a mistake to overlook them. Under such conditions as seen in Chart #22, "Neu-

TACTICAL-STRATEGY CHART #18
FIRST CONSEQUENCE WITHIN OPPRESSOR OF
THIRD OFFENSIVE BY OPPRESSED

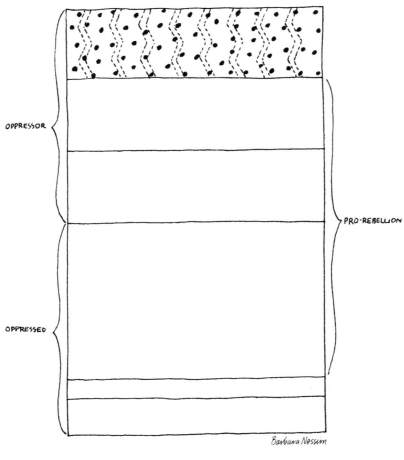

OPPRESSOR

PRO-REBELLION

OPPRESSED

Barbara Nessim

|[[[[[[| ANTI-REBELLION (anti-feminists) | :::: | INFILTRATION |

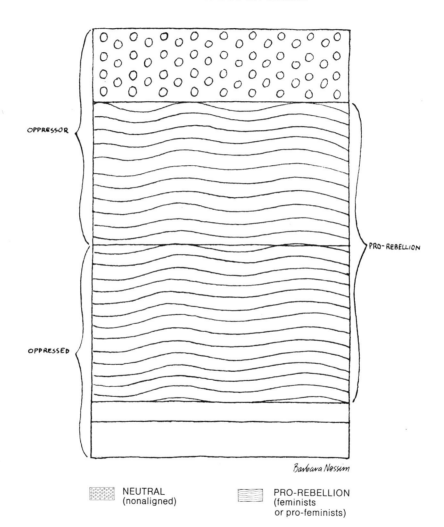

Barbara Nessim

NEUTRAL
(nonaligned)

PRO-REBELLION
(feminists
or pro-feminists)

TACTICAL-STRATEGY CHART #20
INITIATION OF REPERCUSSIONS WITHIN OPPRESSED OF THIRD OFFENSIVE

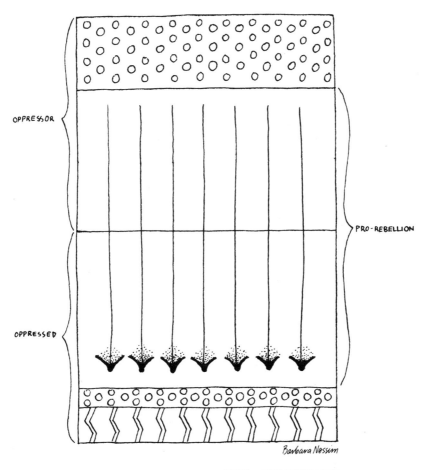

OPPRESSOR

OPPRESSED

PRO-REBELLION

Barbara Nessim

 NEUTRAL
(nonfeminists
or nonaligned)

ANTI-REBELLION
(anti-feminists)

 REPERCUSSION II

TACTICAL-STRATEGY CHART #21
RESULTS OF THIRD OFFENSIVE WITHIN OPPRESSED

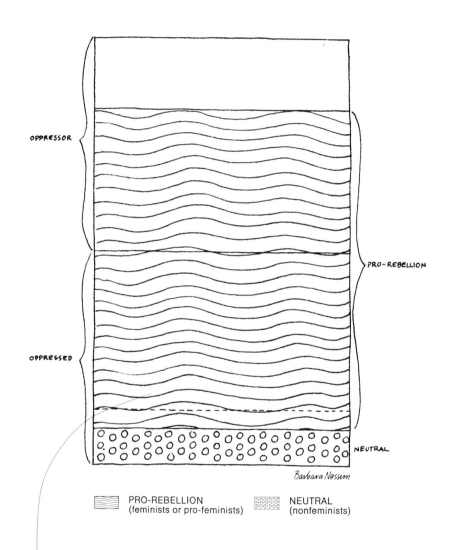

OPPRESSOR

PRO-REBELLION

OPPRESSED

NEUTRAL

Barbara Nessim

≋ PRO-REBELLION
(feminists or pro-feminists)

▨ NEUTRAL
(nonfeminists)

TACTICAL-STRATEGY CHART #22
CURRENT SEX CLASS CONFRONTATION
AND SUPPLEMENTAL POLITICAL ALLIANCES
AND/OR SIMILARITIES

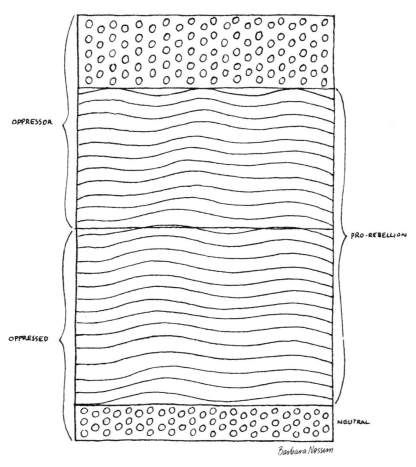

OPPRESSOR

PRO-REBELLION

OPPRESSED

NEUTRAL

Barbara Nessim

 NEUTRAL
(nonfeminists
or nonaligned)

PRO-REBELLION
(feminists or pro-feminists)

trals" must always be viewed as *dormant* Anti-Rebels.

What is left for the Rebels to do after Chart #22 is, in one sense, a cleanup operation. But, in another sense, this stage is crucial. Controls, guarding against the "Neutrals" in both camps, would have to be built into whatever new system is constructed. Within their own lifetimes, these remaining Neutrals would be extremely unlikely to change internally, or significantly.

What is left, for my audience, is to compare Tactical Chart #1 and Tactical-Strategy Chart #22. We are, presently, at best, looking forward to creating the conditions illustrated in Tactical Chart #1. We are far from there, at this point.[13] The value of strategy and tactics should be seen in the discrepancy between these two charts.

There are two points I want you to remember.

First, this paper is an extremely rough suggestion of a strategy for the Oppressed within the sex class system. My purpose has been to introduce these two concepts, "strategy" and "tactics," and to convince you of the significance of these ideas for all of us.

Second, the concept of the "Buffer" is not limited to lesbians. It is a concept including all those who by some distinction manage to escape the iron confines of the classic sex institutions—marriage and the family. Prostitution would be another Buffer candidate.

There are important distinctions between lesbianism and prostitution. Lesbianism would seem more of an option for self-determination. Prostitution is more class determined, in the economic-background sense of "class." But there are many objections that readily come to mind, on either of these characterizations. I could not suggest, exactly, what the clear political and strategic distinctions are between the two. I only stand by the statement that, on its face, there seems to be some strategically significant political distinction between lesbianism and prostitution.

The Buffer concept could apply to other class systems as well, whether the particular system is based on race, national origin, religion, age, or some other pretext

TACTICAL CHART #1
COOPTING THE ENEMY'S STRATEGY
dissolving the front-line buffer zone

TACTICAL-STRATEGY CHART #22
CURRENT SEX CLASS CONFRONTATION
AND SUPPLEMENTAL POLITICAL ALLIANCES
AND/OR SIMILARITIES

[13] [As of November, 1972, I would say we have arrived at Tactical Chart #1.]

used in an attempt to categorize and restrict.

I have one last question. It is both political and personal. How come *I* had to do this. And don't give me the "smart" routine. You're the "smart" ones to be sitting down there, while I'm beating my brains out up here, and screaming my lungs out.

This center is one of the few respectable contributions to the Women's Movement in the last four years of this fucking movement. And, essentially, only four people made it: Ruth Simpson, Ellen Povill, Eileen Webb and Becky Irons.

Now, what are all the rest of *you* going to do? I'm not interested in why you *can't* do this or that. All I know is, if you're not carrying your own share of the load, you're adding to mine. And I'm sick of it. And I'm *un*loading. I'm cleaning house.

We have a center. I'm not sure why, but it's the first women's place I've felt had a positive atmosphere, and hope, and a place where we could get things done. Especially Ruth, and Ellen, and Eileen, and Becky have proven the validity of lesbianism contributing heavily to the vanguard of the Women's Movement. *Now* I'm worried whether these four will survive feminism![14]

Okay. We have a place to meet, now. So meet, damn it, and MOVE OUT!!

189

[14] [None of these four even "survived" D.O.B. Becky left the country. And Ruth Simpson was forced out as President in May, 1971. (Ellen, Eileen, and myself, as well as others, left D.O.B. along with Ruth.) After the final meeting, Ruth's opposition left behind "maps" of their strategy to oust her. Much to my chagrin, I saw the fruits of my "chart" dedication speech. It was the first, and only, influence I know these charts have had, thus far.]

Photo by Matthew Lewis–*The Washington Post*

CATHOLIC UNIVERSITY[1]

First, I wish to express my appreciation to the President and Board of Trustees of Catholic University. They have taken considerable time and trouble to provide a demonstration of my theory of the Catholic Church versus feminism.[2] I couldn't have done a better job myself.

In defense of Clarence [Clarence Walton, President, Catholic University] and charity, however, I feel it is my moral responsibility to make one point clear to the students. I truly believe that, concerning the events of the past week, only Clarence and I fully understand and appreciate each other.[3]

While I do want to get on with my exposé of the Church, there are a few recent details that I should clarify. Fortunately, they're entirely relevant to a proper political understanding of the Church as the greatest organized crime ring the world's ever seen.

I like to think of the Vatican *re* women as analogous to the Pentagon *re* the antiwar movement. The Church (hierarchy) is a sort of Ku Klux Klan. Unfortunately, up until tonight, the Church has not been exposed sufficiently to hide its face. And those costumes they wear can hardly be compared monetarily to sheets. But the *political intent,* not the scale of that intent, is the important point to grasp here.

Why is Catholic University the first institution of higher learning to ban a feminist from speaking? I have spoken at other Catholic universities since my speech at Notre Dame. Why such flattering hysteria only here?

I admit that at several Catholic institutions I have been abundantly preceded by the apparent student public relations representatives of the Church, the Young Americans for Freedom. I saw one of their flyers distributed at Trinity College (in Washington, D. C., for women). It was a selection of excerpts from my October 15, 1970, speech at Notre Dame. Given that the notes for the speech itself (it was also taped by a couple of people, undoubtedly also reporting to their central offices in Washington) covered some six pages of legal-sized paper, the excerpts caught only the highlights and livelier spots.

The vast majority of the Notre Dame speech was a fairly academic attempt to distinguish between political and moral responsibility. My thesis was that this was essentially a false distinction that the Church tried to force on its constituency. The mo-

191

[1] [March 10, 1971; Washington, D. C.]
[2] [I had been banned from speaking at Catholic University, and was only permitted to do so by court order.]
[3] [About how heavy the politics involved were.]

tives are obvious. The individual is morally responsible to follow the Church's authority wherever questions of faith are concerned. On questions of faith, the Church—through the Pope—is infallible.

Now, on those issues concerning the liberation of women, the center of each issue (abortion, for instance) is at deadlock with tenets of Catholic faith. At this point, *political* responsibility ceases to exist for the Catholic, and obedience to the authority of the Church is paramount.

At this point, I introduced a more modern notion. In any society remotely resembling a democracy, every individual is responsible for acts committed in its name. Thus, in any given case, one is an accomplice or a revolutionary. Blood on one's hands or blood on one's head.

It was in this context that the issue of the Virgin Mary was raised. She was impregnated supernaturally, and was, therefore, forced to bear the responsibility and sorrow of her supernatural child more than if he had been conceived naturally. "Knocked up"—she was impregnated; "knocked down"—this son was a source of great grief to her; "with no clues"—without sexual intercourse. My remarks *depended* on the virginity of the Blessed Mother. I was attacking the cruelty of her having to bear this sorrow alone. So much for what I said at Notre Dame.

[It was at this point that Mrs. Bozell struck me.]

Catholic hallucinations, sometimes referred to as articles of faith, are of no interest to me. (Among other difficulties, such articles are not subject to rules of evidence —hardly a scholarly utopia.) I am interested only in the sadistic political practices of the Church, particularly as they relate to women. I'm afraid that the fixation of the University on my challenge (which did not, in fact, exist) to the Blessed Mother's virginity is not understood in its political significance in the community at large.

I said, earlier, that Clarence and I understood each other. I still stand behind that. Clarence understands that it is the political power of the Church, exercised through economic blackmail on individuals and political parties, and sustained by the concept of the Church's "authority," that I am striking at. The source of the Church's infallibility on matters of faith stems from the Divinity, Christ. Infallibility, obviously, cannot be subject to mistakes. Ordinary human beings, because they are conceived through carnal knowledge, are cursed with original sin, that is, they can make mistakes. Christ, through whom the Pope and Church are infallible on matters of faith, could not be created through carnal knowledge (or any other taint of knowledge, one is tempted to add).

This is why Clarence is jumping up and

By Matthew Lewis–*The Washington Post*

down about Mary's virginity. I don't know if, consciously, Clarence is also trying to pit one woman against another (viciousness comes naturally to men like Clarence).

Catholic University has forty-eight trustees, only eleven of whom are lay people. Unlike most universities, the trustees are not listed in the catalogue. However, after some research, Ruth Simpson[4] found that the Board includes all U.S. Cardinals and metropolitan Archbishops, and two Bishops elected by the National Conference on Catholic Bishops. Clarence Walton, Catholic University's president, is distinguished by the publication of a book, in 1968, entitled *Big Government and Big Business*. It strikes me as curious, but not unrelated to the brouhaha over my visit to Catholic University, that one of the richest cartels in the world—tax exempt, and thus rich, on the grounds that it does not function politically—should establish all of its big guns in the U. S. hierarchy in a relatively undistinguished university. The fascinating coincidence is that the government of the Church just happens to be in the same city, otherwise undistinguished, of the United States capital.

The Catholic Church is the biggest corporation in the United States. It has a branch in almost every neighborhood. The assets and real estate holdings exceed those of Standard Oil, A.T.&T., and U. S. Steel combined. And the roster of dues-paying members is second only to the rolls of the United States Government.

The "cooperation" between the Church and governments (the more fascist the government, the stronger the Church) has been recognized as mutually beneficial, but has not been carefully analyzed. Does the Church thrive under the most oppressive regimes because it succors the poor? Or does it thrive in countries such as Spain, Batista's regime, South American countries generally, because it profits and grows rich off the poor, and, thus, increasingly powerful in determining the policies—whether foreign or domestic—of a given country. The political power of the Church depends on its economic strength, thus, leverage. The principle and practices accompanying it, of maintaining property and wealth in the hands of a few, makes the interdependency of dictatorships and the Church especially congenial.

The Church is a kind of vulture on the poor. The Church picks the bones of the poor and is eagerly permitted to do so by them, in exchange for the promise of revenge in the world to come. The fantastic cathedrals are built from the nickels and dimes of the poor and the blood of women. This was true of the pyramids also. But the cathedrals are inhabited, in addition, by the living dead—the women who pray for relief, whether death or the living death of fantasy. Hallucinations come easily and are welcomed under such conditions.

It is for this, this savage and hypocriti-

---

4 [At the time of this speech, President, Daughters of Bilitis, New York City.]

cal abuse and manipulation of humanity, that the Church and institutional religion are hated and despised by free peoples. It is for these conscious and cruel deceptions that in the uprisings of the Oppressed (a miracle, indeed, where the Church exists) the Church is driven out, their properties returned to the poor from whom it was stolen, and the Church's representatives butchered, and butchered, and butchered. And this is just.

At Notre Dame, with every effort I could summon, I brought the indictments against the Church I had heard from so many, before the accused. I had hoped reason and explanation might help. It was I who did not understand. Catholic University, at the orders of the Catholic hierarchy in the United States (perhaps more powerful now than in any other country), has given me my answer to reason. So be it.

The Church sustains itself only through oppression and cannot survive without that political condition. All other groups, with the exception of women, can be rotated into or relatively out of oppressed classes as long as oppression itself is not proportionately challenged. It is only over the class of women that it is necessary for the Church to maintain absolute control.

1. The control of women is essential for population control and manipulation.

   a. population control is necessary in event of ground wars
   b. population control is necessary for Church numbers, especially when the conversion rate is going down
   c. population rate, overpopulation, must be maintained and manipulated for guaranteed unemployment, which maintains a rigid economic class hierarchy, since wages can be controlled through fear of unemployment.

   Obviously, either birth control or abortion, at the discretion of the individual, would jeopardize one of the Church's most powerful political levers.

2. Women are also key in the indoctrination of the youth. The Church has said before, "give us a child until the age of seven, and we have him for life." The mother controls the child through those crucial years. Thus, again, it is crucial for the Church to control the mother.

Unfortunately, from the point of view of women, although apparently not from that of the Church, it is necessary to deny woman free will, and to murder her if necessary. This can be managed through external controls as well as internal ones.

The Church withdraws funds from primary campaigns of a given Party in a given area, if the representative of that area casts an important vote for, say, abortion. This occurs regardless of the denomination of either the candidate or his constituency.

Similar strategy is used in the United Nations whenever issues arise concerning freedom of movement and residence for women, just and favorable remuneration ensuring for women an existence worthy of human dignity, and other issues vital to women. Birth control has never been permitted on the agenda. Even within the United Nations' Commission on the Status of Women, men represent the Catholic countries or those countries whose governments are subject to the Church's influence. Women represent the socialist and Communist countries. The feminist records of the fascist countries are insulting. Most frequently, they cite some one or few "illustrious examples." The countries represented by women cite impressive percentages of women who have realized, more fully, their human potential. The men from the Catholic fascist countries are regarded with scorn by the women—as pimps for their governments.

It is the greatest privilege of my life to be here tonight. For myself, yes, that's part of it. But for all my people, women, whom the Church for two thousand years has slaughtered, and robbed, who were born and died deprived of their humanity, who died in agony without even the right to cry out against their pain, because their agony was at the same time their shame. I remember you—all of you. The mute faces of these women crowd my mind often. Tonight is for them, too. I have not forgotten you. I shall never forget you.[5]

I, Ti-Grace Atkinson, in the name of all women, most especially the deceased victims of the accused, charge the Catholic Church, its government, and all its subsidiaries and members such as Catholic University with murder in the first degree, premeditated and willful.

In the name of all women, I charge the Catholic Church with conspiracy to corrupt the democratic process, by blackmailing the major parties and their candidates, against the interests of women.

In the name of all women, I charge the Catholic Church with conspiracy to imprison and enslave the women of the world, through coercion into such institutions as marriage and the family.

In the name of all women, I charge the Catholic Church with forcing many of our class into prostitution, through the financial greed of the Church.

In the name of all women, I charge the Catholic Church with inciting rape against women, by its degrading and sadistic propaganda against women.

In the name of all women, I charge the Catholic Church with constituting, by its

---

[5] [This paragraph was the only one omitted during the presentation of this speech. I feared that the emotion of these sentences, combined with, by that time, the Bozell incident, might cause me to lose control to the point that I couldn't finish the rest of the speech.]

very existence, an obscenity on the face of the earth.

On the charge of murder. *Guilty!*

On the charge of political conspiracy. *Guilty!*

On the charge of enslavement. *Guilty!*

On the charge of prostitution. *Guilty!*

On the charge of incitement to rape. *Guilty!*

On the charge of constituting an obscenity. *Guilty!*

There is no "justice" for oppressed people. I came tonight, as a woman, symbolically for all women, to confront the Church in all its despicable hypocrisy, and to cry out in public so that all women might hear: "Motherfuckers! We have heard your answer to my appeal for reason at Notre Dame. And you are *right.* The struggle, between the liberation of women and the Catholic Church, is a struggle to the death! So be it."

ON
"VIOLENCE IN THE WOMEN'S MOVEMENT"

COLLABORATORS[1]

I am dedicating my remarks tonight on violence to Sister Joseph Colombo. I am referring to America's latest *super*star, gangster, criminal: Joseph Colombo. You may have heard about how Superstar Colombo, not content with his vertical media image, backed his head up into three bullets at Columbus Circle on June 28, 1971. I fill you in, because, what with reading the *Hanoi News,* the *Peking Gazette,* the *Panther Party Paper, Now, Now and Then,* the *Havana Has-Been* and the *Old* and the *New Guardian*'s, it's understandable that this audience might have failed to notice that their tootsies were slopping through blood on their very own streets. The problem of the "underground" is that it is necessarily "off the street." But the "problem" in this case is, happily enough, also the solution.

I decided only last night to come here and to say something. It's about time this phantasmagoria of "violence" as a tactic of the Women's Movement, directed outside of itself, was given a decent ("adequate") burial. And the superstars of this Movement of ours are the obvious experts on this subject, if on no other, since they are the recipients of the violence, such as it is, from both within the Women's Movement and without.

If my meaning escapes you, consider that recent song hit, "Jesus Christ, Superstar." And a priest recently sent me a book called *The Power Tactics of Jesus Christ.* I immersed it in water upon receipt, but the title alone suggests that its contents reflect the spirit in which I appear here tonight. What some people won't do for publicity!

Now, about "violence." First, let's establish what we're talking about. As a

[1] [August 4, 1971; Panel on Violence, P.S. 41; New York City.]

concept, I think everyone would agree, at least minimally, that "violence" refers to the employment of "*force* used by one party to *maintain* or *further* its own interests *against* the self-interests of some *other* party or object." Thus, "violence" would seem to be at least *an,* if not *the,* primary characteristic of the class *function* within the phenomenon of oppression. "Violence" itself, in this role of "aspect," has at least two characteristics: (first) it is mono-directional, and (second) its purpose is self-aggrandizement. Insofar as the existence of "oppression" is a reality, this self-aggrandizement, that is, the power of one class over another, is already established.

The *use* of "violence," as an instrument or tactic, is determined and restricted by the *concept* of "violence." "Violence," as surplus energy or "force," is available as a *tactic* only to the oppressor class within any given class system. I am not making any value judgment here but simply positing that, in political theory, "violence" is by definition a class function. It is organized weight or pressure to maintain the *status quo.* As such, "violence" is irrelevant as a concept and unavailable as a tactic to the Oppressed.

Some people might suggest that this explains why "violence" is observed as a tactic of the Oppressed *primarily* when it is practiced *within* its own class. But insofar as "violence" is a function *between* classes, another *system* (with some basis for dichotomizing the original class) would have to be posited. The positing of this second system within the oppressed class has been attempted by several movements: the Black, the Women's, and, now, the Italian-American. Insofar as this second positing is successful, the theme of this evening is a viable one: "Violence *in* the Women's Movement." It would also explain the hostilities and charges of "elitism," "superstar," "privilege," and so forth, I expect to hear long before I have any chance to read *this* paper.[2]

But there is at least one obvious clue, to the *difficulty* in attempting to transpose the class function obtaining *between* men and women to that between two or more classes *within* the class of women. In the first instance (the sex class system), a "special" class was perceived, that of "women." *Then,* and with great reluctance and still far from universally, another class was posited to account for the *source* of "discrimination" (the "ladylike" euphemism for "violence") against women. Unfortunately, an analysis of the *nature* and *expressions* of the *activity* of oppression, of which "violence" is one aspect, has been for the most part evaded. The result is that the phenomenon of oppression, itself, has yet to be addressed. Instead, the oppressor *class* has been focused upon and *verbally* assaulted. And in the immortal words of Anthony Imperiale,[3] as witnessed on the six o'clock TV News, December, 1969: "Militancy with the *mouth* is fine."

In the second instance, the second system posited *within* some more primary class system, the *activity* of oppression is focused upon. And, then, an attempt is made to elicit a class *system* from a myriad and somewhat vague list of grievances. This reversal of the genesis of the concept of "violence," or oppression, is the "clue" I mentioned earlier.

If "violence" is a necessary condition to the class function existing between the Oppressor and the Oppressed, and if this condition represents an accumulation or

---

[2] [If only these *had* been the accusations to materialize!]

[3] [Italian-American leader in Newark, New Jersey. While "of the people," Imperiale is moderate in tactics and right-wing in his choice of enemies.]

excess of power on the part of the Oppressor, and the use of same against the Oppressed, we seem to have a sort of "explosion" relationship. If the Oppressed is, by definition, to some degree deprived of strength or power, a sort of benign vacuum (I like to call it "love") is brought into being.[4] "Consciousness," or activation of this vacuum, could turn the benign into the malignant. The combination of the pressure *outside* the class, and the imbalance of power *between* the two parties, could result in a sort of "implosion" or "negative" expression, reversal, of the class function of oppression outside.[5]

IN SHORT, THE "CAUSALITY" OF FUNCTIONS, OR PERHAPS YOU COULD SUBSTITUTE "MOTIVATION" FOR "CAUSALITY" IN POLITICAL THEORY, IS CRUCIAL TO A PROPER UNDERSTANDING OF THE FUNCTIONAL PHENOMENON ITSELF (IN THIS CASE, THAT PARTICULAR ASPECT, "VIOLENCE").

I suspect I am making a mistake. Perhaps I am trying to ingratiate myself with you by considering this subject in a serious manner. In fact, I truly believe the discussion of violence as a tactic for the Women's Movement is, at best, absurd. At worst, it is a feeble and somewhat flattering attempt by the C.I.A. to flush out any potential firebrands. I think that the increasing discussion of violence, as a concept or tactic relevant for us, is a case of "militancy of the mouth." Let's look at some facts.

In the last women's movement, we suffered one casualty in this country. Inez Mulholland collapsed on a speaking tour in California, and expired from nervous exhaustion. The most impressive description I've been able to come up with is this: "Inez Mulholland was struck down by hoof and

202

[4] [See *Radical Feminism and Love*, pp. 41–45.]
[5] [See *Untitled: Some Notes Toward a Theory of Identity*, pp. 109–116.]

mouth disease. The feminists in her Washington, D.C., funeral cortege, in recognition of the dread disease that took Inez from amongst their midst, all rode silently down Pennsylvania Avenue on horseback."

Now, come on. Isn't this gathering tonight sufficient evidence of this subject's absurdity? "Violence" is not a choice for us. Every woman is in it up to, and apparently *over,* her eyeballs. Violence for her friends, we all accept. Our enemies, we worry about.

Consider. We are several hundred, supposedly activist, women "discussing" violence. Action against this meeting from the Oppressor is cool. Now, imagine, if all of us here were to get up and drift over to St. Patrick's Cathedral, and kind of "hang around." Nobody talking. Just "hanging around."[6]

We're in here talking about using violence, because we know we ain't got none

to *use! First,* we got to get out into the street. Then, we got to get some *direction.* Then, all we got to do is *move.* Just lean. To pretend to seriously discuss motion variants without targets, or, even worse, to actively avoid *known* targets, is the most irresponsible sort of self-deception.[7]

Do you think that, if several hundred *Mafiosi* were to hold a meeting like this, it would come off? Anthony Colombo, Joseph's eldest and 26-year-old son, complained, recently, that the F.B.I. picked him and his friends up for standing on the corner. But radicals could stand on the same corner, advocating the overthrow of the government, and nobody bothered them!

Now all of us here know the answer to Anthony Colombo's complaint. Revolution, in this country, is a false rumor. The so-called "Left" has to hold interpretive meetings on the significance of Nixon's visit to China. Me, I understand fine. I understand

203

---

[6] [Women laughed. Women got the point.]

[7] [There was worse to come.]

Women and Blacks better find some new friends. With the possible exception of some Weatherpeople, forget the Left.[8] Nobody dies on a charitable impulse. I want to be in the street with people fighting for their own asses. I won't have to watch them all the time, then, and can concentrate on the opposition.

I came here tonight for a purpose. I want to put a question to you. It is both about "violence" and "the Women's Movement." Where have all you political "heavies" been, who regularly bleed over the white working-class and, in passing (for such a noble cause, of course), dump on the Women's Movement? How come, since August of last year, not one "heavy" has gone and looked over this Italian-American Civil Rights League? You can read as well as I can. Thousands of for-real working-class people, in an organization supposedly founded by *Mafiosi*. Black criminals are revolutionary! So why not Italian-American criminals, with a tradition of resistance?

Several people have seemed quite discomposed over my association with the League. "You're the last person in the world I'd have expected to be working with them!" You'd better believe it! The question is, how come the "last" one was the only one to go look?

I have an answer. I think the Left, or the "politicos" (however you want to style them), are afraid to deal with *Mafiosi* because they're reputed to be "serious." They don't understand "mistakes" that put other people in jail. They don't "understand" blabbing directly or indirectly to the pigs. They don't "understand" compatriots who don't get up in time to make the Revolution.

I had a blow-up made of this picture. I'm taping it up where you can see it. *That* is violence! I suggest, if you're serious, you

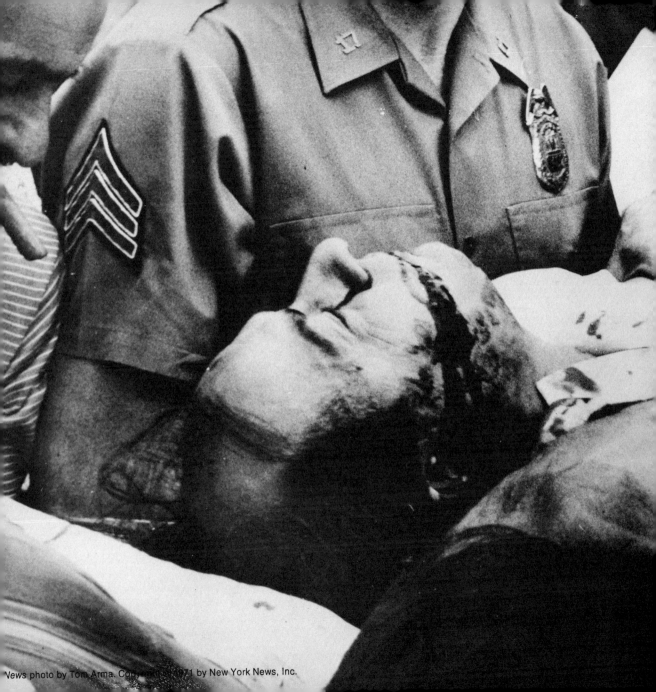

get a copy of this, and pin it on your wall, until after the Revolution. Just so you don't "forget."[9]

I don't know why Joseph Colombo started the League. I don't know why he became "political." I used to tell him he was STUPID! I used to tell him the government was going to kill him. He asked me if maybe people like him couldn't be considered "political prisoners." I laughed, very bitterly, and I answered him. "They assassinate people like you. Shore up your back."

Joseph Colombo did not have the "right" to live. Joseph Colombo fought for everybody else's rights. But who fought for his? As a "gangster," he couldn't carry a gun. As a "gangster," if he had adequate security, it would be called "muscle." So he couldn't protect himself. Because he was a "criminal," even though the threats were coming in well over the really dangerous zone, he had to run around loose in the open—in an uncontrollable security space. I think he knew he was going to be hit. You sense it. I knew it at Catholic University, and there *were* guns in there. I got lucky because I had the "right" to survive.

Everyone asked suspiciously: "What is he *really* up to?" He lost money. He became super-vulnerable to attack from *every* side. He was hideously humiliated. He lacked formal education, so he was filled with even more self-doubts than most people would be. Well, now everyone can stop asking—and they have—only nobody's speaking out the answer. "Joseph Colombo *got* three bullets in the back of the head! And he got them for single-handedly starting the first white working-class movement in this country. The first since the labor movement in its early stages in the earlier

[9] [It was at this point that the symposium became "violent."]

part of this century. He was a 'leader,' a superstar, super-likely to get shot from the back. And we all know who's in back of leaders: followers."

So, cut the *star* shit. Any real star won't last long enough to bother *any*body. And as for democratic! *Any*body can be a star. There's one thing this country has enough of for every single one of us, and that's bullets. This picture is the picture of *our* tragedy, not Colombo's. And a tragedy, not for *his* loss, but for the revelation of the truth about ourselves. We're phonies. We are meeting in a school (a *small* improvement over the usual church) to "discuss" violence. It's dripping off our hands, not only because we are each and all collaborators, but for a much worse reason. We are worse than collaborators because of our pretensions of sincerity, our concern for humanity—the further away the better.

In part, I indict myself with you. For the first few months, I worked with the League in off moments (cursing the Left, under my breath, that I couldn't get to do its job). I abused the League members royally. (Poor babies. They think that it's natural for "radicals" to turn purple whenever an Italian-American male opens his mouth, and for a movement person to shake them until their lapels tear, and heap obscenities on them. "That's just the way 'they' are. Don't act surprised or alarmed in any way. You'll hurt their feelings.") Now, I'm tough to take in the Women's Movement. But this STRANGE and BEAUTIFUL and REVOLUTIONARY *FOOL* and "criminal"—Joseph Colombo—wore a "Freedom for Women" button, in front of the press, and the F.B.I., and nobody dared laugh.

It was only a few months ago as I worked on the Corky Willis case, the Building Service Employees' Union member, whose job the League got back for her, that I was shocked into a very ugly truth about myself politically. You see, I thought the League was "lucky" I would even try to work with them. And I made this judgment on the basis that "I was the last person anyone would expect, and I was doing more than anyone else on the Left." In an arbitration meeting between the company, Allied Maintenance, and the union, the company's lawyer in front of several witnesses baldly stated "we're throwing this woman out of that building because Chemical Bank told us to. *That* woman filed sex discrimination charges with the State Human Rights' Division, and got the *name* of Chemical Bank on television! But we wouldn't care *what* reason Chemical Bank had. *We* (Allied Maintenance) give people like *that* an opportunity to make a livelihood for them-

selves." This lawyer for Allied Maintenance talked like Corky was an animal, that it was a "privilege" for her to survive. I'd promised the union to keep my mouth shut at the closed grievance session, but I had this vision of quietly strangling that pig to death. And then it struck me: Why hadn't *I* thought of Chemical Bank as possibly behind this? Chemical Bank was the super-employer. And I realized that I hadn't thought of the politically obvious, because it was cheaper to distrust this particular union. And I realized that the Left is as Establishment as the Establishment.

I realized that I had been abusing Joseph Colombo and the League because they had no "standing." And for this, I was a phony. *Why wasn't I more afraid of being unjust to even one human being, than of giving one human being the benefit of the doubt?* It was irrelevant *what* anyone else was or was not doing with the League. The only question for me should have been: Am *I* being just to them.[10] The answer to that question was, of course, "No." And that was and is, always, the only issue.

I never told Colombo why I came back and worked differently. Or why I dragged my friends, Ruth Simpson and Ellen Povill from D.O.B., with me. (Ruth and Ellen quickly became members of the League.) But all this *does* belong HERE, and TO-NIGHT. It's my business to tell *you*, the people *I* live with, why I went back to the League and why you—especially you, with your revolutionary claims—should have been with the League from the beginning. Either that, or you too will continue to be phonies, as I was.

You will continue to be phonies to the Women's Movement as well, if you continue to sit around talking about whether or not to do something that you know as well as I do is irrelevant and absurd.

Is Susan Brownmiller here? (Or friends of hers?) In reference to her review of the book about Diana Oughton of the Weather-people, in the *New York Sunday Times* Book Review of April, 1971: that's called fucking over the dead. I quote:

> All the Weatherpeople wanted was to be heroes of the inevitable American revolution, an arrogant wish born of privilege.
>
> But as credit-card revolutionaries at large in the mother country, they could merely extend the American paradox to a further degree. There was one way, finally, to wipe out the white-skin privilege, and the blast on Eleventh Street accomplished just that.

209

[10] [See *Individual Responsibility and Human Oppression*, pp. 117–130.]

And the heading reads: "One way to get the monkey of privilege off your back."

Susan, you are claiming "feminist privilege." You are a despicable human being for that. Diana Oughton is my sister long before you. If you haven't the courage for the truth, at least have the shame to keep your fucking mouth shut!

LONG LIVE THE SPIRIT OF DIANA OUGHTON. LONG LIVE ANGELA DAVIS. LONG LIVE BERNADINE DOHRN. LONG LIVE THE SPIRIT OF VICTORIA WOODHULL. LONG LIVE THE SPIRIT OF THE VALERIE SOLANAS OF THE *SCUM MANIFESTO*. LONG LIVE THE STUBBORNNESS OF SIMONE DE BEAUVOIR. LONG LIVE BIG MAMA FLORYNCE KENNEDY. LONG LIVE SISTER MARK RUDD. LONG LIVE THE SPIRIT OF JONATHAN JACKSON. LONG

LIVE THE SPIRITS, AND THE HOPES, AND THE BODIES, OF ALL THE BEAUTIFUL, REVOLUTIONARY, FOOL, CRIMINALS, WHO ARE STUPID ENOUGH TO FIGHT FOR THE POSSIBILITY OF A HUMAN SPIRIT. LONG LIVE THE SPIRIT OF SISTER JOSEPH COLOMBO, AND HIS BODY, IF ITS CONDITION MEETS HIS TERMS. HE HAS PAID HIS DUES, AND TOO MUCH OF OURS BESIDES.

May we, the women here, make a Revolution.

I have copies of the Catholic University speech here. I promised many of you copies, long ago. I'll leave them here. If you have a quarter, I need food money.

I'm leaving now. I came to say these things, because I should have come before. We all want to be accepted. I am no different from anyone here. I know what I've said will not be liked. But my stomach gets weaker, as my hopes get higher. I no longer have the "right" to cut corners with the truth. I owe you the truth, as best I can make it out. I owe it to you, as well as to myself. And the difference between the two fades more and more.

I'm going up and hang out around St. Patrick's for about an hour. Hangin' in and hangin' out get closer and closer.

SELF-DECEPTION[11]

AN OPEN LETTER TO ALL THE COL-
LABORATORS IN "SISTERS WILL TALK
ABOUT VIOLENCE IN THE WOMEN'S
MOVEMENT"

I've known for a long time that no one
can be both a "revolutionary" and engage
in self-deception.[12] But your actions
Wednesday night taught me that the "self"
in self-deception extends beyond any
particular individual. As a woman in the
Women's Movement, the "self" includes
deceiving oneself about the women in
the Movement, as well as about oneself.[13]

It took close to two years in N.O.W. before the evidence overwhelmed me into understanding that N.O.W. was *not* interested
in changing society to the point that *all*
women would benefit.[14] When I left N.O.W.
in October of '68, I left essentially alone.
In about a year, it was commonly accepted
that N.O.W. was the "right" wing of the
Movement.

It took me nearly three years to catch
on to the "left" wing of the Movement. Personally, I probably should thank you for last
Wednesday night. You liberated me from
you. I left, finally, because you disgust me,
and I would be ashamed to associate with
you.[15]

After three years, I *still* can't figure out
what you're trying to do, *except* for one
thing. You are *not* trying to do what you
say you're trying to do:

> (1) divest yourselves of all class priv-
> ilege, and

---

[11] [August 6, 1971; this statement was intended, at the
time it was issued, as a warning to the Women's Movement. As part of *Amazon Odyssey,* however, it will reach
an audience far outside the immediate scope of this
movement. For that reason, I have deleted the names of
women where my remarks were either particularly biting
or where my remarks were extensive and the names,
herein, serve no purpose.]

[12] [See *Individual Responsibility and Human Oppression,*
pp. 117–130.]
[13] [See *Untitled: Some Notes Toward a Theory of Identity,*
pp. 109–116.]
[14] [See *Resignation from N.O.W.,* pp. 9–11.]
[15] [I never left the "Movement." I threw everybody else
out!]

(2) struggle against oppression it-self.[16]

Your major activity is talking to each other in special sessions, which you carefully label "political." This careful labeling distinguishes "talking" about your lives from the way you spend the majority of your time, which is in "living" them. There is no significantly observable truth connection between the two activities, at least not apparently to the individuals living this double-life.[17] But you consciously and maliciously attempt to deceive others that there *is* a difference, that you *are* political. And you then use this deceit as a weapon against all outsiders. Yours is the conspiracy and apex of self-deception. I was a part of you. I am so no longer.

I must be the dumbest human being who ever lived. I *believed* that you were concerned about the working-class. But the only evidence for this is that you've used a claim to this group (a claim you have been careful neither to examine nor define) to evade your responsibilities as feminists. You have assumed class "privilege" to conceal your cowardice and betrayal of that "other" class you claim to fight in the name of—women.

There is supreme irony in that you exposed yourselves to me, and the you in me, because of a photograph of a dead,[18] 48-year-old, Brooklyn-born, 8th-grade-educated, male "gangster." That a picture could do so much is the measure of the truth you claim.

When Carol Turner invited me to speak, I hesitated for at least a couple of reasons:

---

[16] [See *Juniata II: The Equality Issue*, pp. 65–75, and *University of Rhode Island: Movement Politics and Other Sleights of Hand*, pp. 95–108.]
[17] [See *Juniata II: The Political Woman*, pp. 89–94.]

[18] [Joseph Colombo was no longer breathing when the picture appearing on page 205 was taken. He was "dead." His breathing was restored, shortly thereafter, at Roosevelt Hospital.]

(1) the subject is an obvious absurdity, and

(2) the speakers were chosen, not for any special interest and development of the subject, but for name value alone—a mind-boggling invitation to charges of "elitism" and "superstar."

I agreed, finally, on Tuesday night because

(1) while the subject is absurd, it is not treated as such, gains momentum, and thus encourages our super-plague of "militancy of the mouth," and

(2) I thought I *did* have something to say on the subject.

Imagine my surprise, on arrival, to find the panel and the audience, not in confrontation, but in "sisterhood"! (In spite of the increasing abuse Carol Turner received prior to the event on charges of "elitism.")

I could never quite grasp the distinction made between "leader" and "superstar," between so-called *true* leadership and media-contrived leadership.[19] You finally explained this to me on Wednesday.

I never imagined I was anyone's leader. I have never had followers. But I had never imagined the truth, that I was your slave. You have been content to trade off *my* guts and struggle as your own. As long as the truth of *your* cowardice and betrayal of women is not made public, you permit, are even quite content with, having panels of individuals be your conscience. The distinction between a "leader" and a "superstar" has been the distinction between your secret exploitation of some individuals, and the exposure of you to your-

215

[19] [This distinction, and the issues underlying it, were instrumental in my leaving The Feminists (April, 1970).]

selves via the press. But your "privileged" days are over. I warn you. Think well before you act. From now on, you will be held responsible—before the "people," not under any governmental jurisdiction. You stand accused on moral, not legal, grounds, according to your pretended "standards," and on your own evidence.

I spoke, briefly, last Wednesday night. I heard only Kate Millett and Robin Morgan. I had written out my statement so I would be clear. I have never spoken "well." I admire people, like Kate and Robin, who can mobilize feeling. It amounts to a talent.

First, I explained with some care why "violence" was irrelevant to us, both as a concept and as a weapon. I did this out of respect for any good faith that might have prompted any belief in the subject's relevance. Secondly, I pointed to the facts, the evidence behind this theory, from the last

movement and implicit in that forum. Then, after establishing the irrelevance of "violence" to the "Women's Movement," I began to say something about "violence." Surely, we weren't there to discuss the Women's Movement. The point, or distinctness of this forum, was the topic of "violence."

I taped a 16" x 20" photo on the front of the podium. An example of "violence" that is familiar to everyone, and fresh in all our minds. This photograph is from the *Daily News*. Primarily, it is the head of a dead Italian male in profile, blood still streaming from the right side of his mouth. This image takes up two-fifths of the space. Immediately above and behind is a pig's torso, his badge and three sergeant's stripes are prominent. (The pig takes up one-fifth additional space.) To the far left, a white male profile with fat cigar, savagely intent on the dead horizontal figure being lifted into an ambulance. Newspapers cushion the dead man's head.

I went to great trouble to get this picture for you. The symbolism is compelling as a statement of the political expression of power, "violence."

At first, from the response of the audience, I thought I might have the photo upside-down, or backwards. Somehow, as I have often thought for five years, I thought *I* must not be making myself clear.

Florynce Kennedy, whom I saw later, fled before she caught the disease—the unbelievable ugliness coming from all of you. I stayed long enough to catch enough to be immunized.

I saw and heard ————'s remark: "That's horizontal hostility." (I used to excuse you, ————, because you were "sick." But such obscene and excruciating inhumanity was the norm Wednesday night.)

The Feminists, Pam Kearon and Barbara Mehrhof were two I saw, the originators of the class workshop, the champions of the working class, I couldn't believe what I heard from you. You were in the forefront of the attack. Pam said: "Talk about the Women's Movement." Someone else from that section said, "The Mafia has the power. It has nothing to do with oppression."

I saw and heard women with hate for me on their faces shouting: "You're taking up too much time. Your time is up. It's getting late." Flo Kennedy told me, later, this was a lie. Many had spoken much longer.

Women shouted: "Take her off the stage, if she won't shut up." Women started coming up on the stage, their faces pinched with malice, "You've had your turn."

I tried to explain that this was what I'd heard you were looking for (and certainly abused other women for not being), the "working-class." I gave the dead man's "credentials": educated only through the 8th grade. His father murdered. Working to support his mother and sister from the age of 13. He even lived in Brooklyn.

Someone else shouted, "He's a gangster. That's not violence. That was about power. That's not political. Take her off!"

I kept trying to explain: "But the black revolutionaries you most admire were criminals. Malcolm X and Eldridge Cleaver. And what is politics about, if not about power?"

Another woman shouted: "He was shot by his own people." But so was Malcolm X. A Feminist shouted: "That's a racist remark." But the few black women in the audience understood what I was saying far better than their "champions."

"The Mafia is our Oppressor. Colombo traffics in drugs and prostitution," I heard .from the back. I asked: "Are all black 'criminals' the same? Does every 'thief' steal the same things? Colombo is accused of ripping off Wall Street, not trafficking in narcotics, or prostitution. He picketed the F.B.I. every weekday for a year. He has organized the working class."

You, YOU, my fine "sisters." You dare level the accusation of prostitution? YOU who have whored away the self-respect of the Women's Movement? YOU who speak of violence to men, and continue living with them, sleeping with them, loving them, bearing their children, *eager* to be seen on the street with them? You DARE to speak of prostitution? YOU who have made a mockery of women as a political force?

And my fine "sisters" on the stage. The panel:

You, ———. You who defended the

betrayal of lesbianism as an issue in N.O.W. You who became ugly with fear in jail and supported the pigs—"don't offend them." You who left me to fight them alone. You kept silent Wednesday night.

And you, ———. You asked me only "who's a superstar," as if you'd never heard the word. You who write such eloquent plays about oppression are strangely silent in the midst of the outrages you describe so well.

You, ———. You have not changed since you stayed in N.O.W. and heaped insults and lies on me, because I was the cheapest target. I was told you spoke up for J.D.L.[20] But not the League? You who asked me about the Italian-American League doing your dirty work for you? You who still have not learned that people who lie down with dogs get up with fleas? You, my closest friend in N.O.W.? You were as silent Wednesday night as you were at Gloria Steinem's, when the welfare families in the hotels were being sold out.

And you, ———. You who called a psychologist to find out the proper position on lesbianism. You who love Grape Pickers, Blacks, and *now* Women. You over whom I struggled with my conscience. You who pulled every emotional string in the book to keep me from exposing the Mayor's despicable plan for the welfare families, most of whom were your beloved Blacks. You who wanted me to put blood on the hands of the Women's Movement to keep Pretty Boy Pig clean. You were silent Wednesday night.

And you, ———. You who betrayed Linda LeClair, Valerie Solanas, and me. You who spoke for nonviolence Wednesday night. Where was your voice for the corpse in the photograph? You who use the work-

[20] [Jewish Defense League.]

ing class, the Irish, as part of your credentials. You were silent in the face of the audience—*their* violence. But when I left you tried to detain me, asking solicitously: "Do you think your life is in danger? I have the feeling what you're *really* trying to say is that you're afraid *you're* going to be killed." That sounded like Freudian violence to me.

And ———. You of the poetry. You who wrote "Good-bye to All That" and read on Wednesday "One Last Word." You who were nonviolent when faced with the pigs. You who joined the pigs in pressuring me to betray women. You who urged me to come Wednesday as your lone ally on violence. You of the Proud Monsters. I congratulate you. *You* were the spokeswoman of Wednesday. And you were *all* successful. You are all monsters on such a scale that I could not have imagined it. Or believed, if I hadn't been a witness to it. No,

———, we are not allies. You were loved Wednesday night. The women *there* are your allies. I was not permitted to speak. I was driven away, and I saw hate and violence toward me from the women there.

You all wanted me to stay, but your price was too high—to collaborate in your unspeakable crime. No man has been able to buy me for a long time. Wednesday night marked the end of the sale of myself to women.

The irony of it! I, Ti-Grace Atkinson, who has refused to appear with men who were not Revolutionaries, divorced herself Wednesday night from Revolutionary Women who collaborate with men *in spite of* their being Counter-Revolutionaries. I left alone except for two friends, Ruth Simpson and Ellen Povill, and Flo Kennedy who left before. And I, the Super-Feminist, Extremist, Man-Hater, divorced you over the picture of a working-class, uneducated, criminal, second-generation immigrant, male corpse. I stood by the irrefutable evidence of his Revolutionary spirit, *in spite of* his maleness. And I shall stand by that spirit from now on wherever I find it. If necessary, I shall stand alone. Yes, my "sisters," if necessary, I shall stand even against you.

I was mistaken about the appropriateness of value judgments concerning Wednesday night's topic.

NOW, my "sisters," you shall have my value judgment on Violence and on the Women's Movement. To do violence to the face of violence already done, and in the name of "justice," is shameful and disgusting. Yes, my fine "revolutionary sisters," you are something far worse than "criminals." You are human imposters!

In the Spirit of Equality,

221

THE OLDER WOMAN

A STOCKPILE OF LOSSES[1]

It is appropriate that I make my first major statement in nearly a year at a conference for the liberation of older women. I have not spoken for a long time. About a year ago, I made a serious political mistake. I did not fight hard enough for what Joseph Colombo was about to prevent his near-fatal shooting.

I have had to rethink myself, to find out and correct in myself whatever made such a mistake possible. This conference will be the first group to enjoy the fruits of the new me, although some of you may see the "fruits" as more accurately described as "fallout."

I

OW (Older Women) as the BÊTE NOIRE of WM (the Women's Movement)

I learned a year ago that there is at least one thing more brutal than the truth, and that is the consequence of saying less than the truth. One becomes an accessory to any facts one attempts—however much —to conceal.

The issue of the older woman is the strategic Achilles' heel of Women's Liberation. The definition of her problem was evaded from the beginning, its existence even denied at first. The definition of the "older woman" *is* "woman." This definition exposes the softness of the feminist analysis.

"Woman," bluntly put, means "garbage," waste. Woman is "potential." The older woman is "past potential." A contradiction in terms? Not if you understand the meaning of "potential."

"Potential" means "not actualized," "nonexistent." The non-older woman has "hope." She may still be used. The older woman is use-less, past the possibility of use. She is no longer in danger of, has lost the "opportunity" of, being politically raped by one man. The older woman is *guaranteed* ravagement by the whole fucking system.

The older woman no longer has potential. She's *had* it. Or rather she can no longer *have* it. The older woman has had it. She's been ejected from the system. She is a stockpile of losses, a walking history of lost potentials. She should, of course, have

223

[1] [June 2, 1972; presented an *ad lib* version of this speech, June 3, 1972; Older Women's Liberation Conference, New York City.]

the good taste to lie down and die, like a lady. Be that as it may, for better or for worse, the "older woman" hangs in. And I say, "As long as we're gonna hang in, we might as well hang *out,* too."

II

History of OW in WM

In 1966, OW *was* WM, only OW wasn't *in* WM. I was *one* of the, if not *the,* youngest active members in N.O.W. (the OW of "Never"). But most of the women prefaced nearly all their major statements with: "It's too late for me. I'm fighting for my daughters." Charitable kamikazes have always seemed a dubious lot to me. These proved no exception.

The OW in WM didn't "care" enough for the future of their daughters to fight for it in the only way the future can ever be fought for—on the battleground of your own present. If OW isn't worth the fight, then neither are women as a class worth the fight. My thesis here is that the older woman is the conceptual nub of the class of women.

The conveners of the present two days have had the tenacity and, yes, the courage to hack out the area of "older women" as a special section within the Women's Movement. My question is: "Do you have the guts to take it over?" It is only when the OW becomes WM that we will have a Movement. It's only when you're all the way in the shit, that the shoveling is worth it in the long run.

Do older women care enough about all women to hammer home within the Movement that the truth about the older woman is the truth about *all* women?

I have heard for many years now, particularly from so-called "leaders" within the Women's Movement, that Simone de Beauvoir's work on old age gives the lie to her feminism. No feminist, the line goes, could be concerned with old age.

I am one of the few feminists I ever met who did not become aware of her feminism before the age of five years. I did not become a feminist until I was old enough (about 18) to fix my beady little eye on my prospects at age 70!

III

Significance of OW to WM

I have already suggested the ideological significance of the "older woman" to Women's Liberation. Her *tactical* significance is no less important.

I used to say that, "Come the Revolution, I want one housewife for every ten Revolutionaries on *my* barricade, [since] the middle-aged housewife has no place to go but revenge." The OW of WM is liberated from any false hopes. And hope is always a political extravagance.

One can see the older woman as a reject. Or, one can see her as a true leader of women's liberation, because she is free of her womanhood.

I am aware that few older women, even women here, take that position of "liberation." Most, still, see their age as politically negative. *Outside* the Movement this negative view, as it affects their lives, may be valid. But *within* the Movement, this outside condition places the older woman in a natural position of leadership. *If,* that is, the Women's Movement wants radical, that is, sufficient, changes in society for *all* women.

The OW in WM has always interested me. I had thought my final realization of this issue had arrived last May. I was the keynote speaker at the New School's graduating exercises of their Continuing Education program. Elinor Guggenheimer opened with some bright and cheery remarks about the burgeoning possibilities of the After-Life.

My speech was entitled "Where Can You Go When You've Been There?" I had studied the New School's Continuing Education program, the oldest in the country, with considerable care. I attempted to raise certain questions.

(1) Why spend time and money on "diplomas" without academic value?
(2) What kind of "education" prepares you to "assist" in a job you required *no* education to "boss" in? for example, that occupation of glorified mother's helper.
(3) What kind of "education" led to, almost without exception, "volunteerism"? Jobs, with no loot.

All these seemed like sound questions, before I arrived at the auditorium. But it was immediately clear upon my arrival that the two years of "continuing education" had been spent on preparing physically for this event of presentation. Ladies in blue hair arose amidst much applause to accept diplomas in lavish leather folders, each of which had the name of the recipient embossed outside in gold. Several of the diplomas, as it happened, had their contents misplaced in the wrong folders. These "errors" were greeted with much high-pitched giggling.

Prior to my arrival, I had been looking forward to the presentation of my speech, as a kind of shared enlightenment. I began, instead, to cringe at giving the death blow to cripples. To make matters worse, I tried in the end to soften the blows. This resulted, of course, in an agonizingly slow and painful death for all.

My speech was received first with shock, then stolid resentment. Needless to say, there was little applause.

Only months later did I get any feedback. The consensus appeared to be that I was not at all well, and obviously addicted to a mixture of speed and heroin. This puzzled me, at first, until I translated this ladylike curse properly. "Drop dead as fast as possible!"

I hope, today, that my remarks are received more happily. But I think it's appropriate here to repeat what I said earlier.

I have spent the past year learning a bitter lesson. The consequences of the truth left unsaid are far more brutal than any facts stated, however raw. I fear such a year, as this past one, far more than the most negative temporary response of the combined energies of all those present here today.

I leave you on a note of optimism. You may or may not be familiar with the cliché of Women's Liberation that "all women are treated like a joke." I say, "If women are to be a joke, let's make older women into a bloody riot!"

Acknowledgments

•

Afterword

ACKNOWLEDGMENTS

Part of the feminist theory that I projected very early (and that was rejected as blasphemous for so long) was that "women" were the beginning of the political notion of class, and, as such, were the foundation and contained the conceptual essence of oppression as a phenomenon in its totality. If feminists had taken oppression apart *as a phenomenon* (as I have been doing in *Women and Oppression*), perhaps we would enjoy insights into many more of its manifestations than is now the case. But feminists have so far chosen the limited route. And it is *we* who shall pay the most for this error.

For example, the publishing industry. As early as the spring of 1968, I was receiving offers from publishers. Feminism had surfaced, and they wanted a piece of the action. But it was also immediately apparent that publishers wanted to determine the *character* of that action as well. From the outset, I offered *Women and Oppression,* but the publishers wanted *Rapists I Have Known,* or *How I Became a Freak.* And so I held out. Writing feverishly and "publishing" odds and ends by mimeograph.

Publishers like to project the image of disinterested intellectuals. When pushed to the wall, they anoint some editor their House "radical." They even promote women prominently, to prove they are "with it." But the women are *with* the House first. I must have tried just about every woman editor in New York.

Publishers have their own cabal. They suppress the guts of Movements, thereby contributing heavily to their cooptation. By 1973, I admitted discouragement. Here I had written as much as any feminist in the country (without financial support), and I couldn't get it out. Not on my terms. And as I told one publisher, I can't *afford* to publish *your* book. I tried to be content with the influence of my work within the Movement itself. My ideas were published by others, but always with the punches pulled.

Jill Johnston, an old friend of mine, kept urging me to see a new publisher, Links Books. She kept saying it was *made* for me. But the head of it, Danny Moses, was a man, and I had to try every woman first. In the end, Jill was right. And my first thanks must go to her.

It seems there has been dissatisfaction *within* the big publishing houses for some time. At least some editors have felt the hypocrisy and Establishment base of these Houses are ultimately insuperable obstacles to publishing as it should be, and now there is an organization, Bookworkers, made up of people searching for a new way.

I can only speak about Links Books, which *is* new, and radically different from the other publishers I've seen. One aim of Links is to be the "connection" between an "idea" and an audience. The author's politics are not even *breathed* on. At no time were my ideas or writing interfered with. I received support and information and considerable forbearance at all times. (The publication date was originally September 1973 and was delayed due to my explorations, to be explained in the Afterword.) There have been no "games." Wow! what a change and what a shock.

These acknowledgments are in the back because, above all, they belong to Danny Moses. And because he's a man, he has to still ride in the "back of the bus." Danny, you have my admiration and respect as a political comrade. And my personal appreciation, which is secondary.

Carol Fein works with Danny Moses. I have not mentioned her as prominently since the impetus was Danny's. Together they have created Links Books, and Carol has been a special support and feminist eye for me and for this book. Carol and I have practically lived together through the production process. I know it's been difficult, especially in the last months, as the *physical* properties of the book required interminable changes. But the book is what it *is* now, what it *should* be, *because* of these changes.

The Afterword is about the last of those to whom I'm indebted—Barbara Nessim. Together we transformed a "collection" into a book, and my work with her gave me great joy. Oppression, as a subject, *is* a downer—as Jill once wrote. But I hope the Afterword will convey the excitement and pleasure of constructing the proper environment in which these pieces could live.

This book requires an Index. But there isn't time for me to complete one for the first printing.

I have been surprised at the enthusiasm expressed by women over this publication. If this enthusiasm holds up through a second printing, the Index will appear there. This information is of especial importance for those women in academia. Hopefully, the second printing will be available for fall 1974 classes.

February 25, 1974

AFTERWORD

"This is a book. . . . A 'book'. . . .

"A book is like someone's 'home'. . . . 'Someone' *lives* inside here. . . . The 'idea' of someone.

"A book is the home of an idea."

I heard these words over thirty years ago. From my maternal grandfather. He was very old then. Retired from the railroad.

He was what people nowadays call "weak," because he was gentle. Part of the heritage of a certain class of Southern gentlemen. A gentle man.

We were all living in Baton Rouge at the time. He and my grandmother, whom I was named after (and *took* after in her "wild" spirit), lived across the street from us. And I used to go over and hang out there whenever I could.

John Cook Broadus. Every day I'd find him sitting in his rocking chair, by the front windows of his bedroom, rocking gently. Always there was a "book" in his hands, often just resting on his lap. Sometimes he'd be "reading" it; sometimes he'd be staring off into a place I couldn't see.

One day, when I was about five years old, he saw me hanging about near him, watching him, staring with curiosity at this funny, boxlike object he never seemed to be without. It seemed so "flat," so closed, so impenetrable, so empty—so *meaningless*. Why did he always have it with him? And how could it be so much a part of his existence.

He saw the questioning in my eyes—"what is that object you treasure each day, the fragments of which you touch and turn over so carefully? It must be about *some*thing. But why can't you 'see' it all at once? Why does it take up so much time? What are you *doing* with it? What is it doing *to you?*"

And so, in his Southern way, John Broadus tried to explain to me what a book was. That it wasn't what it *appeared* to be at all. That it was very real. The pages might *look* small or flat, but that was an illusion.

He made the idea of a book more real than reality. A book contained many realities. And each one was as intimate and warm and revealing as someone's home—the Southern sense of "home."

And a book wasn't empty or flat. That was an illusion too. It was alive with "people"—people moving about—like they do at home—busy and natural.

Every book was, of course, unique. Just like the spirit of every individual is unique. And like the environment each individual builds about itself, to reflect its especial spirit, is unique. He made books seem thrilling and delicious.

I had forgotten this incident until recently. It was, after all, just a moment out of a day—so very long ago. But, among other things, it gave me a very definite conception of what a book "is." When I made my first one, I stumbled over this memory and couldn't fall short of it.

A BOOK IS THE HOME OF AN IDEA.

"Picturing" Ideas

But what is an idea? And since we're speaking in terms of books, and books are "read," what would an idea look like?

(I always *did* have an eye for the "easy" questions! What is an idea!! The entire discipline of philosophy is basically a haggling over the answer to that question!)

An "idea" is an object of knowledge or thought; it's an "object" of the mind. The problem is that this object is *unique* to each mind; it is subjective. A difficulty arises in comparing any two such objects as the same, or at least as similar enough to be common objects of discussion or communication. Ideas, in short, are intangibles. They must be *objectified* to have any place in the "real" world.

Words are the obvious attempt to the resolution of the objectification of ideas. But words themselves are imitations of intangibles, and thereby become circular definitions of ideas. "Words" are a code that must itself be translated into either tangible forms or imitations of such forms. By tangible forms, or imitations thereof, I'm referring to those forms accessible to at least one of the five senses: sight, touch, taste, smell, or hearing.

Ancient Greece was not only the source of what we know as Western philosophy; it was also the cultural crossroads of East and West. It neither saw man and nature as totally separate entities, nor did it separate the "arts" into our present compartmentalized forms. Man and nature were the "world." And the "arts" (drama, music, painting, poetry, etc.) constituted the culture of some particular civilization.

Our word "idea" derives from the Greek word *"idea"* (df. of *"idea"* = "a form, look, or appearance of a thing as opposed to its reality"). Our word "idea" is also reflected in the Greek verb *"idein"* (df. of *"idein"* = "to see").

"Seeing" and "knowing" are often used interchangeably in everyday usage. But these terms are also often used together in a more stringent philosophical sense as "perception" and "understanding." What you cannot perceive, you cannot understand. And without *common* perception and understanding, *meaningful* communication or dialogue is impossible.

The origins of the word "idea" clearly concern the sense of sight. Ideas must be communicated visually. Words—because they are symbols for ideas (themselves nebulous)—are necessarily ambiguous. No *quantity* of words can ever entirely resolve that paradox.

But because ideas are *images* of the mind, in the subjective, they are obviously best translated into the *objective* via images of the world. Art, in the sense of visual art, is as much an imitation of reality as are words imitations of ideas. But the language of art—color, form, line, shape, texture—opens up a repertoire of nuances, and thus precision, designed to communicate *meaning* accessible to the organ of reception—the eye. Words, without art as their conscious and meaningful extension, must pass through an organ, the eye again, which is relatively insensate to their form. Words have little visual "form."[1] The ultimate target of apprehension for any idea is the mind, but the object of knowledge must *reach* the "other mind" in its intact form (with some precision), and this is simply not possible via words alone.

Words are, of course, never "alone." They always appear in context, or as my grandfather used to say, "in their homes." But most writers seem to view the visual, in terms of their books, as the enemy—and, naturally enough, prefer as little as possible. Books are presented "pure" or as visually "blank." But books are not read with one's toes, usually, and John Cage is only one of the more recent musicians to observe that a silence can be the loudest sound of all.

I've come to the conclusion in doing this book that most writers suffer under the delusion that words *mean* something. That ideas can be communicated through these symbols. This delusion may help account for the appalling lack of communication within political Movements. Misunderstandings abound, at least in part, because one party's idea was never clearly presented in any understandable form, in the first place, to the second party trying to perceive, that is, understand it.

Art as Symbolism

Consider, for example, *Strategy and Tactics: A Presentation of Political Lesbianism* (pp. 135–189). Imagine that piece without those 35 charts. How in the hell could anybody understand that piece, in terms even close to what I was trying to get at, without them?

(1) The charts make it clear that I'm talking about units of political commitment in relationship to and in interaction with each other;

(2) the linear symbol for each political unit characterizes precisely my vision of their separate natures.

To be even more specific, take Strategy Chart #3 (A). The "theme" of this Chart is the "Oppressor" reaction (His "offensive") to the theme of Strategy Chart #2 (the appearance of a rebellious faction within the Oppressed). The class character of the Oppressor in action is symbolized by short staccato lines, each culminating in a ball (or fist) of force. The Oppressor is not simply an indistinguishable mass of pressure, but, instead, is made up of individuals, each of whom can be held responsible for His part in any action His "class" undertakes. The "Oppressor," in Strategy Chart #3 (A), most resembles a rain of blows directed downward.

CCXXXV

The "Buffer," in Strategy Chart #3 (A), shows line developed into texture. While mono-directional and also pointed downward, thus to that degree supportive to the Oppressor as a pressure on the Rebels, the elliptical character of these lines suggests shape— albeit abbreviated. The pattern chosen also suggests an attempt at individualism. The density of the pattern clarifies the class nature of the Buffer, as well as giving the effect of a cushion. One can almost feel the elasticity margin within this crucial band.

(A)

---

[1] Words lack "plasticity": they have neither the *appearance* of reality nor any *imitation* of such an appearance.

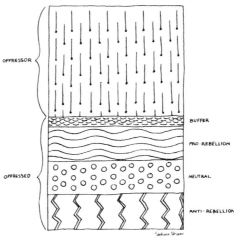

OPPRESSOR

BUFFER

PRO-REBELLION

OPPRESSED

NEUTRAL

ANTI-REBELLION

(A)

"Pro-Rebellion" is represented by horizontal and continuous wavy lines. When analyzed as an aesthetic form, in its symbolic aspect, this is perhaps the most distinctive pattern within this chart. Each line indicates unity, albeit a wavering unity. But the lines are also *demarcations* of *degrees* of political radicalness. The closer to the Buffer, the more front line. The closer to the Neutral zone, the easier to fade into non-commitment and irresponsibility.

(A)

The "Neutral" symbol I saw as an "egg" pattern. Flo Kennedy loved it, because, as she said, "that's just what they're like—*ZEROS!*" As part of the plastic[2] language within this one statement, however, the circles represent closed, free-floating forms, within an apparently inner, non-defined space. Those units closest to borders have different views of the reality of the situation, but can still *imagine*

themselves as uninvolved. As discussed in the main body of *Strategy and Tactics,* it is just that undefined character of the space *surrounding* the "private" figures that renders this zone so potentially dangerous.

The "Anti-Rebellion" zone uses line and shape. The zigzag suggests the strange bedfellows a common enemy often throws together. The units created by these jagged lines are distinctly separate. They are united only by their common *function* of shoring up the Rebellion from behind, and even this function is suggested only by their initial pressure up against the "Neutral" zone.

Much more could be said in the translation of this Chart, but the few remarks made already should suggest the potency, immediacy and brevity possible within the visual language—especially within its "symbolic" aspect.

---

[2] In aesthetics, "plasticity" refers to the *use* of some *means* peculiar to the visual arts, such as color, form, line, shape, texture, etc., to *objectify* (or reify) some *essence* observable in the external world.

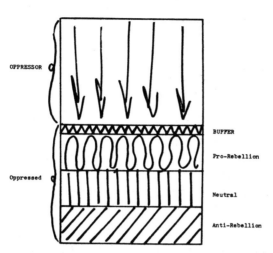

OPPRESSOR

BUFFER

Pro-Rebellion

Oppressed

Neutral

Anti-Rebellion

Form, shape and texture were all created with the use of line. And "color" must also be included here in terms of the revelation of emotional character.

Each of the 35 charts saved me pages of explanation. But, more important, each one brought pages of text together into one unit of explication. Relationships can be taken in at a glance that simply could not be explained adequately in any other way. Proportions and character must be *seen*. Especially when juxtaposition, as in tactics and strategy, means everything. In short, life or death.

Strategy Chart #3 (B) is the original Chart drawn by me. Strategy Chart #3 (A) —composed by the artist of this book, Barbara Nessim—is a *translation* of that same Chart. (Chart (A) can be found in the first of the three series of charts in *Strategy and Tactics,* pp. 135–189.)

I was trained for years as a professional painter, but I have not painted for over ten years. It shows. My hand is no longer an extension of my mind.

A comparison between these two charts will serve several purposes. It will demonstrate the potential importance of symbolism within art—especially when that art is essentially "abstract" in character ("abstract" art simply attempts to capture the *essence* of an idea, whereas "representational" art tends more to delineate a specific *instance* within the scope of a particular idea). In addition, it should be noted that Nessim quite often evolves the "abstract" *into* a representation of an object that does not in *fact* exist in the "real" world. This "object" is conjured up from the imagination *into* reality. (See especially the "landscape" on the cover, supposedly representing the "form" left by the tracks of an Amazon's odyssey. Often, this image resembles, to me, a hulking catlike animal—scarred from many wars, resting its chin on a bloody paw with claws still extended (!), its guts hanging out and weighted down with bloodsuckers, maggots on its back—but all in all, STILL ALIVE. Just resting and thinking things over before the next bout.)

But back to *my* failure. In fairness to myself, I was using two colors in "my" charts. The *status quo* (defined as the conditions shown in the chart prior) was defined in red, and the new action—the theme of the chart in question—was defined in black. In the case of Strategy Chart #3 (B), the "Oppressor Offensive" was in black ink. Because of production costs, Links explained to me from the first that the two-color method of distinguishing stasis and action would have to be somehow modified. With that one excuse, I must stand by this Chart as I made it.

My translation of my own text, as seen in Strategy Chart #3 (B), into visual form is not only mind-bogglingly inadequate, but seriously misleading as well. Because of the lack of diversity of symbols used within the separate zones, the bulk of the meaning of this chart is lost. Strategy Chart #3 (B) is static. The unbroken arrows representing the *"Oppressor* Offensive" are barely distinct at all from the pattern representing the *"Oppressed*-Neutral." This weakens the idea of confrontation.

My representation of the "Oppressor Offensive" indicates a *unity,* and a similarity of degree of hostility to the Rebellion, among the factors/factions comprising the Oppressor.

(B)

(B)

Nessim's representation, from Strategy Chart #3 (A), indicates the *diffuse* and individual character of these blows and of the motivations *behind* them, in this early stage. These two statements are radically different (*and have* radically different implications). This is especially significant since the "Oppressor" is the primary zone at issue in this particular Chart—the *agent* behind *this* action.

(B)

(A)

The "Buffer" design, in Strategy Chart #3 (B), is too sharp and powerful in appearance for its textual description as cushion and/or maneuverable margin for the "Oppressor." My *chart* suggests that the "Buffer" *blocks* the "Oppressor Offensive" to some degree—or, at the very least, blunts it. But, in *fact* (that is, according to my *text*), I describe the "Buffer" as no less than a *"conductor"* into Rebel lines. In contrast, *Nessim's* chart,[3] Strategy Chart #3 (A), illustrates my idea, as it appears in my text, perfectly. My own shapes and patterns at best mislead, and, at worst, contradict my words preceding the illustration.

(B)

(A)

The "Pro-Rebellion" zone, while not the primary factor in *this* particular chart, should be compared for statement of meaning, first, as represented by me, and, then, as "translated" from the text by Nessim. *My* pattern suggests forms or units operating *parallel* to each other. This represents the statement that all the organizations within the Movement are roughly parallel, in both their revolutionary aims and in their mobilization of forces to achieve these aims. Such a "statement" is obviously insane. (The downward loops simply make no sense at all in this context. All I can offer as excuse is that I was concentrating on keeping the zones

(B)

---

[3] For an illustration of Nessim's "Neutral" zone legend, and a discussion of its political symbolism, see p. ccxxxvi.

as a whole a documentary history (or *reflection* of this history) of the Movement itself. But this chronological thread and common authorship simply were not enough, in my opinion, to comprise any kind of coherent statement. For this reason, this book I originally entitled *Bites and Pieces*. I renamed it *Amazon Odyssey*, when I considered the suggestion that my original title gave no indication about the subject matter of the contents.

At the very least, there were three strikingly sore thumbs to be dealt with—all similar in nature. Within the collection are three "mini-books." That is, three pieces have several separate parts *within them*. Obviously, this was a "design" problem that *could* not be handled verbally. I kept pinning frantic notes to my manuscript, as I handed it over—in sections—to Danny: *"Attention!* this is a design problem. Please resolve." Never having published a book before, I imagined the author contributed the idea/s in written form, and the publisher contributed (or rather designed and *built*) the proper "home for the idea." After all, I assumed everyone *knew* "a book is the home of an idea." (Df. of a "publishing House" = "a company that makes houses for ideas.") This all seemed simple, straightforward, and obvious enough.

The manuscript was in on time. I had added many footnotes (separated from the pieces, as they had originally appeared, by bracket enclosures). I hoped these additions would be of some little assistance in gluing the separate entities a little more closely into a unit. But I did not deceive myself about the *adequacy* of this—as a solution. I started get-

ting impatient for the "house" to show. So far, I'd seen no "walls," no "roof," no "furniture" —no shelter or accommodations for my ideas *what*soever.

IDEA AS "IMAGE"

The Cover

Ah! the cover. Naturally, I wanted a woman designer. Links' designer was a man, so they went outside the House for a woman who had designed a book for them in the past. (Everyone had been very happy with her work.) The woman read the entire manuscript.

The first cover Links didn't dare show me. The second cover, which I went to view with great anticipation, I didn't recognize as being for my book—until I was told. The visual statement bewildered and baffled me. It wasn't remotely connected to the *meaning* of my book. The "idea" of the second cover, represented in *absolutely* realistic form, was "a long hard climb—with a sunset at the end of the struggle." I thought maybe the lady had read the wrong book. Then I thought maybe I had been having delusions about what I had been saying—as an overall statement. *One* thing, I knew for sure. If this book, in *fact*, said "guaranteed rainbow at the end," I was long past ready for the loony bin.

I asked an artist friend to take a crack at it. She was studying textile design at the time. But, while she got the *idea* of the book's theme, she wasn't sufficiently trained to execute it.

By this time, I'm desperate. I suggest the House designer give it a try. He agrees, some-

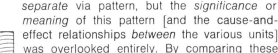

(A)

(B)

separate via pattern, but the *significance* or *meaning* of this pattern [and the cause-and-effect relationships *between* the various units] was overlooked entirely. By comparing these two separate illustrations of Strategy Chart #3, it's possible to see that this "oversight" on my part wiped out any point or effectiveness this visual representation might have had.) *Nessim's* abstract representation of the Movement as *"spectrum"* is accurate. Individuals, in *actuality,* link up to form lines or positions, whether or not these individuals fall within the same formal organizations.

The pattern for the "Anti-Rebellion" zone, while not as ambiguous as that of the "Neutral" *linear* representation, lacks any direction relevant to the action supposedly in process. The lines run diagonally off to the side, instead of aggressively buttressing the "Neutral" zone. Without "function," the "Anti-Rebellion" zone has no character, and, in effect, ceases to exist.

I have but scarcely touched on a few points that could be made concerning these charts. But I hope I've said enough to demonstrate one rather shocking fact. Art is as special a language, and as distinct, as Chinese is from English. That only I could have written the words in this book has no bearing on my ability to translate this same book into Chinese. Barbara Nessim, approaching my ideas from the vantage point of her *primary* language, could translate a hundred times more accurately and effectively what I had just explained.

A book is in two languages, the visual and the verbal. All books are "duets." But nearly all the ones I have seen so far are simply *un-*successful duets. Either because one voice—the extension of meaning, or the visual—was "absent." Or because the writer made the fatal error of imagining its visual partner as an accompanist instead of co-producer.

. "ORCHESTRATING" A COLLECTION[4]

I am not suggesting that finding the right partner for such an enterprise is easy. On the contrary. After three individuals and four covers, I consider myself miraculously lucky to have found Barbara Nessim. She not only understands what I'm trying to say, but usually turns around, and in her "translation," says it better. We have made this book together. The work on *each* of its parts was a unique experience, and each experience added to and evolved the variety of statements (or "duets") we've managed to produce. Each time my heart was in my mouth. Each problem seemed nearly insurmountable.

The Problem

From the beginning of this book, I knew I had a problem: it wasn't a book. It was a "collection." This collection had only one common thread: all the pieces were written by me. But the *purposes* of these pieces, thus their styles, were wildly disparate. There were formal philosophical presentations, harangues, press releases, pieces written for large-circulation magazines, college speeches, intra-Movement essays, "think" pieces, and, finally, an "open" letter. The collection had a chronological structure, 1967 through 1972, which gives the pieces

---

4 I am indebted to Lila Karp's article, "The Sociology of Women's Literature." (Unpublished, September 1972. Pp. 18.) Her work with literature convinced me that art and politics can be legitimately unified. This *Afterword,* however, takes a somewhat different tack: that art and politics are a "unit" of *necessity.* It questions both when separated.

what reluctantly. But he has a condition: whatever "art" is used must be by a fantastic woman artist he knows—Barbara Nessim. He says she's always painted women and does excellent "commercial" work as well. (Rubens and a lot of other artists always painted women, too, so I wasn't overwhelmed by this recommendation. But this cover obstacle had already thrown our production schedule way off, so I wasn't going to argue. And, besides, this book was supposed to have been a *means* to an end, namely, *Women and Oppression. Amazon Odyssey* was turning into a major project.)

Round four. I arrive, with some anxiety, to view the fourth try. Everyone is getting a little nervous now, and eyeing everybody else. I go into Danny's office. The designer shows me his solution. The lettering is nice. The size and shape of the cover are nice. The white space is nice. The cover texture is nice.

The figure. I squint my eyes. It looks like a Balinese dancing girl, bare-breasted, swinging into the bottom grind of a hootchy-kootch. And what is that above? on her *shoulders?* It looks like some kind of milkmaid's yoke!

I look at the designer. I stare at Danny. What is *this?* Links promised me political freedom. Didn't they *know* books are in two languages? Why are they *doing* this to me?

The designer starts talking fast. A *beautiful* cover! Just *look* at that figure—a *liberated* woman! *Bare*-breasted! And such a nice *Oriental* quality. Get it? *"Amazon"*—the figure looks "foreign." (I planned to *keep* it that way—*all* the way.) And she's *dancing! Move*ment! An *"Odyssey"*!

I said—the Amazons *fought,* not danced.

Well, says he, there's all kinds of ways of fighting.

I can't figure it. Only one conclusion makes sense. The designer's doctor just told him he has incurable cancer, and he's looking for a one-way trip out the window (we're six floors up).

I mutter to Danny: "just give me some lettering. Forget it." Danny says the artist, Barbara Nessim, wants me to call her—if I don't like the image. She wants to try to make something special. I look at the hootchy-kootch, in "chains," and think it's hopeless.

The designer gets Barbara on the phone anyway. I say, "no way" on the dancer. She asks me to her studio, to see if I like something else. If I don't see anything that's "right," she'll try something—special—for *this.* I don't believe for a second it will work. But I like her voice. I just liked her voice—and couldn't refuse to give it a try.

I go down several days later. I look at her work—for several hours. She has a lot. She paints women, alright, but as *individuals,* not as a class or "oppressed." I go through everything she has, explaining why this and/or that wouldn't be "right" for the "idea" of *Amazon Odyssey.* Three or four hours go by—looking, looking, looking. Nothing.

The "Translation" Process

Barbara Nessim refuses to get discouraged. She says, "come on over and sit by me while I work. Let me give it a try." I'm frantic. How *can* she do it? I've seen nothing that would indicate she'd understand. She doesn't know *my* work. I ask her to give me a few minutes, to let me try to explain to her what the "idea" of *Amazon Odyssey* means to me.

I tried to explain about the Movement. That it wasn't like the media said it was at all. That, to me, it wasn't even what most Movement women said it was about either. *Amazon Odyssey* was the story of *one* woman's journey through this Movement. This particular woman's evolution was relevant, first, because she'd been in the Movement from the beginning, and second, because she'd trail-blazed so much of it. *Amazon Odyssey* was a "collection" of the tracks, or "traces," left by this woman. These "tracks" had left a residue, which in itself formed a *reality,* a "story," of its own. This collection was a documentary of the Movement, as well, because this particular individual had been so much involved in the midsts of its evolution.

The "picture" of *Amazon Odyssey,* therefore, must be a kind of landscape. But a "landscape"—only in a metaphorical sense. It *had* a reality, a solidity; this odyssey had occurred. But it was not like any landscape ever seen before. It was a landscape of *events*—of the residue *left* by these events. This THING, this Movement, was not pretty. It was a scene of struggle—struggle within itself. It had a beginning, and it must "end" (in any "representation" of it) with the time the "art" of it was finished.[5]

The word "Amazon" represented darkness and struggle to me. The Amazons were probably only a legend, and, in any case, from the far distant past. Even those once said to exist, either lost their own wars, or picked "losers" with whom to side. If any got away or survived, their fate was like Odysseus'—but their journey covered centuries, not ten years.

The word "Odyssey" was used here metaphorically, too. It was a voyage begun in high hopes, after the victory of the Greeks over the Trojans (the Amazons are said to have fought beside the Trojans). Odysseus was going home, but his ship was thrown off course, and he stumbled from one "adventure" (or nightmare) to another. His ship lost direction. Homer's *Odyssey* is a saga of struggle over time and space. The adventures vary in quality; the journey is uneven—in every sense.

Amazon Odyssey must "picture" the impossible—a lie. That it was an Amazon who escaped (note my first dedication page) and sailed the voyage of the Victor. The image must be, thus, of *both* the Victor *and* the Vanquished. It must be the truth about reality, not as it has ever actually happened—all together, in any one time or place—but the idea of many events compressed together, *some*how, *some*way, into one image. The cover "statement"—the visual image that represents the words of my title, that gives this title its *meaning*—must be more than truth. It must be art.

A small request! Barbara sat down on her high stool, before her work table—a bright light beaming down on the large white board. Oh my God! Watercolor paper? I nearly fainted. You can't make mistakes in watercolor. The worst medium, for the most difficult of projects! Barbara said, "I see this in Payne's Gray; I've always loved Payne's Gray." (I've always *hated* Payne's Gray; it always seemed like *no* color at all!)

---

[5] In this case, June of 1973.

Not a promising beginning! I sat down beside her. Dejected—but, then, it could only be for a few minutes anyway. She picked up her pen. (My God! she wasn't even going to sketch it in pencil first?) And then Barbara Nessim started to draw—the pen scratching its way, from left to right—over the heavy textured paper. After the first few lines, I knew we were "home." I couldn't believe it. I watched the "idea," that idea I had come to despair of anyone else *ever* "seeing," emerge with apparent effortlessness. I'll never forget the experience of seeing the thought of my mind's eye, made *real, palpable,* on that paper. It seemed miraculous. But, then, I started worrying: she'd spoil it! In that damned medium, one false move and it's all over.

I'll never really understand how Barbara "knew" all she said in that cover image. She painted events she never knew about, and in their proper order. She wasn't there, and yet she was telling it better than I could. The red claw was abortion. The purple peaks—lesbianism. The dark shadows (within that Payne's Gray!!) were the periods of loneliness, doubts, despair, wrong turns—the shipwrecks over the years. The figures around the cauldron—peering into the darkness, *down*—was consciousness raising, organizing, many possibilities. And the threads running up from the outside were all the influences, mostly political, that had fed into this Movement of ours. The Student, the Black, the Antiwar, the various political philosophies within each. The black *circles* are *sources* of influences—or, as we have come to call them, now, at Links—the "bombs."

The right side shows pointers of hope—

jets springing off yet again into space.

I kept saying, "yes, yes, *that's* it, *that's* what it looks like. That's *it!* Oh my God, you're getting it. How did you know about *that?*" Barbara didn't know "how," or even *what* it was, that she knew. She just "knew" and "heard" what I was saying, and answered me in *her* language, "speaking" *her* thoughts, about what I was saying. We *sang* together that night. Jesus! did we sing. I was so happy! I kept hugging her. I *hadn't* been crazy! There *were* such things as "pictures" of "ideas." There were "pictures" of images and of "concepts," too. Maybe even of "theories."[6]

Responses and Re-Actions

Links' response, to what I refer to now fondly as "the animal," surprised me. Carol Fein loved it. Immediately. *"Now* I understand why you were so dissatisfied before. You were right. *This* is beautiful." She meant it was hideous and magnificent. The truth. About the Movement, about the messages within this collection—when seen as a whole.

The men were put off. The designer thought it repulsive. Now I *knew* we were home free. The response to this cover really broke down along class lines: the women loved it; the men were horrified.

But the end was not in sight yet. I had underrated the power of both the visual and of the subconscious. First, the designer turned the figure on its back. More elegant, he thought. I was so happy I was prepared to be broadminded, and agreed to come look at it. But Barbara Nessim knew, without seeing it, that this reversal would "gut" the message.

[6] Essays on theory construction usually include drawings of theory structure. All my statements in this collection were drawn in visual form first—to check the accuracy of the general idea, the *theory,* itself.

AMAZON ODYSSEY

THE FIRST COLLECTION OF WRITINGS BY THE

POLITICAL PIONEER OF THE WOMEN'S MOVEMENT

TI-GRACE ATKINSON

(A)

AMAZON ODYSSEY

THE FIRST COLLECTION OF
WRITINGS BY THE

POLITICAL PIONEER
OF THE WOMEN'S
MOVEMENT

TI-GRACE ATKINSON

(B)

She was right. The "animal" is taken off its back.

The visual representation—interpretation, "translation"—of *Amazon Odyssey* depends largely on the use of *form* for the *power* of its message. (The use of color is the most powerful instrument within the two-dimensional medium to express mass.) But the *scale* of that mass, or color form, can determine the *nature* of the "statement" itself. By "scale," I refer to the *size* of an *image, in proportion to* the rest of the *space,* within that *image's* respective *"frame."*

"Cover (A)" is a "true" statement, while "Cover (B)" makes a "false" statement. All on the basis of *scale.* In "Cover (A)," the image is powerful and massive. It indicates the impor-

tance I give to the Movement. It "says" that this Movement, or Odyssey, is the dominant feature of my life and of this book. It indicates weight, importance, staticity—but, above all, *actuality.*

A "cover" is a *spatial* problem. It depends for its impact on painterly plastic methods. The "type" is secondary, because it is not in the "language" required by the *mode* of the problem, and *its* demands. A cover has no temporal aspect—as do chapters, made up of pages. A cover is a one-shot chance for communication. The "idea" must be in "image" form, and "say" *exactly* what you mean. The words are "seen," necessarily, second.

Some 7,500 copies of "Cover (B)" were printed by "mistake." *On the basis of scale alone,* "Cover (B)" makes an entirely different statement about the message of this book than does "Cover (A)." The image "floats" in far too large a space. It has little "presence." This book is *not* about the *title* at the top, or about the *name* at the bottom. It's about an *idea!* A cover *image* must carry the *burden* of whatever that *idea* might be. The *image* on "Cover (B)" is "decorative," and *secondary*. It is "lightweight," and, thereby, states that *that* is the *nature* of *this* book. The character of "the animal," as described on pp. ccxxxvii – ccxxxviii, and pp. ccxlii–ccxliii, is wiped out by at least half.

The *second* 7,500 softcover copies, and the hardcover edition, correct this error. I include this comparison, because I have come to understand how unaware both publishers and writers are of the significance of these "details." The ignorance I've encountered *everywhere* so far, about the *fact* that books are *read* and therefore *depend* on the *visual* for *communication,* is absolutely *staggering.*

In no part of this *Afterword* is it my intention to criticize Links. We have struggled through the evolution of this book—as an art object—together. *I* have delayed production for close to a year, for reasons the publisher has not often understood. I doubt if any other publisher would have accepted such delays.

The "art" of making books went out with Gutenberg and specialization. Mass production further alienated the human means for expression and communication into rigid compartments. I am certain "communication" has paid too high a price for whatever could have been gained by "distribution." At this point in history, I see no technical, or even commercial, reason why expression and *meaning*—in *all* its significance—must continue in its present crippled and adumbrated state.

IDEA AS "CONCEPT": "FLAT" FORM

The Charts

Next, Barbara Nessim and I did the Charts for *Strategy and Tactics: A Presentation of Political Lesbianism* (pp. 135–189). Three series of "maps" appear within that piece: (I) in the "Strategy" series—ten "maps"; (II) in the "Tactical" series—three "maps"; and, (III) in the "Tactical-Strategy" series — twenty-two "maps." Each "map," or Chart, is an "idea" by itself (see pp. ccxxxv - ccxxxix). But an "idea" in the sense of "image." The *temporal* aspect is minimal.

Within this *Afterword,* I discuss the visual "translation" of an "idea" in terms of three categories: idea as "image"; idea as "concept"; and, idea as "theory." Idea as "image" is the representation of *one* object of knowledge. *One* thought that can be taken in—frontally—at one "look." There is no shifting of attention from one "thought" to another. No *first* "image" must be, to any significant degree, set aside to attend to any *second* "image." Idea as "image" does *not* include the notion of *process.* Idea as "concept" *does* involve process. A "concept" includes *at least two* images, two particular thoughts. Both "strategy" and "tactics," in that paper devoted to these ideas as central to our Movement, are *each* discussed as "concepts." These "concepts" are, then, reified as *series* of "moves" (Charts, or "maps"). For example, the ten Strategy charts comprise only one *example* of the "concept" of "strategy." (Actually, here are *two* examples, if you want to count the "Strategy" outlined in Charts #6–#10—presented as an alternative "Strategy" to that outlined within Charts #1–#5—as a separate "concept.")

Within each series, each Chart depends in part for its *meaning* on the Chart, or "map," preceding it. The concepts of "strategy" and "tactics" both include the notion of *"cause and effect." This* notion obviously includes a primary *temporal* factor. And it is this *temporal* dimension that leads me to designate "concepts" as *"flat" forms,* as opposed to simple "images." While "images" constitute the *parts* of *"flat" forms,* "concepts" and/or "series" are distinguished as *forms* via their ordering.

"Concepts" are *multiple* images, *extended* images. While they are "seen" separately, these *serial images* are also always viewed *consecutively* over time. The temporal factor *unites* the parts; and, while not perhaps dominating a "flat" form over the primarily spatial factor, the temporal dimension at least holds its own as of equal importance.

Aesthetically, these Charts (or "maps") can be appreciated singly.[7] But the Charts also form distinct aesthetic units as *series.* Their characters, as *serial units,* are quite separate and distinct. (For reasons of space, I won't elaborate on that here.) But I feel I must, *at least,* point out Nessim's extraordinary use of line to express movement. As an artist, she was under extreme restrictions to express a wide range of meanings. To appreciate the richness of vocabulary Nessim managed for a problem generally viewed as insurmountable ("motion" restricted to line as medium, *and denied the use of perspective,* or "depth"), see her symbols for "Oppressor Offensive I" (p. 143), "Cooptation" (p. 156), "Oppressed Offensives I, II & III" (pp. 163 and 181), "Infiltration" (p. 163), "Boomerang" (p. 166), "Bombardment" (p. 171), "Repercussion I, and II" (pp. 177, and 185).

I should mention that *each series* of Charts obviously work together *as series*—within the *Charts* (all three series *together*) *as a whole.* This reference is to that over and above the individual charts *within each series* working together. These are the sorts of plastic problems which must be constantly juggled within any book as an art object.

IDEA AS "THEORY": "FULL" FORM

By early 1974, we had all the pieces: the writings, which are representative yet discrete; the photographs; the cover; the charts. All we lacked was a "book"!

How did these pieces fit together as a whole? The cover represented the "idea," but there was no aesthetic design, no "unity," past that. A book "speaks" visually with every inch and from every angle. It's two-dimensional *and* three-dimensional, with various "forms," (such as "flat") gradating in between.

The Problem of the Problem

How were the mini-books to be made im-

---

[7] Some of the Charts remind me of Jasper Johns' numbered lithographs, which, by the way, I'd like to see some of *these* Charts become.

mediately distinct to the eye? These were key pieces—historically, as well as within the evolution of my own thought. I had the idea that, if someone wished, such as a Women's Studies class, these three "little" books could be read as a summary of the *thought* of this Movement. But how to make these mini-books stand out? And in accurate proportion, in terms of *significance,* to the rest of the book?

I had seen this as a design problem from the first. It never occurred to me that book *designers* depended primarily on *letters* for the plastic material of the structure of a book. Every book, but above all a "collection," has to be orchestrated. Every *note,* every *pause,* counts.

The solution presented to me for the set problem was, essentially, to use larger type for each main heading. At *this* point, I freaked out. I countered with colored paper—and a different color—for each of the three sets.

(1) Each set had to be cohesive within.
(2) Each set had to be distinct from the rest of the book.
(3) Each of the three sets must be distinct from each other.
(4) All three sets must work together, somehow, to balance the *unity of the edges* of all the white (straight) pages.
(5) Each set had a two-dimensional aspect (the page) and a three-dimensional aspect (the edge, or "bleed," of the page, translating into distinctive striping on the edges of the book when closed).

The Sets

We discussed each set, and its character. *Radical Feminism* (pp. 46–63) and *Juniata II* (pp. 64–94) formed the mid-section of the book. Since one follows the other, their "colors" must be sharply distinguished to stand apart. *On "Violence in the Women's Movement"* (pp. 198–222) falls at the end of the book. It is the dénouement—in effect, of the *"Odyssey."* *"Violence,"* although standing alone and of relatively few pages, functions as a finale of sorts.

Radical Feminism was conceptualized and begun in 1968. *That* mini-book, appearing herein, was distributed in early 1969. It marked the beginning of a formulation of the *dimensions* of the problem of women. (I nicknamed it *"Genesis."*)

Juniata II was produced in 1969 and presented in early 1970. It was the first major *breakdown* of the Movement into primary foci. (I nicknamed these four subsets the *"Apostles,"* because the pieces represented initial thrusts of evangelical missions.)

On "Violence . . . ," which has two parts, was written in late 1971. It marked the disintegration of all my prior certainties, and a very painful recognition that everything must be rethought. It was a period of devastation and wrath. (I called it—*"Revelations."*)

But what "color" is the "beginning"? What "color" is "structure"? What "color" is the "end"?

Carol, Barbara and I met to discuss this quandary. No one of us could quite follow what the other was trying to get at—although I was certainly the one posing the problem.

ccxlvii

Barbara thought color unnecessary. That tones of gray would be more appropriate. I could see her point, in terms of picking up the Payne's Gray on the cover, and also in continuing the "documentary" character of the book as a whole. But the plastic restrictions worried me. (I should mention that my own work as a painter depended almost entirely on color for expression. Naturally, the elimination of this element in its most obvious form [tone can translate into color if juxtapositions are sufficiently sensitive] made me feel deprived of the use of the most important tool of visual language.)

Barbara offered to try the "art." This "book" was becoming such a problem, even Nessim was becoming intrigued. The cover had been a "job," the Charts, a "favor" to me. But now we were starting to talk "art." When the colored paper was ruled out (the paper shortage, and our time shortage, made the necessary color subtleties out of the question), Barbara and I sat down at her place for another marathon.

The "House"

This time we had to make the whole fucking house! Floor, walls, ceilings, hallways, lighting, windows, doors. Then, furnishings! crowded or airy? dark? period? contemporary? varied or consistent? And whose spirit should be captured and reflected?! those living inside? or contemplated guests?

I had thought that explaining the *cover* idea had been difficult. But *that* was general. *Now* I had to get down to specifics, and, yet, characterize "details," or moments, as meticu-

lously and thoroughly as I had a generalization. How to do this? And how to be so specific, about so much, in terms that could be grasped easily, and translated visually? How could all the necessary factors be successfully juggled, so that everything worked in the end? And with only *tone* to work with?? I was a nervous wreck before we even began. I felt like a fifth-rate juggler with fifteen balls to keep rotating in my hands. I could see them flying wildly apart, totally out of control. Already.

I went to Barbara Nessim's loaded with "mood" materials. Mainly poetry and music. What she had to do couldn't be explained by words alone. I knew I'd need all the "outside" help I could get.

I could only figure one way to do this project. I had to tell Barbara the whole story. From the first piece, *Abortion: Paper Number II* (pp. 1–4), to the end. She had to understand the *feeling*—the *rhythm* and *pattern*—established even before *Radical Feminism* was written. The pieces are quite short to begin with. They get progressively longer, as my perception of the dimensions of the issues expands. All the pieces are strong. In a sense, "black and white." I always reach for the jugular. But there is a distinct political evolution of increasing doubts—about just how well conceived this whole Movement has been. By 1968, I realize nobody has a plan, a "map," or a direction. Nobody *knows* what the fuck they're doing!

SET NUMBER I

Radical Feminism, pp. 46–63, picks out

the enemy (the outer dimensions of the problem), and begins at the beginning of a philosophical analysis. We've decided, by this time, that the "house" will be half text, half art. (Throughout the sets, each "voice" is balanced in strength. The art reinforces the text —slips under it, so to speak—thereby supporting, and adding "body," to the *meaning* of the words.)

But what is the *theme* of this set to be? What is the central "image"? The first part of *Radical Feminism* is *Declaration of War* (pp. 46–55). It marks the end of the massacre, and the beginning of "war." There must be battlefields and explosions. Signs of resistance. Signs of women *fighting back*.

Explosions

Barbara started with thumbnail sketches, fragment (A). The first idea was to open each set, and subset, with a full page of art. This "art" would appear on the left, and introduce the visual theme. At first, I didn't understand the "bands." But slowly they became recognizable as "horizons," and I began to feel the desolateness of deserted battlefields—no man's land, "mined" against all trespassers.[8] But the dark patches on top of these horizons horrified me. They looked like desert scrub brush. *This* wasn't *action!* It was too *diffuse.* But, more than that, I sensed something was seriously wrong.

Barbara and I started discussing violence. And I saw our problem right away. To Barbara, "violence" was sad, tragic, deplorable— even if necessary. Her images on the horizons were low-key, and, in the introductory section,

the "explosions" *looked* regrettable. As if she wished they'd go away!

"Hey, *Barbara,* they're on *our* side. When an oppressed people rise up and resist injustice, their blows are *beautiful!* They're *celebrations!* Like fireworks. *Especially* for women, when our humanity and dignity have been questioned for so long."

For six hours, we struggled over the *meaning,* and "character," of violence. And how that character changes—according to context, and justification. When "violence" appears *against* "oppression," it is a *negation* of *institutionalized* violence. "Violence," these opening blows, are a positive humane act—under such circumstances. Such acts are *acts of bravery,* such as those Camus describes in his essays, *Resistance, Rebellion and Death.* It is a betrayal of humanity, and of hope, to represent such acts as shameful, or regrettable.

I wasn't getting too far. I tried to get literal. I searched Barbara's art library—*frantically*— for pictures of explosions, especially of the land mine variety. Nothing. Then I remembered my art history. Such representations are always avoided, because of the impossibility of capturing the *feeling* of the physical *shock* of such events. And because, by definition, explosions are less *spatial* (they *destroy* staticity) and more *temporal.* (They are *action, faster* than the eye can follow. One follows the *result* of the action.) As I said earlier, I always could pick the *easy* problems!

Explosions are diffuse, in their rapid change of movement. But they also have *"forms,"* in the sense that they are able to cause *effects.* Fragments (B), (C), (D) and (E)

---

[8] The "horizons" as "units" repeat a motif in the Charts. *Sections* of action ("commitment") are ruled ("cordoned") off. Keep in mind that the Charts are "abstractions" of "maps." The "terrain," appearing on most such battle strategy maps, is deleted to clarify the *political* action between conflicting interests. In *Radical Feminism* and *Juniata II,* the "terrain" begins to emerge *representationally* from the "pure" abstraction of the Charts.

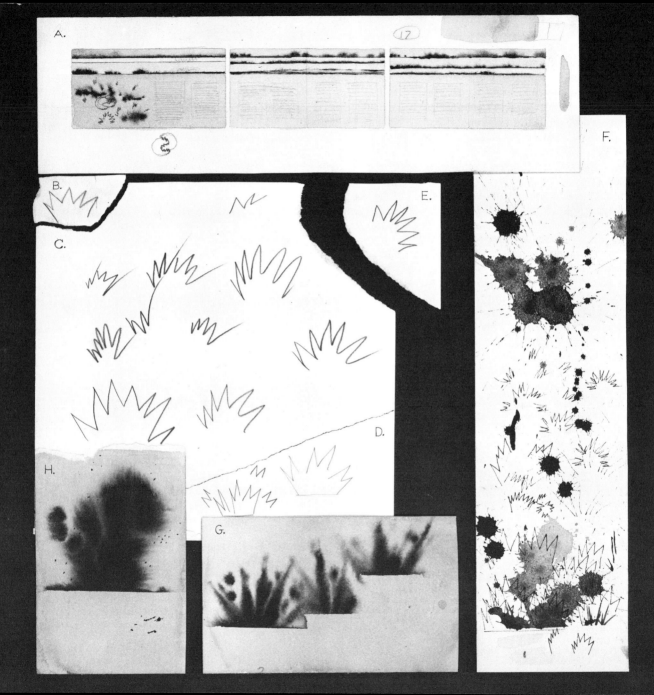

represent attempts to define the formal "character" of "explosions." But this form *disperses* —as it *causes* its *effects.* The form *"echoes."* And these echoes (in the simplest, non-successive detonating devices) decrease in potency—as they spread out from their source. These "echoes" are notoriously subject to environmental conditions: the placing of mines; the geological composition of the land strata; the cause and direction of the triggering of detonation; the weather and wind conditions. In short, the *representation* of *any* and every *explosion* must be *unique* and idiosyncratic.

Fragment (F) shows some of the technical experiments we attempted—for repercussion effects. Density of ink, height from which it was splashed onto paper, quickness with which form was superimposed over "echoes" (the *actual* temporal sequence of reality is not necessarily followed in the *re-creation* of that reality).

Fragment (G) was an attempt to re-create the accidental effects of (F) under controls— brushwork. But the results were too stagey.

Fragment (H) would have been my choice for a thematic opening. I find the form and aftereffects so beautifully integrated that, even though the spirit is still too "dark," I would have found the aesthetics hard to resist.

We worked straight through, nonstop, for four days. When wiped out, Barbara and I would collapse on couches, and sleep until able to start again. The first night ended without resolution, and I was beginning to despair of conveying the *spirit* of the joy of "resistance" to Barbara's heart. Her *heart* must reach her head. *Then,* I knew she could find the technical means to express that "form." But *how* to convince her? I knew from years of political activity, how deep such convictions went, how deeply rooted they were in the *need* for security, how much I was asking of Barbara to express herself—on the line, alongside me—in this. I knew it could bring her trouble.

The "Character" of Violence

I woke next morning to Ravel's "Le Gibet," from his suite *Gaspard de la Nuit.* I had brought it the night before—for "mood." I think the horizons of the sets,[9] and *their* mood tones, were greatly influenced by this music. It accounts, I believe, for much of the eerily personal feeling of the "forms" created by the ruled units. In "Le Gibet," death is suspended in a vast landscape. One death extends into many, as the Angelus tolls them off. The bells continue to "sound" through the hours—through and *over* time. In Nessim's "horizons," the *lines* mark off the *bands*—mark off *space.* The lines are like Ravel's bells, marking off *time,* and "life" with it. The "lines," *the demarcations,* the "beginnings" and the "ends," are erratically drawn, yet inexorable.

In *Radical Feminism,* both in *Declaration of War* (pp. 46-55) and *Metaphysical Cannibalism* (pp. 56–63), the bands *are* the forms. They vary in *width,* although never in number, *within* each double-page sheet. The gray tone, on which the text appears, is a consistent 20% throughout the first set. But the *tones,* within the *upper* forms, vary within each sheet, and are used in each *combination* only once.

ccli

[9] Especially those of *Radical Feminism,* but, also, to a degree, those in *Juniata II.*

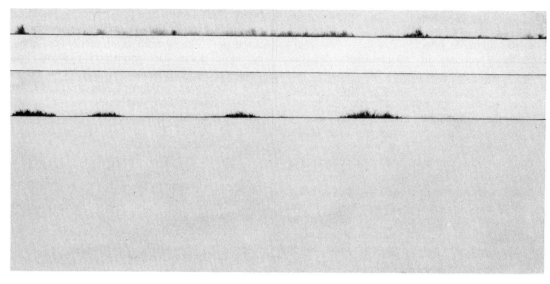

Barbara Nessim and I had become friends over the months. In November, I had learned that an old friend of mine from Philadelphia, Charlotte, had killed herself. This news hit me very hard, and started me thinking about my past, and sharing some of these thoughts with my friends. My character is such a replica of my maternal grandmother's, and she was so deeply Virginian, that certain memories—ways of thinking—flooded back over me. I rediscovered the Fugitive poets, and had taken a newly acquired volume of Donald Davidson's down to Barbara's, just for my own enjoyment. I hadn't thought to "use" it to any purpose.

But, suddenly, I thought maybe I should try reading a little to her. I had noticed, before, how she had seemed to understand my stories about my grandmother—her strength, and pride, and how she gave me to myself, made me *believe* in myself.

I selected, at random—*Redivivus*

Thin lips can make a music;
Hateful eyes can see;
Crooked limbs go dancing
To a swift melody.

The probing knife of madness
Can start a dullard brain;
Cold cheeks feel kisses
And warm with tears again;

The surly heart of clowns
Can crack with ecstasy;
Rootbound oaks toss limbs
If winds come fervently;

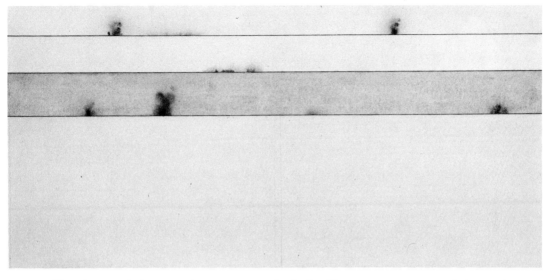

Then let my skeleton soul
Writhe upward from its loam,
Drink red morning again,
And look gently home.[10]

Something shook Barbara's heart free from her fixed idea, from the night before, of the nature of the violence. Maybe it was *Redivivus.* Maybe that line, from *Soldier and Son:* "Wounded, captured, rescued—there is the scar." Or, maybe, those lines, *Written for Allen Tate:* "Earth/ Is good, but better is land, and best/. A land still fought-for, even in retreat."

The "explosions" flowed down on the paper—fast and sure. And "right." They have "character"—*human* character. They're sparse, but that's faithful to the truth. The "explosions" rise up from the horizon edges—slowly, tenta-

tively. There are moments of increasing exuberance. They "work" across, and throughout the pages. But the "images" ("explosions") in *Radical Feminism* are still secondary to the "forms" (horizon "bands") against which they appear.

The motif of bands and diffuse images continues in *Metaphysical Cannibalism,* pp. 56–63. But the "images" appear as isolated instances, larger in "form," and often in pairs. The subject has changed from Oppressor/Oppressed, as class confrontation, to Oppressor/Oppressed, in one-to-one relationship. The destructiveness of the explosive motif is still appropriate, and, indeed, appears more menacing in the second subset, *within* this first set.

[10] Donald Davidson, *Poems: 1922–1961* (Minneapolis: University of Minnesota Press, 1966), p. 109.

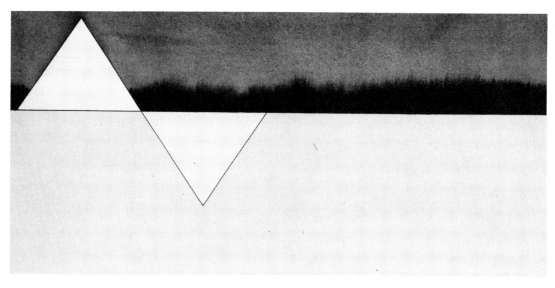

SET NUMBER II

Juniata II, pp. 64–94, represents the Movement in 1970. The year between these first two sets was critical—for *all* the Movements. Only in retrospect, and in part through the "translation" of this book, do I begin to understand the significance of the changes which took place at that time. The years 1968 and 1969 were highpoints for political exploration. The Black, the Youth, the Antiwar, Women came alive with an awareness of themselves as movers and shakers. It was a time of unlimited hopes, of seemingly endless horizons. If "we" were *here,* surely hordes just like us were right behind. Obstacles seemed to tumble before us. Romanticism was rampant! We were naïve; we ignored our backs. And we *paid* for it!

Juniata II shows the Spring of 1970 as it *really* was—although I didn't "see," or "understand," it like this—at the time. Neither did my friends—some of whom are dead, now, because of our naïveté.

Juniata II, pp. 64–94, is based aesthetically on a horizon "form," as was *Radical Feminism,* pp. 46–63. But, in *Juniata II,* there are significant changes *within* this "form."

In *Radical Feminism,* the horizon "form" contains a series of three bands. These "bands" represent *battlefields*—points of *contact* between the Oppressed and the Oppressor. But these "bands," for all their variations in width and tone (signifying duration of engagement and outcome), are essentially *determined* by the Oppressed. *Radical Feminism,* as a set within

this book, represents the "oppressed offensive."

The explosion "images," within *Radical Feminism,* appear *against* and *within* this background—even though the "battlefields," themselves, could not have existed without the *actual* occurrences of these "images." These *battlefields* are, consequently, *"echoes"* of the *explosions.* "Form," in this sense and case, follows "image"—that is, "theme" or "content." Still, the "image" in *Radical Feminism* SEEMS to stand out sharp and distinct *against* its *"field"*—seems to *follow* the landscape, instead of being its *creator.*

In *Juniata II,* the "form" changes. The base *horizon* remains. But the "bands"—as "war" zones initiated, defined, and shifted by the Oppressed—have disappeared. The "battle-field" is now monolithic. And *held* by the Oppressor!

What functioned as "image" in *Radical Feminism*—the "explosions"—is now *integrated* into the horizon *landscape,* as part of the "form." But the "explosions," in *Juniata II,* have an altogether different character than those found in *Radical Feminism.* In *Juniata II,* the "explosions" (or *"violence"!*) form a *continuous* band'—dark, looming, and ominous. *This* "band" is without restrictions. It seems to rise slowly, inexorably, from its base. It is Ravel's Angelus, but without "measure."

In *Radical Feminism,* the "violence" appears *within* a "field." In *Juniata II,* the *"violence"* IS the "field." The "form" of *Juniata II* is *not* static, as is the "form," essentially, of the prior set. *Juniata II,* as a set within this book,

represents the *response* of the Oppressor to the isolated instances of resistance seen in *Radical Feminism.* It is a "response" without joy, without hope. It is "Le Gibet," *Gaspard de la Nuit*—for us all, and for all time. It is "death."

Shape as Motif

The triangular *shape* is the primary thematic "image" used throughout the four parts of *Juniata II,* the second *set* within *Amazon Odyssey.* In *Juniata II,* the right-side-up triangle represents the Oppressor class. The upside-down triangle represents the Oppressed. In the first part of this second set, *The Equality Issue* (pp. 64–75), the triangular opposites never confront each other directly. And the tips of their far corners just barely touch, even though these

triangles are obviously on opposite "sides"— in terms of their conflicting interests.

In the second part of this set, *Metaphysical Cannibalism or Self-Creativity* (pp. 76–81), the triangular forms *do* confront directly. But *this* confrontation does not have the *significance* it might have had, in the context of *The Equality Issue.*

The shift of focus, seen in the two subsets of *Radical Feminism,* is repeated here. This second part of *Juniata II* concerns the concept of *identity:* the individual as opposed to the political mass. The white, or "empty," triangle represents "identity" dependent on the external. The grayed-in triangle represents "identity" constructed from within the individual: free from the need for power and control over others.

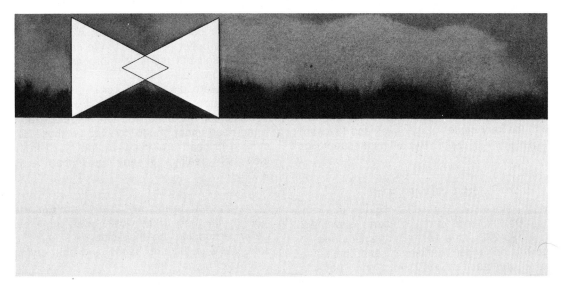

The closing sheet, of this second part, shows the *externally* dependent "identity" (the Oppressor)—as *shriveled* in size. The *internally* created "identity" is *now* on a *par* (standing on the same horizon line) with the Oppressor. The *formerly* Oppressed has, *also*, unlike its counterpart, *retained* its *original* size.

The third part of *Juniata II, Lesbianism and Feminism* (pp. 82–88), *repeats* the triangular *motif*. But from this point on, since the subject matter concerns women only—only upside-down triangles are used. In addition, all *action* occurs *on* the regular horizon line—heretofore, reserved for the occupation and action of the Oppressor.

Lesbianism and Feminism is introduced, *thematically*, by these two issues *interlocking*.

This motif, then, *shifts* to the two issues standing *side by side*, but distinctly separate. The final "image," *closing* this third part, represents the two issues as interlocked and *in confrontation*.

The *last* page of *Lesbianism and Feminism* appears on the *same* double-page sheet as does the *first* page of the *fourth* and *last* part of *Juniata II*. Because of this, *The Political Woman* (pp. 89–94) "shares" the last *confrontation* "image" closing *Lesbianism and Feminism*. These third and fourth parts of *Juniata II* are more closely related than are any of the other parts, within this set, to each other.

As the triangular motif continues throughout *The Political Woman*, the "theme" *shifts* to the *bases* of the units being *back to back*

—but still attached. The ostrich approach.

In the *last* figure, the triangles *intersect* with each other *completely*. This *"fusion"* is from point to base. In so interacting, these two triangles (apparently unwittingly) *re-create* the same triangular pattern of *base* confrontation —just seen prior. But *now*, the *double triangular* "form"—a *"diamond,"* in effect—is *absorbed* into the very *center* of the *class* and *functional* "identities" of both! The ultimate cooptation!

SET NUMBER III

On *"Violence in the Women's Movement"* (pp. 198-222). Late 1971. By this time, the *horizon* is no longer "darkening" and "ominous," as in *Juniata II* of 1970. And any "pockets" of "resistance," seen in 1968-69 (as in *Radical Feminism),* have long since been wiped out. "By any means necessary."

When I confronted my "sisters" on the subject of "violence" that evening of August 4th (it seems like a million years ago now), I lost the last of my illusions. About them, about myself, about what I had thought was "reality." Darkness swallowed my universe.

It was only by gathering every vestige of strength I still had, that I formulated an answer (*Self-Deception:* pp. 212-222) to the horror I had witnessed that "August" year of truth. If I had not struck out, I should have had to destroy myself. It wasn't possible to live, and to "accept," the errors. The "errors" which *we* —*all* of us—have participated in, over the last years. How blind! How superficial! How irresponsible!

How little *any* of us knows of the "real" world! We can't help that. But we *can* help keeping a better perspective. We *can* help trying to reach out more, to more and *different* kinds of people.

There were always enough signs for us to find out about ourselves—before it was too late. Too late for the dead, too late for those now living deep underground, too late for those destroyed in heart and mind—by too much truth, too much "reality," for any one human being to bear.

I finished telling my "story" to Barbara Nessim—the story of my Odyssey. By this time, we were huddled together—side by side—on a sofa. We were holding hands, and both crying —for all of us, for "life."

Finally, Barbara said, "well, there's only one way to 'say' *this*. Black paper and white type. *This* is the 'end,' except for some little sparkles of 'light.' The text, the words, will be the hope. The will to keep fighting. But *this* is the only way to 'say' *this*.

"I knew this was where *all* this was leading. I saw it coming in *Juniata II*."

I knew Barbara was right. It *was* the only way. I had thought originally of a funereal border. But that would have been for Joseph Colombo. And it was not Joseph, but "Márgarét I mourned for".[11] Colombo, and his people, were the last of the big movers (and by "big," I mean organizing large numbers successfully). We let them go down. And we couldn't afford that.

We are the problem. And we have been

cclviii

---

[11] "Márgarét," *Spring and Fall*, Gerard Manley Hopkins.

left with ourselves as the solution. *That* is our justice. And sufficient revenge for anyone who wants it.

Charlotte

Barbara and I made the "Charlotte" page last (p. xi, the *second* dedication page). It's a darkish gray—35% tone. (How *cold* it seems to "measure" tragedy. And yet it must be done.) Charlotte's death had fewer political. ramifications than did Colombo's attempted assassination. Realistically, Charlotte's death lacked the tragic scope of Colombo's, in effect, "elimination."

But Charlotte was my friend. Her death *was* political. And she had a proud heart. I can't leave her unsung.

Poor Charlotte. She fought too late. She never got completely away. And she made the mistake of going home.

"A BOOK IS THE HOME OF AN IDEA."

The "book" is finally complete. The "idea" of my odyssey has a "home" at last. It's a personal story of an education in violence. It culminates in *Götterdämmerung.* But it *need* not have been so. To "understand" the mistakes of the past is to have a better chance at changing the future.

Amazon Odyssey is now an art object. The edges of this page show its three-dimensional aspect. The work on the sets, the "orchestration," demonstrates "idea" as "theory"—*full "form."* The "art" structures the relationships of, and principles underlying, the concepts and images—the pieces—that already exist in visual "form."

This *Afterword* is long. But it is really the only "new" part of this book. "New" for me—at any rate. And I feel it is at least of as great importance as any other part within the collection itself.

Barbara Nessim made a cover for this piece. It is so beautiful and perfect; I got chills when I saw it. I could almost "hear" the last words of my *Foreword* coming from the figure's "presence":

"I hope the shores I have touched since 1967 will deepen my insights." The past surrounds me. I forget nothing. But I am older, wiser, and much sobered.

March 12, 1974